CHARLIE HURLEY

CHARLIE HURLEY

"The Greatest Centre Half the World has Ever Seen"

Mark Metcalf

SPORTS
BOOKS

Published in Great Britain by
SportsBooks Limited
PO Box 422
Cheltenham
GL50 2YN
Tel: 01242 256755
email: info@sportsbooks.ltd.uk
www.sportsbooks.ltd.uk

Cover design by Alan Hunns

A catalogue record for this book is available from
the British Library.

ISBN 978 1899807 69 7

Printed and bound in England by
Cromwell Press

Mixed Sources
Product group from well-managed
forests and other controlled sources
www.fsc.org Cert no. TT-COC-2082
FSC © 1996 Forest Stewardship Council

This book is dedicated to Noble Metcalf, who died in June 2004, and his grandson Charlie Metcalf, born January 2008.

CONTENTS

Acknowledgements

This book would not have been possible without the help of many people. Special thanks must go to Brian Leng, Dave Hillam, Andy Forsyth, Gordon Sharrock, Chris Bethell, the staff at Colindale Library, London and at Sunderland Social Studies Unit, Plunkett Carter of the Cork *Evening Echo*, Gavin Reardon, Jim Fox, Norman Howe, of the Sunderland ex-players association, John Harvey, Ross McKee, Gordon Taylor – chief executive of the PFA, Roger Pugh, Paul Days, Paddy Crerand, Tom O'Shea, and former players from Sunderland and Millwall, among them contemporaries of Charlie such as George Mulhall, Stan Anderson, Ambrose Fogarty, Len Ashurst, Malcolm Finlayson, Stan Anslow and John Shepherd.

Finally a special thanks to my wife, Ruth Jones, who never tired of telling me to "get on with it" when I looked like running out of energy.

Foreword
by Niall Quinn

Charlie Hurley is as important to Sunderland now in 2008 as he was during his heyday in the 1960s when the supporters who would vote him to be the "Player of the Century" in 1979 considered him to be 'The Greatest centre half the world has ever seen". The players joining Sunderland today only have to look at the way Charlie Hurley is still known as "The King" to know that they are signing for a club that is very special and that if they produce the goods here they will always be revered.

In 2007 Charlie honoured the club by travelling with the team on a tour of Ireland taking in his birthplace Cork as well as Dublin and Galway. Wherever we went Charlie was hailed as a hero. Earlier in the year he'd joined Johnny Giles in becoming only the second soccer player ever inducted into the Irish sporting hall of fame. Winning thirty-eight of his forty caps for his country while with Sunderland makes him the club's most capped player and with 400 games in red and white he served his club and his country as royally as it is possible for even a king to do.

What helps to make Charlie as great now as he was in his heyday as a player when he inspired Sunderland back to the first division after the club's first ever relegation is that for Charlie adoration has never been a one way street. As much as the supporters have admired Charlie his appreciation of them has never wavered. For every time I've heard a supporter extolling "The King's" virtues I've also heard Charlie praising the loyal and unstinting support he always benefited from. Charlie understood that to play for Sunderland needed a special kind of player and for all the heroes the crowd have had none have surpassed Charlie Hurley in their affections.

Always composed and in control on the pitch, Charlie retains that regal air now. He's never short of a smile and neither is anyone who meets him. Even supporters far too young to have seen him play know all about Charlie because they've heard the stories passed down across the generations. Charlie Hurley is one of the most important figures in the history of SAFC, one we all love and admire as much now as people have done since he was the towering presence of that great team of the early sixties.

Niall Quinn
2008

Prologue

Was Charlie Hurley, a player who never won a League or Cup winner's medal, who never played in the World Cup and who played mostly in the second and third tiers of English football ,"the greatest centre half the world has ever seen"?

Well, he was certainly the best centre half playing in English football between 1960 and 1965 with numerous man of the match performances for Sunderland, including games against 'double' winners Spurs in 1961, Leeds in 1963, First Division champions Everton in 1964 and FA Cup winners West Ham in 1965 which earned him the title 'King Charlie' among the Roker Park hordes.

Hurley is also a very strong contender for the best player to have played for Millwall even though he left when he was only twenty-one. For the Republic of Ireland, Hurley had a series of tremendous performances. These included matches against England in 1957, Poland a year later, West Germany in 1960 and Czechoslovakia in 1967. He played international football for more than twelve years in teams often missing key players from top clubs.

These are the only conclusions I can draw from my attempts to provide a fair examination of the playing career of the man voted in 1979 the best player in Sunderland's first one hundred years.

They were not, in fact, what I expected when I first set out more than two years ago without Charlie Hurley's knowledge to write this book. We had never met and I believed that the views of Sunderland supporters from the '60s, including those of my late father, were tinged with romanticism.

However, as I delved into thousands of match reports from local, regional, national and international newspapers, and then spoke to Hurley's former teammates and opponents, it became clear that he was an exceptional footballer whom I wish I had been able to see at his prime rather than at the very end of his career.

Hurley was not only brilliant in the air in defence or when Sunderland forced corners; he was also a great tackler and defender. A celebrated leader of players, a natural captain and a determined opponent, Hurley was the ultimate professional who always gave one hundred per cent when he turned out on the field. And he certainly knew where the goal was, scoring twenty-six times for Sunderland and also grabbing seven for Millwall, Bolton Wanderers and the Republic of Ireland as well as creating numerous opportunities for others to cash in.

This alone would have endeared him to football fans but when he combined all this with an extraordinary ability to control the ball, even in dangerous areas, and at times direct the play from centre half he was marked out as an immense talent.

Hurley's weakness was that he was not the quickest. This was partly the result of his career-threatening injury in 1955 from which he never really recovered and towards the end of his top-flight career some of the best players exposed him for pace, particularly Geoff Hurst in 1968 when he rattled home six at Upton Park as Sunderland slumped 8-0.

But it was typical and to his immense credit that Hurley had the last laugh, playing a superb game a few weeks later when Sunderland gained a measure of revenge with a 2-1 victory over the Hammers.

So does all this make him "the greatest centre half the world has ever seen", a chant which can still be heard chanted whenever Sunderland are playing? Possibly not, but if there have been better ones they are very few and far between, that's for sure.

Charlie Hurley, of course, would never suggest he was the greatest centre half the world has ever seen. Indeed when he agreed for this to be an authorised biography the only complaint he had was about the title, feeling that it might lead to some of his friends and ex-teammates giving him stick.

We should of course leave the last word to the big, genial Irishman.

"I loved being a professional footballer. It has given me, my wife and family a great life. All I have ever wanted is to be recognised as a good footballer on the pitch and a decent bloke off it. I continue to enjoy and be thrilled when people praise me but I am also a 'fan of the fans' and always will be," says Charlie Hurley.

Mark Metcalf,
2008

Introduction

Who's the greatest centre half the world has ever seen,
Who's the greatest centre half the world has ever seen,
Who's the greatest centre half the world has ever seen?

This was the cry from 40,000 fans as the tall, dark-haired elderly man emerged from the tunnel at half-time. They provided the answer themselves.

Charlie Hurley is his name,
Charlie, Charlie, Charlie Hurley

This despite the fact the vast majority could not possibly have seen the man play for their beloved club, his last game for Sunderland having taken place in April 1969.

"Who's he, Granddad?" asked the small boy.

"He's our best player ever," was the reply. No arguments against could be heard.

This book is the first ever on Charlie Hurley, someone who can still bring grown men to tears, so fondly do they think of the man they refer to simply as 'the King'.

Of players of a similar vintage only Sir Bobby Charlton at Manchester United comes close to winning as much admiration from his supporters as Charlie Hurley. When Sunderland won promotion to the Premier League with a 5-0 win at Luton in May 2007 the final chant of that match and the season was for the Irishman.

This was only weeks after Charlie Hurley had been selected by Millwall fans as their "best ever player". This award was in honour of his outstanding performances during the 1950s before he went north.

Hurley was best known as a man-mountain of a centre half but he could also play a bit, being able to pass the ball with accuracy out of defence and, when the occasion demanded it, make foraging runs from the back.

And if anyone thinks that Cristiano Ronaldo's trick where he flicks the ball across goal by moving his kicking foot behind the standing/supporting foot is new then they should think again – Hurley was using just such a technique to clear his lines and bring his full-backs into play as long ago as 1958!

Not for nothing was Hurley chosen to kick-off Niall Quinn's testimonial match between Sunderland and the Republic of Ireland in 2002. Hurley is one of the greatest players ever to play for the Republic, winning forty caps for his country, twenty-one as captain. He was certainly his country's best player throughout the 1960s. Ironically, after his birth in Cork on October 4th 1936, he lived there for less than a year, his family seeking to escape poverty by moving to Rainham in Essex in 1937.

After surviving the London 'Blitz' that killed one of his best friends, Hurley's talent as a footballer was soon recognised but his commitment to the welfare of his parents and six brothers and sisters meant he refused a professional contract at West Ham because the money on offer was a lot less then he was earning as an apprentice toolmaker at the Ford Motor Company.

Salvation came in the form of Millwall who offered the sixteen-year-old a route into the game, which he gratefully accepted. He repaid 'the Lions' by making more than one hundred appearances for them over the following five years, endearing himself to one of the most partisan crowds in England.

Although Millwall were in the Third Division South, Hurley commanded wider attention with a brilliant performance in October 1955 for a London XI which met Frankfurt in a game to introduce Wembley's floodlights. He played alongside Spurs and Northern Ireland legend Danny Blanchflower. Two years later he made a sensational 'man of the match' international debut when he blocked out Manchester United's Tommy Taylor during a World Cup qualifier against England.

The persuasive tongue of Sunderland manager Alan Brown took him north at a fee of £18,000 but the Irishman began disastrously, losing 7-0 and 6-0 in his first two games. He was then forced to suffer the indignity of being part of the first Sunderland side to suffer relegation from the First Division.

As the Wearsiders struggled to recapture their place in English football's top flight, Hurley became the rock around which an inexperienced side gradually found its confidence. In March 1961 Tottenham Hotspur, en route to the League and FA Cup 'double', were fortunate to grab a sixth round FA Cup draw at Roker Park. Hurley was the outstanding figure on the field.

Having proved himself as a no-nonsense defender prepared to play the ball around, Charlie Hurley became a cult figure with Sunderland supporters when, encouraged by Stan Anderson, his teammate and England international half-back, he became the first centre half in Britain to go forward for corners and set pieces. He was often unstoppable. 'King Charlie' was born.

As the Roker Park crowd roared "Charlie, Charlie, Charlie", his power in the air was to bring dozens of goals during the 1960s, either for himself or for forwards such as Brian Clough, Ambrose Fogarty, George Herd, Nick Sharkey and Neil Martin as they knocked home rebounds from the 'keeper.

After Sunderland were twice denied promotion on the last day of the 1962 and 1963 seasons it was Hurley who rallied the troops in 1963–64. With more than a million spectators cramming into Roker Park during the season, Sunderland beat League champions Everton (another game in which Hurley was the best player on the field) and took the holders Manchester United to three games in the FA Cup. When promotion came Hurley's joy was unconfined.

Dragged from the dressing room in his underpants and shirt, Hurley's wild celebrations were a recognition of his delight at having provided so much pleasure for the shipyard workers and miners who made up the majority of Sunderland's support and with whom, because of his background, he could strongly identify. Hurley was to finish second behind Bobby Moore in the Football Writers' Player of the Year Award. In the opinion of this writer, he should have won it.

Back in the top flight during a period when English football was at its peak, Hurley played in numerous big games for the next five seasons against Britain's best such as Bobby Charlton, Bobby Moore, Jimmy Greaves, Billy Bremner and George Best.

Performing in front of massive crowds and alongside quality players like Johnny Crossan, Martin Harvey, Len Ashurst, George Mulhall, Cecil Irwin, Colin Todd and goalkeeper Jimmy Montgomery, Hurley enjoyed the adoration of Sunderland fans now proudly proclaiming in song that he 'was the best centre half in the world."

However, in 1965, Hurley suffered the disappointment of being unable to prove it at the World Cup in England the following year when he was injured and missing as Ireland lost a play-off match to Spain in Paris.

Meanwhile the animosity between him and Sunderland's record signing Jim Baxter grew until, reaching its peak – as this book reveals – Hurley injured the Scottish ball player in training and threatened him in much the same way he had earlier dealt with the Leeds and Scotland midfield hard-man Bobby Collins.

Dropped by manager Ian McColl at the start of the 1967 season, Hurley then played perhaps his finest game, leading as player-manager a makeshift Irish side to a famous victory in Czechoslovakia in November 1967. He then forced himself back into a Sunderland side which ended the season by winning 2-1 at Old Trafford to deny Manchester United a second successive league title. Ironically Manchester City won the League that season by beating Newcastle 4-3 at St James' Park in their last match. United, however, went on to win the European Cup at Wembley.

It was clear Hurley liked playing against the Old Trafford club, for the following season he was the man of the match at Roker Park in a thrilling draw with Matt Busby's side.

It was, therefore, hardly surprising that in 1979, when Sunderland celebrated their centenary, the fans voted Charlie Hurley as their 'Player of the Century'.

It was not just his home fans who had a high opinion of Hurley. In 1963 Leeds United legend John Charles called him 'the best centre half in Britain and a world class player.'

And a short selection of comments from the newspapers of those days shows that Charles was far from alone in his assessment.

"Charlie is Britain's best" – Ken Jones in 1959 in the *Sunday Mirror.*

"For my money Hurley is the best centre half in Britain today" – Stanley Ford, in *The People* in 1961.

"Hurley is perhaps the most cultured centre half in the League" – the Arsenal v Sunderland programme for September 12th 1964.

"He was a colossus in his time; a player of rich ability and a man who, though he loved all that his great football ability brought, never forgot his family values or the fans that put him on that pedestal" – Tom O'Shea of *The Irish Press*.

"Charlie Hurley was easily the best centre half I've ever seen playing" – Johnny Crossan, who played in the European Cup for Standard Liege against Real Madrid before joining Sunderland.

And yet outside of the north-east of England and parts of south London and Ireland Hurley has largely been forgotten and that's a shame. He was one of the most gifted players of his generation and this book is in part intended to rescue him from relative obscurity.

It brings to life Hurley's career at Millwall and Sunderland plus his two seasons at Bolton Wanderers from 1969 to 1971 and his five years as Reading's manager shortly afterwards.

It is not, however, only about football. It's about Hurley the person, his background and his family life. He reveals some of his own experiences which, combined with his footballing ability, made him a genuine 'people's hero'.

Set against the background of the political and cultural era in which he played, this book draws on extensive interviews with Charlie Hurley, his teammates, opponents and fans, as well as archive materials and Hurley's own extensive scrapbooks.

Welcome to *Charlie Hurley: "the greatest centre half the world has ever seen"*, an authorised biography of Charlie Hurley.

Chapter One

Growing up in Essex and a lucky escape from a V-1

Charles John Hurley was born in number 10 [*] Devonshire Avenue in Cork in the south-west of Ireland on Sunday October 4th 1936 to Patrick and Christina [née Creedon] Hurley. His birth took place just as the storm clouds of the Second World War were approaching.

Meanwhile, a day later, in the north-east of England, where Hurley was later to find fame, people were taking to the streets to watch 207 Geordies set off from Jarrow on an ultimately unsuccessful crusade to London. They aimed to persuade the then national government led by the Conservative Party to do more to alleviate unemployment and poverty. Prime Minister Stanley Baldwin said he was "too busy" to see the exhausted walkers when they got there.

Escaping poverty was the reason why Charlie Hurley soon ended up living in east London. "I was six months old when I left Ireland. My father went over to Fords for work and then my mother brought over four children. There was nothing in Ireland except big families. I finished up as one of eleven kids and that's a lot of kids; it was a very tough time for the seven that survived. We stayed briefly in Gainsborough Road before moving and settling down to live at 157 Southend Road in Rainham in Essex.

"Money was always tight but there was also tremendous affection for all of us from our Mam and Dad, especially my dad as in those days dads took no rubbish from anyone. You couldn't talk back to your mother or father. If you did you got a slap. We had loads of friends and my mates and I played football morning, noon and night. It was great fun."

This was not necessarily the view of all the neighbours as balls crashed into their gardens and at times through their windows. "Oh yes, parents frequently came out. We often played with a tennis ball if we didn't have a football. I remember Mrs Connolly. She often came out to chase us. We used to smash some windows," remembers Hurley

When Hurley was three months old momentous events were taking place in Ireland. The country had been divided in 1921 when the House of Commons had passed the Government of Ireland Act. This partitioned the country into a six-county Northern Ireland and a twenty-six-county Southern Ireland or 'Free State.' But in late December 1936, the Free State President Eamon de Valera struck. While British political affairs were in a period of significant upheaval with the abdication of Edward VIII following his decision to marry the already twice-divorced American, Wallis Simpson, the Dail [the Irish Parliament] passed the Constitution and the External Relations Act.

At a stroke these laws removed the new and any future king's authority within the twenty-six counties. In 1937 a new Constitution significantly altered key elements of Irish affairs including the State's name, thus bringing into existence 'Eire', or in English 'Ireland'.

Edward VIII's abdication saw his younger brother George VI, the Duke of York, become king. This meant it was his wife Elizabeth who presented the Sunderland captain Raich Carter with the FA Cup at Wembley five months later after a 3-1 victory against Preston North End.

That was to be Sunderland's last major trophy until the famous defeat of Leeds United at Wembley in 1973 when an Ian Porterfield goal denied a Yorkshire side managed by Don Revie, a teammate of Hurley in his first two seasons at Roker Park.

By the end of the Second World War Charlie Hurley's father had been working alongside thousands of his fellow countrymen at the Ford plant in Dagenham for almost ten years. The factory had opened at the end of the 1920s and was to remain an important source of work for local people and immigrant workers until car production finally ended in 2001. [In 2008 transit vans were still being assembled on the now much smaller site.]

Estimates suggest that around 250,000 crossed the Irish Sea between 1936 and 1945. Some, like the 40,000 or so who joined the British Army – joining up with a similar number from Northern Ireland – became part of the war effort. For others it was an attempt to escape unemployment, poverty and an uncertain future.

It was an uncertain world into which the young Charlie Hurley was thrust. The Second World War started when he was only two and he lived not far from the East End of London which suffered from intense bomb raids. From mid-September to mid-November 1940 an average of two hundred bombers attacked London every night but one.

Whole parts of London were flattened, some 250,000 people losing their homes in the first six weeks of bombing. Gas-mask practice was made compulsory in schools. Children, the elderly and disabled, pregnant women and the sick were evacuated to friends and relatives, or to homes in the countryside.

On December 29th the raid was so severe that it was dubbed 'the Second Great Fire of London'. The images of an embattled St Paul's Cathedral provided a lasting legacy of London's resistance. The attacks on London ceased in May 1941 when Adolf Hitler, the German chancellor, decided to switch to an eastern front and invade the USSR.

However, the Luftwaffe, the German air force, continued to attack ports throughout Britain. They included Sunderland, where the shipyards were working flat out, providing much-needed employment in a town that had suffered badly from a lack of work during the mid 1930s, to produce new vessels to replace those that had been sunk. The bombings presented a daily threat to the workforce. In August 1940 six bombs were dropped, hitting the yards of Sir James Laing and Sons and killing two men.

One of the most severe raids occurred on May 16th 1943. Enemy planes dropped flares before attacking in numbers. Houses were destroyed, people killed and several fires burned furiously for a considerable period of time. The Luftwaffe was back the following week; some people taking shelter in air-raid shelters were killed. A German High Command Communiqué was quoted as saying: "Last night the Luftwaffe again attacked the shipbuilding town of Sunderland with strong forces. Large fires were started in the city and harbour area."

The attacks did have the effect of forcing the miners at Wearmouth Colliery, lying alongside the shipyards close to the River Wear estuary, to demand that they were brought to the surface during the raids. They knew that a direct hit to the shaft area would have brought disaster and the deaths of many of them.

Sunderland largely built ships for the merchant navy. During the war the shipyards of Sunderland produced almost two hundred and fifty ships, totalling over one and a half million gross tons. This was more than a quarter of the total for British yards during this period.

And although the war was coming to its conclusion by June 1944, if by no means over, the assault on London was resumed with V-1 bombers and an eight-year-old Charlie Hurley was lucky not to be one of those killed. It was the discipline instilled by his father that saved him.

He remembers: "The bombs the Germans dropped were called Doodlebugs. They had a particular noise and it was when they stopped that you got worried because you then knew they were going to hit the ground. I was playing out with Gordon Smith, a good friend of mine, at the corner of Jersey and Southend road. My father was a very strong character; you got a whack if you didn't do as you were told. We had our air-raid shelter in the house. It was corrugated – it was in the lounge. The air-raid siren would go and you'd dash home.

"Gordon and I were actually playing on an old bogey-cart, a wooden thing with a piece of rope to help steer. We were pushing each other up and down the street. My father had said to me on many occasions – 'whatever you do boy, if you hear the air-raid warning then come home, don't go anywhere else'. My dad had this whistle, not an actual whistle, just blowing through his fingers. I was nearer Gordon's that day when I heard his whistle. My first thought was to go to Gordon's and he was suggesting I did. But I thought my dad would murder me. So I told Gordon I would see him later and off I ran.

"I got into the shelter at home and the doodlebug dropped in Gordon's back garden and killed him. This was towards the end of the war; it was wintertime but I am not actually sure what year. I would have been killed as well if I had gone with Gordon. London was decimated by the bombings. We lived near Hornchurch aerodrome and the Germans wanted to bomb it and put it out of operation so our area got bombed quite a bit."

Hitler's bombing campaign from 1940 onwards was estimated to have killed 43,000 British civilians, the majority from London.

The joyous celebrations in the city at the end of the war in May 1945 temporarily obscured the severe problems that had to be faced in the years to come, particularly if London, and especially the eastern part of it, was to be restored as a place for people to live and work. Whole areas of housing had been flattened; 'bomb sites' remained a legacy in the area for many, many years afterwards. It could hardly have been otherwise.

Charlie remembers the carnival atmosphere. "On VE [Victory in Europe] Day we had a party in Jersey Road. We had all the tables right down the middle of the road; we had athletics races along the road and you got a couple of cakes if you won. I got a couple."

The end of the war was a time of radical and historical change with the Labour party winning a landslide election and introducing the welfare state. But life has to be about bread and circuses and competitive football returned, although the 1945–46 league season retained the regional league format it had used during the war.

Sunderland, of course, were not even in Charlie Hurley's consciousness in those days and he would not have known that on January 5th 1946, before a crowd of 12,050 at Blundell Park, they could finally be said to have returned to competitive football. They defeated Grimsby Town 3-1 in the first leg of the 1945–46 FA Cup. It was a first leg because that year in the cup each round was played over two legs until the final, the only year it has not been a straight knock-out.

This was a day which started with a north-east tragedy when the overnight express from King's Cross to Newcastle crashed near Durham at 5.40am after it ran into a derailed goods wagon. Ten people were killed, including a soldier who had survived the war only to die shortly afterwards, a particularly cruel fate.

Four days later 18,500 passed through the Roker Park turnstiles to view a 2-1 home victory in the second leg. Sunderland then beat Bury over two legs after extra time before crashing out on aggregate to Birmingham by 3-2 in a tie that attracted aggregate crowds of 82,820 to Roker Park and St Andrew's, including many soldiers just back from the war.

The end of the war gave Charlie Hurley, then a pupil at Blacksmith Lane Junior School, the opportunity to visit his hometown of Cork for the first time since early 1937. "We originally intended staying only a while but we ended up staying the full six weeks holiday. Danny, my eldest brother came with me and we stopped at my dad's parents' place. I only saw them once. I never saw my mother's parents and because of this I have always said I would be a good granddad and I have done my best.

"One daughter, Tracy, who lives in Macclesfield, has three, two boys and a girl, while my other daughter Joanne has two and I like to think that I am there for them if they need me. I recall that my grandma was short but my granddad was a big lad. They lived at 4 Devonshire Avenue, Cork. She was a lovely woman, but that was sixty or so years ago."

Charlie Hurley's grandfather, Daniel, had served in India with the British Army for many years. On his return he obtained employment with Cork Corporation and along with his wife Julia Cullinane, from Crosses Green, they settled in Devonshire Avenue. It has long since been demolished. Julia's father had worked as a stonemason, a skilled trade of some standing at the time. They had four children, two boys, Patrick [Charlie's father] and Charlie, and two girls, Mary and Eileen.

Patrick Hurley, a labourer, married Christina [Dina] Creedon, who was originally from Rope Walk, Sunday's Well, in Cork and they moved to live close to his parents' home before they emigrated to England in 1937.

[*] Until recently Charlie believed he was born at number 4 Devonshire Avenue. However, during research by Plunkett Carter for the Cork *Evening Echo*'s magnificent supplement for Sunderland's match against Cork at Turners Cross on July 30th 2007 it was discovered that it was Charlie's grandparents who lived in number 4.

Chapter Two

Rebuffing West Ham but signing for Millwall

When League Football returned in August 1946 it enjoyed enormous crowds. Against a background of austerity, the game provided a relief for millions of people. So too did the cinema: this was a time when that art form had a regular audience of thirty million in Britain.

With admission prices ranging from around 1 shilling and 3d [7p] to stand on the terraces to between three and five shillings [15–25p] for seats, football grounds between 1946 and 1950 were packed. In the 1949–50 season seventeen teams had average gates of more than 35,000. These included Notts County, then in the Third Division South along with Millwall, who averaged 20,753 per game.

Those watching did not include Charlie Hurley, as "We were too poor. Every penny had to be well spent. None of us had anything, no one had a car. Tony Woodhouse's dad had a motorbike and sidecar and it was Tony who had the football. He wasn't very good but he always got first pick as it was his ball."

[It seems, too, that Charlie's brother Danny was not that good either. He had a different attitude to his younger brother when it came to football. "Danny thought that by hitting the ball very, very hard then you were a good footballer. I thought differently even then. I thought skill was the thing," says Hurley. A younger brother, Chris, was to play four games as a centre forward for Milwall between 1963 and 1965. He scored twice. Says Charlie: "Millwall were hoping that Chris would be able to do for them what I'd done, but he was more of a cruncher. I never saw him play a first team game for Millwall as I was playing for Sunderland at the time. Arthur, my older brother, was a very good player at wing half. I think if I hadn't gone up to Sunderland he would have made a professional footballer. He was skillful, determined and confident. I would have got him trials at various clubs but I was too far away to do that. I could have helped him a lot".]

"I was captain of the primary school side but I used to have to play with plimsolls because we could not afford a pair of football boots. I was eleven years old when I got my first football boots. A guy up the road who wasn't much of a footballer decided to sell his boots and I bought them – they cost 7 shillings and 6d [37p] for the pair. That was a lot of money in those days. I played in them for four years and they were my pride and joy. My mother gave me the money and she always said it was the best investment she ever made.

"I was at Sutton Secondary School and I played for Essex County as well. I had a schoolteacher called Mr Mumford and he said I was going to go further. He got me a trial at Arsenal. I had to go to Highbury. I was fifteen years old while all the other players were around eighteen. It was quite frightening because I'd never had any experience of playing at somewhere like that in a trial and they were big lads. Don't forget that from fifteen to eighteen you put on a bit of muscle.

"After the game Arsenal's manager Tom Whittaker said, 'Well done Charlie, I'll send for you in a couple of years' time'. This was a very polite brush-off and when I went home to my dad, he was desperate for me to be a professional footballer and asked how it had gone. I said it was quite frightening. I said I'd not done very well and I explained that I was only fifteen and they were eighteen. I said, 'I'll tell you one thing, Dad: when I am eighteen I will be better than any of them'. It wasn't a cop out. I meant it and I proved it in those three years.

"I was fairly decent at school. But the only way out of my standard of life was through sport. I saw it as a way out of really working for a living. I used to hang around with the brother of a West Ham player called Petchey. We went to his house and I saw him putting a golf ball in the back garden. It was during the day and I asked 'Why aren't you working?' He told me that during the summer players didn't work, that they got three months off. I asked if he got paid during the summer and he said he did. That was another sign that football was the profession for me."

Nevertheless Charlie Hurley was forced to decline his first professional offer, which came from West Ham United of Division Two when he was sixteen. "I had played a few games for West Ham's youth team and Ted Fenton, the manager, came to my house and asked me to sign on as an apprentice. It was not really an apprenticeship; you were just a boot-cleaner and he offered me £3 10 shillings [£3.50]. I'd left school and was earning £4 10 shillings [£4.50] a week at the Ford Motor Company in Dagenham. As one of the first workers from the seven kids that extra pound was an awful lot of money.

"So I could not afford to sign for West Ham. I wanted to but there were also rail and bus fares to get there. It just wasn't practical. People thought I was mad and West Ham always regretted it because they used to speak to me about it afterwards.

"My father worked in the foundry at Fords, as did my brother and my brother-in-law and it was like working in hell. I was an apprentice toolmaker for nine months and in the foundry they had free lemonade. I used to go down and see my dad and get some lemonade and also to escape from doing any work.

"I didn't like it at all. I worked on the top floor of the building. It was all glass. In the summer it was hot and in the winter it was freezing. When I got the chance to turn professional I always remember the foreman, Paddy Downham, coming up to me and saying [in Irish accent], 'Charlie, you'll have to be very careful boy, you could get injured and then you've no career behind you'. I looked at these Irish guys flogging their tails off and I said 'I'd rather take the chance on the broken leg than spend the rest of my days working like the rest of those guys over there'."

Most of 'those guys' clearly agreed because as he said his farewells they were all cheering and wishing him good luck. The chance came courtesy of West Ham's great rivals Millwall.

"I was playing in a County Cup match for Rainham Town Youth Club. Training at the youth club was fairly rudimentary with lots of running. We also played a lot of five-a-sides, I was a good tackler so I got put at the back. There were no tactics as such; someone who was good on the ball got put up front.

"I always played as a defender, I regret that now. I got twenty-six goals for Sunderland as a centre back and I scored for Ireland as well. Now if I had played centre forward I would have got some goals because I was frightening in the air and I could play a bit. I never went in and asked to play centre forward, I liked centre half. But when I look back I should have been a centre forward.

"The County Cup was a big match and we had a double-decker bus of fans who went with us to Walthamstow. We lost 1-0. The lad I was playing against I didn't rate. Maybe I played well but anyway I found myself being followed by this old bloke, who I now know was Bill Voisey. Bill asked how I was and I said I was a bit sick because we'd just lost and all those mums and dads had come to watch us and I was going to get some stick after the match.

"He said he'd been there to watch the player I was against and that I seemed to have him in my pocket. I wasn't particularly interested in this old boy; I didn't know him from Adam. He kept walking behind me and I asked him who he was and he told me he was a scout from Millwall and he asked me if I wanted to sign for them.

"Now I was sixteen and three-quarters and he'd just seen me play in a County Cup match, which to me didn't seem enough to warrant getting a contract at Millwall. But I agreed to meet him and he brought round the manager Charlie Hewitt and the trainer Ron Gray to my parents' house. I was on a tour abroad with the Essex Youth team so when I came back my dad asked me to ring Millwall because they wanted me to sign.

"I just could not believe it. I was offered £10 a week if I was in the first team, £7 otherwise. I'd get £2 a win and £1 a draw, half if I was in the reserves. It was a lot more than I was getting at Fords. It was very, very exciting. I phoned Millwall as soon as I could. This was my opportunity. I signed and was delighted" – not least because it also meant the end of working at Fords.

Millwall Football Club was formed in 1885 by workers at Morton's Jam Factory on the Isle of Dogs and turned professional eight years later, reaching the semi-finals of the FA Cup in 1900. At the time the club played its home games on the Isle of Dogs, on the north side of the River Thames approximately eight miles east of the City of London. The name "Mill–wall" sprung from the mills which stood on the marsh walls in the seventeenth and eighteenth century that were used to drain the low-lying land. These were actually removed in the nineteenth century when industrial premises were erected along the riverside, the most notable of which was John Scott Russell's shipbuilding yard at which Brunel's *Great Western* was launched in 1859, the largest vessel built in Britain.

In 1902 an underground tunnel had been constructed linking nearby Greenwich to the Isle of Dogs so that workers could cross from the south to the West India Docks for work. Eight years later, Millwall Athletic – the Athletic was dropped in 1925 – went south, crossing the river to New Cross, then part of Deptford but by 1953 in the borough of Lewisham. The tunnel meant, of course, that dockers from the north could continue to support their team and the club retained its reputation as 'the dockers' team'. Its nickname was 'the dockers' until giant-killing exploits in the 1900 FA Cup earned it the current nickname, 'The Lions'.

Because it was a densely populated area, the site chosen for Millwall's new ground, 'The Den', was only four acres in size. Three railway lines formed its boundaries and this meant only one side could be accessed by road, the appropriately named Cold Blow Lane End. Designed by Archibald Leitch and built at a cost of £10,000, the ground was badly damaged by Luftwaffe bombs in 1943 and then a discarded cigarette caused a fire in the main stand shortly afterwards.

Unable to play at The Den, Millwall found a temporary home at the nearby Valley, headquarters of Charlton Athletic, and it was during this time that they reached Wembley for the first time. Charlton also provided the Lions goalkeeper as well. Millwall manager Joe Cock had been short of players for the Football League (South) Cup semi-final with Arsenal and had approached Sam Bartram, born and bred in South Shields and who as a youngster had watched Sunderland from the terraces at Roker Park, to play in goal. The 1-0 victory meant that eight years after losing 3-1 to Sunderland in the 1937 FA Cup semi-final the New Cross side lined up at Wembley against Chelsea. In the opposition side as a guest was a recovering George Hardwick of Middlesbrough, later to manage Sunderland and Hurley in the mid 1960s, and although he failed to score Chelsea did win 2-0.

The Den was rebuilt after the war ended with compensation money from the War Damages Commission. It was typical of league grounds of the time, consisting of a main stand with seats, with terracing on the other three sides.

Entrance to the pitch for the players was from underneath the terrace at the Cold Blow Lane end. From there spectators could just see the nearby New Cross Speedway and Greyhound Stadium sticking above the roof of the Iderton Road Terrace directly opposite.

Finding the ground was difficult. The floodlights, first used for a friendly with Manchester United on Hurley's seventeenth birthday, were so low they could hardly be seen among the scrapyards and warehouses that surrounded the ground. The approaches were so twisted and awkward that it felt like the ground was on an island and with cobbled streets and a series of low tunnels it made a perfect setting for a Jack the Ripper, or any other horror movie.

"They were one of the best crowds to play before. They had a passion for the club and if you gave one hundred per cent they'd give it back to you," says Millwall forward John Shepherd, who played for the club throughout the 1950s.

Before he even appeared in front of those spectators Charlie Hurley was relishing his new world. "At the start of my career as a Millwall footballer I got a luncheon voucher for 2 shillings and 6d, [12$\frac{1}{2}$p]. After we went training that first morning we went to a nearby café and we had soup. They asked what I wanted. And I said I thought that was it; soup was the main course. So I had a steak and they asked if I wanted a sweet. I'd never had one before, so I had a three-course meal that day. Before that my idea of a three-course meal was breakfast, dinner and tea.

"After the meal we went back to the ground and they said 'we don't train after dinner'. I replied that I was a professional footballer. I had to train in the afternoons. But the players said during the season they didn't train in the afternoons and I looked up to heaven and thought this was going to happen to me in the rest of my career as long as I made it. I have never moaned since the day I became a professional footballer.

'I went home and told my mam they had given us steak in that little café. I'd never had one in my life before and this was beautiful steak. The owner sold me some; I gave some to my sister Sheila. She'd never had any either before. She looked at it and said there seemed to be yellow fat around the steak. As I had never seen a steak I assumed that was always there. I went back to the café and asked and the owner said it was horsemeat. Sheila stopped eating it immediately. The players knew but they didn't care; my brother went mad because he loved it."

Sheila was later to marry well-known Ballymore cyclist Danny Leahy.

After signing as a professional Hurley was quickly pitched into the reserves. "I played six games in the reserves before my seventeenth birthday. Fulham reserves was my first match. I was quite pleased. I played against a first teamer coming back from injury and we drew 1-1. After the game I heard some of the older players saying 'Who is this kid we've got here?'"

Charlie Hurley made his league debut for Millwall away at Torquay on January 30th 1954, a game that finished 2-2. He had originally been due to play against Headington United [now Oxford United] in the FA Cup second round tie in December earlier in the season but injury delayed his debut.

The Millwall side at Torquay that day was: Finlayson, Jardine, Fisher, Short, Hurley, Heydon, Johnson, Stobbart, Shepherd, Saward, Hazlett. Millwall's scorers were Stobbart and Johnson.

"Going to Torquay on the bus for my debut was like heaven. I was due to play in the cup against Headington but I had a strain. I'd never had one before. When you're young you just play, but now this was my living.

"I was told on the Monday that I would be playing. The manager called me into the office. I was playing well in the reserves but I didn't think when I signed in the October that I would play in the first team that season. Talk about butterflies – more like eagles in my stomach.

"My parents couldn't afford to travel to see me, but everyone was very proud. I was in the first team! I always understated myself, but I was personally quite pleased, as the talk afterwards was all about 'Who's this new centre half we've found?'

"I didn't want to be clever in my first match. I got the ball and got rid of it, and I played it very simple. I had Alex Jardine, the captain, on one side. He was very good for me. [Jardine made 321 League and FA Cup appearances for Millwall, scoring 26 goals.]

"Before the Torquay game the players were saying 'Come on kid, you'll be all right, it will take you a few games to find your feet', that sort of thing, 'We've all been there'. It wasn't bullshit. They were trying to encourage me and I thought 'Well it's up to me' and after the game it was me they were all talking to with 'Do you think you can play like that every week?'

"I said very little but I thought I would play better than that. We went to Torquay on the same day, there and back. There were no complaints. It was one of the best days of my life. I was a professional footballer; marvellous, absolutely marvellous!"

The crowd took to Charlie Hurley from the start, which was just as well. The Den had a fearsome reputation. By 1953 it had seen its fair share of trouble and no other ground had been closed more times – in 1920, 1934, 1947 and 1950.

Hurley remembers: "The Den in those days was quite a vicious place for the opposition to come to. In fact just before I signed for Millwall it was closed down for six months because of the violence among the fans.

"The one thing about the dockers is they either liked you or they didn't. There were no grey areas. The fact that I was a young lad who had come up through the ranks and I was a footballing centre half – used to play a bit, taking risks as they would call it today but I just thought that was how you played – then the dockers fell in love with me. I could never do any wrong at the Den.

"The ground had a very narrow edge between the touchline and the terrace wall. There was a guy called Des Quinn and his mate Stan Anslow, two monster full backs, and I saw them hit so many people into this wall. But that was all par for the course. The Millwall team was hard, especially Stan Anslow.

"It was, however, an unbelievable experience. Some games we got 20 to 22,000; even some reserve games got 8,000. It was a very exciting time for me; you got adrenalin from the crowd pumping you up when you were on the pitch. There were players who told me years later how frightened they were to turn out at the Den. We had some very hard players, as well as some very good ones. I loved them as long as they were on my side."

Unfortunately the Den was rarely anywhere near full to its capacity of around 40,000. At the end of Hurley's first season the average gate was only 13,502 for a team that had been relegated from Division Two at the end of the 1947–48 season and was now playing in Division Three South alongside Watford, Crystal Palace, Southampton and Norwich City.

Hurley made an immediate impact on his home debut as Millwall overcame neighbours Southend and was singled out for praise by the *South London Press* reporter who wrote: "Only the determination of Brian [sic] Hurley, making his home debut and the brilliance of 'keeper Finlayson enabled Millwall to hold out against persistent Southend pressure for both points on Saturday. Hurley kept so tight a grip on opposing centre forward Grant that the visitor was given few openings."

Charlie says: "I played a lot of games in front of Malcolm Finlayson the 'keeper. He was a great goalkeeper who helped me a lot when I got into the first team. He was big and strong, brilliant at crosses and very brave.

"I was very young when I got in the side and he was a big fella, bigger than me. He told me he'd seen me in the reserves and in training and that I'd nothing to worry about. That gave me an awful lot of confidence. He was very important to me at the start.

"I wasn't surprised he later did well at Wolves because he was big and he wasn't frightened. Also when he came out for the ball you got out of the way or else you ended up on the floor."

Finlayson was 6' 1" tall and weighed 13½ stone.

Finlayson remembers that "Charlie was only a young boy when

he started playing, but he grew a lot in the three years I played behind him to become a big strong lad. He came in for Gerry Bowler, a ball-playing centre back who didn't tackle very much. You'd be playing on a muddy pitch and he'd be the only one who'd come off looking immaculate. Charlie, however, was a never say die player, always tackling people. And you could see as a youngster that he had this great ability.

"I went to Wolves in 1956 and then, in '57–58, I played against Charlie when he was at Sunderland. We were at opposite ends of the pitch then after we'd been in the thick of it at Millwall; we won 2-0. It was the season Sunderland got relegated. He looked a good player even that day but he wasn't fully developed, as he was still only about twenty or twenty-one. He didn't dominate the game the way he did later on when he got more experience and became physically intimidating for opponents as well.

"He was a good lad. A goalkeeper has to command his area and one thing that can happen when you're playing is that you're giving instructions and someone's taking no notice of them – you're coming for a ball and they also go for it. Charlie always did exactly as he was instructed to do.

"I saw Charlie at the 'Dockers Day' that Millwall organised before their match at the New Den in February 2007. It was the first time since I played against him at Roker. Don't forget you're talking fifty years ago and I greeted him exactly as I did then: 'Hello, Charlie son how are you?' and he said 'Hello Dad'. Football is a funny business, you meet so many people but it's often for not very long. When he came to Millwall he was very quiet but he was a very young boy. I'd joined the club when I was young myself and you think 'I'll listen first before I start to give any opinions out' and that was what Charlie was like – he was trying to work out what was happening. Millwall had some good players even though we didn't do that well. Pat Saward went to Villa, Charlie to Sunderland, and I went to Wolves and won two championships and an FA Cup.

"I played behind Billy Wright and then Bill Slater at Wolverhampton, both excellent, but I would rate Charlie as a very, very good centre half. I wouldn't like to compare him with Billy Wright or Bill Slater, as they were different eras. Billy Wright wasn't the hardest tackler in the game but he had the ability to know where the ball was going before it was kicked. If Danny Blanchflower had the ball and was going to put it down the inside track Billy Wright could see him trying to do that and would get across to cut it out. He was the best reader of a game I ever saw."

Hurley, of course, was not the only Irish man, or woman, earning his corn in south London as demonstrated by a whole series of letters in the *South London Press* at the time under the heading of 'IRISH EXODUS'. Typical of them was one from Norah James of SE14 saying: "The Irish are quitting their country because their large families could not find proper housing accommodation or sufficient work to keep them. As conditions are better in Britain emigration is the only solution to the Irish problem."

There were certainly plenty of jobs for them, with the paper reporting that 'NOW THERE ARE TOO MANY JOBS' with men wanted in all major trades including bricklaying, carpentry, welding and in the police. Women workers were urgently needed as shop assistants, bus conductors, domestic servants and shorthand typists where the pay was £7 and 10 shillings [£7.50] a week.

After a two-game absence Hurley was back for the home game with Norwich City where the local paper reported that he 'never looked comfortable against Johnston', the centre forward. Despite taking a seventh-minute penalty lead Millwall lost 3-1.

At Bristol City, Hurley faced a man who he was to line up against in his first international match three years later. John Atyeo, the centre forward, not only scored himself but forced Hurley into conceding an own goal as the Lions lost 2-1. Hurley did, however, play much better when Millwall beat Newcastle United in a friendly under floodlights and when the season ended he had made sixteen league appearances for a team that finished twelfth. He had done well at seventeen and he started the next season in the first team.

Sunderland, Charlie Hurley's next club, were doing well. In the 1954–55 season they finished fourth, just four points behind first-time winners Chelsea. One particularly thrilling match was the 4-2 victory against that season's FA Cup winners, Newcastle United.

The ground was so full that Argus wrote in his match report in the *Sunderland Evening Echo* that "youngsters were rolled over the heads of the crowd to the front where they were allowed to sit on the running track".

There was major disappointment in the FA Cup when on a waterlogged Villa Park pitch Sunderland lost the semi-final by a single goal to Manchester City, thus failing to take their place against Newcastle United at Wembley for the final. This is the nearest there has been to a Tyne–Wear FA Cup Final.

One of that team, Stan Anderson, is still bitterly disappointed about that season: "We should have won the league as we were the best side. But we got to the semi-final of the cup. I was desperate to win the league, but how things have changed, because in those days getting to the FA Cup Final was the big thing – it was top of the bill. If you could win the cup, even if it was only six matches, you were going to Wembley. It was the biggest game, probably, in the world at the time. But winning the league – one week you're great and next week it's all forgotten. Different now because you get to enter the European Champions League.

"We took our eye off the ball. We had players saying never mind and thinking they were not getting injured because the semi-final was coming up. The result was we lost 2-1 to Charlton and 1-0 to Arsenal, both at home. We could have murdered those teams – we'd already beaten them both 3-1 away from home.

"I always look at the book I kept and I always think 'God, I could have had a championship medal that year'. It still upsets me. We played Chelsea at their ground late in the season and we had to win to get back into the title race. But we lost 2-1 and they won the title. It was the week after the semi-final."

Hurley played an impressive thirty-eight league games in the 1954–55 season, as well as three FA Cup ties, including appearing at Burnden Park in front of 40,501 in a 3-1 defeat by Bolton. Finishing fifth in the league did not raise the Londoners' average gate, however, and Charlie Hewitt, the manager, was constantly bemoaning the small crowds. Not surprisingly it was reported that the club was losing money despite doing fairly well, particularly before Christmas when they rose as high as fourth on the back of a marvellous run of form by new boy Denis Pacey who hammered twelve goals in fourteen league and cup matches.

Pacey was unlike Hurley in that he was not desperate to play professional football. "I didn't turn pro until I was twenty-three. I was quite a good amateur and I just wanted to play at the highest level I could. I came good at Leyton Orient and I started playing professionally during the 1951–52 season, including at Everton in the FA Cup, within six weeks of turning pro."

He recalls fondly the first time he came across Hurley: "I was playing for Leyton Orient and I was quite surprised at how good he was. I was playing centre forward in the days when you had proper positions, and he was playing centre half. I didn't get many kicks that day, that's for sure. What always struck me about him was his confidence more than anything. He had very good ability on the ball; I think he could have played in any position he chose. He chose centre half and yet he had so much ability in both feet.

"I went to Millwall from Orient where the manager was Alec Stock and he knew how to handle players. They had a good team spirit there. That wasn't the case at Millwall; we had a bad manager in Charlie Hewitt, and he was a bit of a tyrant. He didn't treat players right, he seemed at times to be from a different world. There were several who came after him – Jimmy Seed was one – in the same mould. Being a rather sensitive person I suffered a little bit from this. I was surprised the directors put up with Hewitt."

The Den proved a difficult place for away teams that season, only three winning. Millwall, however, were never really in with a chance of promotion as only the top team in Third Division South were promoted, joining their counterparts from the northern section in the Second Division the following season. Such a system had proved especially harsh on Plymouth Argyle when it was first set up, as from 1921 they finished second on six consecutive seasons. Not until they actually won the league in 1929–30 did they go up.

Hurley had started the season in fine form, being "far too good for Brighton leader Whitfield" in an opening day 2-0 victory and playing particularly well in a dull single-goal victory against Leyton Orient. He also saved a point by heading off the line a last-minute Walsall effort in a 1-1 draw.

However, John Atyeo again showed Hurley a clean pair of heels by knocking two past Finlayson in the Millwall goal as Bristol City won 5-1 on their way to becoming champions of the division. Hurley, now eighteen, also had a hard time against ex-Millwall man George Stobbart on Christmas Day 1954 when Brentford won 3-1 at Griffin Park with Stobbart grabbing two.

Hurley's worth was shown towards the end of the season when he was forced to miss the match at Vicarage Road because he could not get leave from his two-year period of National Service in the Army, which he started in February 1955. The deputising Gerry Bowler had a poor game which saw Watford's centre forward Maurice Cook score four in a 5-3 win.

Of course, south London in 1955 was well known for trouble with numerous reports of fights between various gangs labelled 'the Teddy Boys' who first caught the public's attention when a youth was murdered on Clapham Common in 1953.

Some of the racial tensions that were later to arise were just starting to come to the surface and there was even a 'NEGRO IMMIGRANTS: SOUTH LONDON PLAN'. This proposed to establish a chain of port transit camps to process black arrivals from the West Indies coming to fill the large number of job vacancies.

Nationally among Hurley's teenage generation, the launch of 'Rock Around the Clock' by Bill Haley, following its appearance under the opening credits of the film *Blackboard Jungle* in 1955, proved a sensation. The record became the first rock and roll recording to hit the top of the American record charts, a feat repeated around the world, including Britain, where it was greeted with wild enthusiasm among the young and with horror by the old.

Chapter Three

Representative honours but a career-threatening injury

The 1955–56 season was to be the worst ever for Millwall and Charlie Hurley, starting with the first forty-five minutes of the season at Vicarage Road, Watford racing into a 3-0 lead and ultimately winning 4-2. It meant there were only just over 8,000 at the Den for the first Lions home match, a 2-0 win against Exeter City.

Desperately short of cash, Millwall wanted to use their floodlights for the Brentford game on Monday September 5th but the Football League management committee, as it did with other games at the time, refused permission. The League had become concerned that if they sanctioned floodlights they would be unable to prevent the successful clubs from participating in the new European Cup, matches being played during the week late at night under floodlights.

The seeds of such a competition had been sown after Wolves played a series of highly successful friendly games under floodlights from 1953. Following their defeat of the Hungarian side Honved, the Wolves manager Stan Cullis had proclaimed them as "champions of the World". Gabriel Hanot, the editor of *L'Equipe*, who had long campaigned for a European-wide tournament under floodlights, challenged Wolves and by implication every side across Europe by saying "before we declare Wolverhampton are invincible, let them go to Moscow and Budapest, AC Milan and Real Madrid."

In 1955–56 the new tournament was launched, but for League champions only. The English holders, Chelsea, were persuaded by the Football League not to take part.

The 'genie' was released from the lamp as clubs recognised the financial benefits that could accrue from the use of floodlights and pressure to change the rules became so intense that the League management committee were forced later in the season to drop their restrictions. The first league game to be played under lights took place on February 22nd 1956 at Fratton Park between Portsmouth and Newcastle United, thus starting midweek football at night.

While it was reported that Millwall were on the lookout for new players, a large overdraft meant they had little money with which to buy them. In late September and October the London side had a disastrous run, losing six games in a row, including a 6-2 hammering at Ipswich.

Hurley's form, however, was so good during this period that he was picked as part of the London XI side that became the first English team to play in a European competition, the Inter-City Fairs Cup. In Scotland, Hibernian, by entering the European Cup, became the first British club side to play in Europe.

The London XI game took place at Wembley against Frankfurt on Wednesday October 26th 1955 when the floodlights at the stadium were also employed for a match for the first time.

The line-up gives some idea of just how good Hurley already was at just nineteen:

Ted Ditchburn [Tottenham], Peter Sillett [Chelsea], Stan Willemse [Chelsea], Danny Blanchflower [Tottenham], Charlie Hurley [Millwall], Cyril Hammond [Charlton], Vic Groves [Orient], Bobby Robson [Fulham], Bedford Jezzard [Fulham], Roy Bentley [Chelsea], Charlie Mitten [Fulham].

Hurley and Vic Groves, both from Division Three South clubs, were the only players selected from outside the top flight.

Hurley's teammate John Shepherd recalls: "It was no surprise that Charlie got selected to play at Wembley as he was a great player. He was very good in the air but he was also good with his feet. He'd get the ball down and look up and play it; in those days you didn't see many defenders do that.

"Also nothing got by him. He'd knock it down off his chest. You could see he was going to be a special player. I played against John Charles when I was in the forces; Charlie was on a par with him in my view. He was a class act, but he was no stuck-up git and off the pitch he's a nice bloke," says a man who made 170 League and Cup appearances for Millwall, scoring an impressive 82 goals.

At Wembley, London recovered from going two-nil down before half-time to win the match 3-2. Hurley had an impressive match with Roy Peskett, writing below a massive 'HURLEY HOLDS GERMANS' headline in the *Daily Mail*, proclaiming that "cool, elegant, at times almost classical in his action, Hurley I think is going to figure among the great ones of soccer within a few years."

Charlie Hurley remembers: "The fact that it was reported I had a good game at Wembley was great. I saw being picked for the London XI as my first honour in professional football. I'd gone from playing for Rainham Youth Club to running out at Wembley in less than two years. It was mind-boggling and I was a nervous wreck before the game. I believe that Alan Brown was at that match and I think my performance must have planted a little seed in his mind that led to him later signing me for Sunderland.

"I played alongside Danny Blanchflower, a quiet man. He had tremendous vision. It was said of him that he rarely tackled and he was frail, but he was the best one-touch player I ever saw and I learnt a lot from playing next to him."

Despite this performance at Wembley, the *South London Press* reported, in what turned out to be a remarkably astute piece, that for Millwall at least "too many games in a week, now that he is in the services, have taken the edge from Hurley's game."

Hurley was being granted permission by the Army to play for his club on a Saturday but was due to miss the match on November 26th at home to Queens Park Rangers after he was selected to represent his country for the first time in a match at Dublin's Dalymount Park on Sunday November 27th against Spain.

This would have meant Hurley making just his second trip to Ireland since his move to London in 1937. Disaster was to strike, however. "I was overjoyed, I was only nineteen years of age, and it was a marvellous honour. The catering corps had a good team. Major 'Speedie' Evans suggested that I drop out of the match for them on the 23rd.

"He really wanted me to play against Spain, as he knew it was great for the Army Catering Corps that I did. But I said it would give me a nice little workout before the game.

"I did my cruciate knee ligaments. I knew it was serious from the start; I was devastated at missing the match. They sent me to hospital in Aldershot where I had treatment and then home to recover but there was no playing football. I stayed at home a lot longer than I should have because I couldn't stand the catering corps."

Hurley did not just miss the Spain game or matches for Millwall. The injury meant he was absent as the London XI side fought its way through to the Inter-City Fairs Cup final against Barcelona. They lost 8-2 on aggregate. Groves, who played in both matches in the final, had joined Arsenal by then.

On New Year's Day 1956, the Millwall manager Charlie Hewitt was sacked controversially and replaced by Ron Gray. Hewitt had managed Millwall in two spells, from 1936 to 1940 and from 1948 to 1956, clocking up 509 games in charge of which 220 were won, 120 drawn and 169 lost. On January 17th the *South London Press* reported that "last week a writ was issued against Millwall FC on behalf of Mr Hewitt who had a contract with several years to run." Despite hammering Gillingham 5-0 on January 14th the paper reckoned the Londoners' revival could depend on the recovery of two star invalids, Charlie Hurley and Dennis Pacey.

There was, therefore, good news when Hurley was declared fit to play for the Army in a friendly at Crystal Palace. The home side put up an impressive display against an Army side which included players with First and Second Division experience and it was reported that "Charlie Hurley and 'keeper Hodgkinson of Sheffield United had a hard evening against the bustling Palace forwards." The Army won 2-1.

Hurley was able to turn out for Millwall two weeks later at Gay Meadow where the away side raced into the lead before eventually losing 3-1 to Shrewsbury but he was taken off on a stretcher early in the game, returning later to limp out the rest of the match on the wing – no substitutes in those days. This was to be his seventeenth and final appearance of the season as a knee operation took him out of action.

"Millwall were great, they really looked after me but it was bloody hard work getting fit enough to play again. I did my cruciate ligaments; nowadays they can treat it, but not then. It was one hell of a long haul. I was sent to a rehabilitation centre for six weeks where I put in twelve to eighteen hours' work a day. It was to music. It was my last chance. I heard rumours that I was finished. I had to ignore them; you have to self-heal and that's both physically and mentally. Millwall stood by me during the hardest weeks of my football life. They were brilliant.

"I am an optimist, but I did fear the worst. Bill Voisey was also great. Funnily enough he had the title of physio by then. He, Charlie Hewitt and Ron Gray encouraged me to get better.

"From then on, however, I always played with a handicap. I would have been a slightly better player if I'd had two perfect knees. I had to be a bit careful at all times, especially when taking on a slide tackle. For one and a half legs I didn't do too bad. The physiotherapist at Sunderland, Johnny Watters. kept my left knee going. It used to go up like a balloon after matches."

Since retiring Hurley has been forced to have operations to replace both his knee and hip.

Already dangerously near the foot of the table, Millwall could ill afford the loss of a player just starting to find his feet in league football and they went on to finish twenty-second, just two places off the bottom. This was just enough to ensure the club did not have to apply for re-election to the football league for the first time.

South London Press – May 4th 1956
LIONS RETAIN 20 BUT MAY BE SELLING MORE

"And what of Charlie Hurley? If the cash box is as empty as Millwall records, it seems almost a certainty that Charlie will be sold in the summer."

Up at Roker Park in the First Division, Sunderland had faded to finish ninth. After a good start they were top of the league when they went to Luton Town on November 19th, and had played a very well-attended high-profile friendly match against Moscow Dynamo in midweek under floodlights, losing 1-0.

However, an embarrassing ninety minutes at Kenilworth Road saw them crushed 8-2. Sunderland conceded a whopping 95 league goals that season. These included nine over Christmas against Newcastle; a 6-1 defeat that remains the worst ever home result in Sunderland's history, and 3-1 away.

Considering the Christmas results it was therefore something of a surprise when Sunderland went back to St James' Park in the sixth round of the FA Cup and won 2-0, both scored by Billy Holden. It is doubtful whether Newcastle fans would have agreed with the "Results sound better by REDIFFUSION" adverts for new televisions within the programme for the day. By the end of 1956 around one third of people in Britain owned a television set. In comparison only one household in twenty had the benefits of central heating.

Once again in 1956, however, the semi-final brought heartache as Sunderland were well beaten 3-0 by Birmingham City at Hillsborough.

A still injured Charlie Hurley failed to start the following season, 1956–57, for Millwall and there was then a shock when the London *Evening Standard* reported that "Millwall would try a 'John Charles' move'" whereby the Irishman would copy the Welsh centre half by moving to centre forward. This was at Torquay where, after going a goal down, Hurley scored his first league goal on seventeen minutes – "banging home the ball from a pass from Summers". Little good did it do. Millwall were hammered 7-2. The experiment was continued in the following game at home to Aldershot although again Hurley's second league goal was not worth celebrating. All it did was reduce the deficit from 5-0 to 5-1 in the final minute of the match.

Hurley was back at centre half for the next game where he found himself playing in front of debutant William [Bill] Lloyd in goal. Finlayson had left for a fee of £3,000 to go on to great things at Wolves, having played 247 League and Cup games for Millwall. After a promising start his replacement AP Brewer had shipped in nineteen goals during the four previous games and so Lloyd, twenty-three years old and signed from Bromley in the Southern League, found himself promoted.

According to Bill Lloyd, the move was not universally popular among some of the older players who were friends of the replaced man. "I didn't go there to be the first team 'keeper, I felt I would be in the reserves. So it was a surprise for me to get into the first team as Brewer was the 'keeper then. I had upset a player during a training game where there were no 'keepers. I was eager and was tackling everybody. Somebody took a punch at me.

"The first few games of the season had gone poorly. They'd just lost 5-1 and that's how I came into the team. Results seemed to pick up when I got into the side. It wasn't just because of me; the team just seemed to rally. But I never found Millwall a happy place," says Lloyd, who later turned down a chance to move to Coventry City, preferring to play semi-professionally for Canterbury while working during the day.

He was to appear behind Hurley for most of the Irishman's remaining Millwall games. On his debut things were going well for Lloyd before local rivals Crystal Palace pulled two goals back to pinch a point in a 2-2 draw.

Lloyd speaks highly of Hurley, stating that "he was a good centre half. He could soar up into the air and he just seemed to hang there before he headed the ball. He was also a character and people seemed to like him. I must say we never really got to know each other and when I met him for the reunion at Millwall in 2007 it was a great time to say hello and I think I spoke more to him that day than during my playing time at the club."

In September 1956 Hurley was still not fully fit and was forced to stop playing until he finally returned to a team that had just recorded a famous victory by beating Newcastle United in the FA Cup. The Magpies had arrived at the Den with a magnificent FA Cup record in the 1950s; they had won the competition in 1951, 1952 and 1955 and were one of the favourites to win it again. In front of Millwall's biggest post-war crowd of 45,646, hundreds of whom had climbed up the floodlights to get a better view, two goals from Anslow were enough to send the north-east team home defeated 2-1. The full-back had been pushed up front when Torquay went to The Den and had snatched three goals when, in a complete reversal of the earlier Plainmoor match, Millwall triumphed 7-2. Anslow was to knock in five FA Cup goals in six matches, just two less than

John Shepherd, and at the end of the season he had sixteen goals in all. Nevertheless he returned to full back "because I thought I had more to offer there than up front".

According to Hurley: "Jimmy Scoular was playing for Newcastle. He was no oil painting even in those days, no teeth and balding, but he was some player. He frightened me even sitting on the side.

"It was a very muddy pitch. You've got to remember there weren't screw-in studs in those days, there were nails and studs were banged in. So if you lost your studs you were sliding all over the place. It was pretty archaic. The ball was absorbent and had a lace in it. I am lucky to have a forehead at all, the times I headed those great big leather balls. You finished up dizzy at times. During my career I went down a few times, the ball was so horrendously heavy. At Millwall the little lad on the wing couldn't reach the box from corners. We had to get one of the heavies to take the corners."

The large crowd for the FA Cup tie with Newcastle was in direct contrast to the League attendances at the Den during the 1956–57 season. The Boxing Day fixture with Swindon Town, for example, attracted only 3,209 through the gates. Poor weather had forced the postponement of the previous day's fixture at Swindon and although Millwall's ground was found to be playable the surrounding areas were almost impassable and few spectators could or even tried to get to a match that should clearly have been called off.

This was to be the last season in which there was a full Football League programme played on Christmas Day, thus ending a tradition where local sides played derby matches against each other over two days. Pressure to stop matches on December 25th had come from players and employees who wanted to spend the day with their families. The last Christmas Day fixture in England took place between Blackpool and Blackburn Rovers in 1965, which was won 4-2 by the home side.

Millwall, with Hurley in the side, beat Gillingham 2-1 the week before the fifth round FA Cup game at The Den against the previous season's losing finalists Birmingham City. The *South London Press* reported that "after a long lay-off through injury Hurley looked almost back to international form."

There then followed one of the strangest episodes in Hurley's career, which resulted in him missing the cup-tie. Lance Corporal Hurley, no. 23113593, was presented with a typewritten slip at 6.00am, twenty-four hours before he was to be demobbed at the end of his two years' stint of National Service. Hurley had gone to watch a friend, Terry Pickett, in a match that decided that season's Aldershot and District Reserve Section Championship and afterwards he and Pickett had been having a private conversation about the worth, or not, of the referee, who, unknown to both, overheard their remarks and decided to report them to their superiors.

One month later, a day before his demob, the slip informed Hurley that he was "Confined to Barracks" for fourteen days. After what at the time constituted a media frenzy, the Army agreed to release him to play. Millwall, however, had other ideas and had decided to keep faith with the team that had done so well against Newcastle, with chairman Mickey Purser stating after the game: "Charlie had not had a lot of training and had played only two or three games."

This is a similar view to that of Stan Anslow, who when interviewed fifty years later, stated "the club were right to play the same team. We were on top of the world after the Newcastle game and felt confident we could do it again. Unfortunately I was injured early in the game against Birmingham, so we played them with only ten men."

Millwall were heavily beaten by Birmingham City, a late consolation goal reducing the four-goal arrears, and the following weekend's gate for the Coventry City home match was down by 37,000 to just 5,000. At least they had the pleasure of seeing their favourites recover from a two-goal deficit to win 3-2. Although out of the cup, the gate receipts gave Millwall a financial lifeline.

When Hurley later learned that Purser had also said that the Lions might have to let him go to raise urgently needed funds he was quoted as saying: "The chairman hasn't mentioned it to me, but if he does then I shall tell him I am willing to go."

Hurley meanwhile feels that "National Service was a waste of time. I tried to get out of it at the start. When they did my medical they said I had a big heart and I said that was what people told me! I said I couldn't join up because what would happen if there was a war; I'd be no good as I could die of shock if I had to go to the front! It did me no good. I never went anywhere near any front as I was stuck in the catering corps. And I couldn't cook!"

Despite the Coventry result, Millwall's season fell away after the cup defeat, the side slumping down the table and winning only three of the remaining thirteen matches, losing six.

One of the drawn games was at Brentford – 1-1 – in which Hurley made a heroic attempt to prevent the Bees' goal by diving to try and head the ball away from the foot of Jim Towers. Finding his feet slowly after his injury, Charlie Hurley had one of his finest matches for Millwall on Easter Saturday when promotion candidates and division leaders Colchester were well beaten 3-1. His performance must have impressed the two Eire selectors who'd been sent along to see if he was, at last, ready to make his international debut. Match reports afterwards concentrated on how attack after attack had been broken up by the young Irishman.

Millwall finished seventeenth in Division Three South that season with Hurley making twenty-five league appearances, during which he'd scored his first two league goals. Much more importantly, however, Charlie Hurley's hard rehabilitation work and Millwall's support meant that he had saved his career.

For Sunderland the 1956–57 season had proven to be a disaster. It started with a 6-2 hammering on the first day of the season at Kenilworth Road to Luton Town where entrance cost 2 shillings [10p] to stand on the terraces (half-price for children, although in those days they would all have been boys) and five shillings and sixpence [28p] with no concessions to sit in the main stand. This was at a time when £10 was regarded as a good wage.

The highlight of the season was the 8-1 defeat of Charlton Athletic. At the end, which came a few short weeks after a two-week national strike by shipyard workers that brought work to a halt on the River Wear, everyone associated with the club was probably just happy not to be relegated. The twentieth-placed finish only just kept intact the record of Sunderland never having played outside the top flight.

In fact it was something of a miracle that Sunderland managed to stay out of the bottom two and avoid relegation, such were events off the field throughout the second half of the season.

In 1956 Trevor Ford's autobiography had lifted the lid on the under-the-counter payment system some clubs were operating to attract and then keep their best players. Sunderland had been named as one of the guilty parties.

Then in January 1957, a letter, from someone signing themselves 'Mr Smith' who has never been identified, was sent to the offices of the Football League at Lytham St Annes. It clearly came from someone with an intimate knowledge of affairs at Roker Park. Sunderland, it was suggested, were making under-the-counter illegal payments, thus breaking League rules on signing-on fees and maximum wages.

At first, when the Football Association and League examined the club's books they could find nothing of substance. But when Alan Hardaker, the League secretary, found a receipt for £3,000 for straw, to be used to cover the pitch in the winter and ensure games went ahead, he rang his brother. Ernest Hardaker was chairman of Hull Rugby League club and he suggested that at that price the straw would have lasted twenty-five years!

Later it was uncovered that they had also paid a lot more for tarmac. The club were paying for the two items up front, not using all of them, receiving credit notes, cashing them and using that to make illegal payments. The full amount came to £5,427 and when it was divided by the number of players who had benefited it was clear none of them had got rich. But the rules had been broken.

After two enquiry meetings at York and Sheffield, it was obvious that Sunderland were going to be punished. On April 10th *sine die* bans were imposed on four directors – chairman Bill Ditchburn and Stanley Ritson, Laurie Evans and Bill Martin. Ritson was a magistrate. The club was also fined £5,000, a considerable amount in those days.

Sunderland were probably fortunate that the Football League did not punish them with relegation to Division Two, or dock them a number of points, which would have produced the same effect. At the same time they were unlucky enough to get caught.

It is known now that most, if not all, major clubs were indulging in similar practices. Sunderland's past reputation as "The Bank of England" club did not help during the whole affair.

Meanwhile five players from the club were informed that they were to appear at another joint FA–Football League commission meeting in Manchester on April 25th. It could have done nothing to inspire a team struggling to hang on to a place in the top league.

On the day, Ray Daniel, Billy Elliott, Willie Fraser, Johnny Hannigan and Ken Chisholm refused to incriminate themselves, remaining silent after advice from the Players' Union, in the form of Jimmy Hill and Cliff Lloyd. They were also suspended *sine die*, an incredible decision and one that was found by a clerk at the Manchester solicitors of George Davies and Co to be both against the rules of natural justice and the rules of both the FA and Football League.

It transpired that those involved in the enquiry did not possess the powers to suspend players; only member clubs could do that. The enquiry had also been set up to enquire into events, not to impose sentences. Those involved had overstepped the mark.

The Players Union, ably led by Hill and Lloyd, were to fight an impressive campaign that was the forerunner to the smashing of the maximum wage in the early 1960s. The players' bans were overturned, although they were forced to admit to obtaining illegal payments.

As such they were allowed to re-register as players and the directors too, after a time, became eligible to take up their previous positions. The whole affair, however, had a demoralising effect on manager Bill Murray, who quit after eighteen years in charge.

While all this was going on Hurley had made his international debut for the Republic of Ireland. This took place on Saturday May 19th in a World Cup qualifier at Dalymount Park in Dublin against the hated foes from across the water, England.

Despite a flurry of press speculation that he might be picked, the first the twenty-year-old knew of his selection for the match in Dublin came when he read a brief article in the *Daily Mirror* which stated: "Millwall's Charlie Hurley will be Eire's centre half in Sunday's World Cup game against England in Dublin."

No one from the Irish FA contacted him or Millwall in advance of the announcement.

This was expected to be something of a stroll in the park for the away team, who eleven days earlier had easily beaten an Irish team playing its first game at Wembley. The Irish had been cut apart by a rampant England side led by Duncan Edwards and Johnny Haynes with Stanley Matthews and Tom Finney out wide. Five goals to one – a hat-trick from Manchester United's Tommy Taylor, against whom Hurley would be in direct opposition at Dalymount Park, and two from John Atyeo, of Bristol City, against a single reply from Dermot Curtis.

Ireland's selectors – this was in the day when the team was picked by a group rather than a single manager – had thrown caution to the wind and made wholesale changes in defence. Even the captain at Wembley, Peter Farrell, the scorer of one of the memorable goals back in 1949 when Eire had beaten England 2-0 at Goodison Park, was dropped. Tommy Godwin, another of the Irish heroes eight years earlier, took over from Alan Kelly in goal. Hurley replaced Gerry Mackey.

The teams were:

Ireland – Tommy Godwin [Bournemouth], Seamus Dunne [Luton Town], Noel Cantwell [West Ham] capt, Ronnie Nolan [Shamrock Rovers], Charlie Hurley [Millwall], Pat Saward [Aston Villa], Alf Ringstead [Sheffield United], Liam Whelan [Manchester United], Dermot Curtis [Bristol City], Arthur Fitzsimmons [Middlesbrough], Joe Haverty [Arsenal].

England – Alan Hodgkinson [Sheffield United], Jeff Hall [Birmingham City], Roger Byrne [Manchester United], Ronnie Clayton [Blackburn Rovers], Billy Wright [Wolverhampton Wanderers] capt, Duncan Edwards [Manchester United], Tom Finney [Preston North End], John Atyeo [Bristol City], Tommy Taylor [Manchester United], Johnny Haynes [Fulham], David Pegg [Manchester United].

The Republic's selectors were criticised for making a young inexperienced player the kingpin of their defensive system and there was talk of an even bigger rout. Millwall manager Ron Gray, however, was confident Hurley would do well, being quoted in the *Daily Express* as saying, "Charlie is just the boy for Tommy Taylor – he's so good in the air. He can hover like a helicopter."

Playing alongside him was another Cork-born man, captain Noel Cantwell, then of West Ham, who later moved to Manchester United and managed Coventry City and Peterborough. Unlike Hurley, who had moved to England while still in his nappies, Cantwell had waited till turning eighteen before taking a boat across the Irish Sea in the hope of securing a professional contract.

Football had not been played at Cantwell's school, being regarded as "foreign", which largely meant English. Funnily enough, however, cricket was played! The Gaelic Athletic Association prohibited anyone from playing or watching the game of football if they also wanted to play hurling or Gaelic football. Many people ignored such instructions but others took them very seriously.

Outside of school, Cantwell was always kicking a ball around and he ended up playing for a youth club side called Western Rovers in a minor league. The ground on which he was playing cricket one day was on the left-hand side of the road and Cork Athletics' ground was on the right.

"I was batting in the nets on the cricket ground one evening when someone rushed over from the football ground and said 'the Athletic are a player short. You'll have to play'. I ran across the road, got changed, signed the forms and found myself playing at left half for Athletic in a League of Ireland fixture against Sligo Rovers. We won 2-1. It transpired later that my brother Frank, who played left-back for Athletic, had suggested I was a good player."

His brother was right. When Noel moved to Birmingham he found himself transferring quickly to London after being signed by West Ham.

By far the largest crowd ever to assemble at Dalymount Park – 47,600 – saw the Republic of Ireland start in thrilling fashion when, following a flowing move involving Arthur Fitzsimmons, Liam Whelan and Joe Haverty, Alf Ringstead of Sheffield United was able to knock the ball into the empty net from a few yards out.

England, whose only change from the first game was David Pegg, later to die in the Munich air tragedy, for Stanley Matthews, were piqued and Godwin was forced to make brave diving saves at the feet of Atyeo and Taylor. It was not all one-way traffic. Hurley's ex-Army teammate Alan Hodgkinson in the England goal had to be alert to prevent Ireland scoring the crucial second goal and he was grateful to the covering Billy Wright for clearing Haverty's shot off the line.

Ireland hung on to their lead. Those present knew that if they won, a victory in the next game in Denmark would mean that England and Ireland would be forced to play a third time. The winner would take their place in Sweden at the following summer's World Cup tournament.

Preston North End's brilliant winger Tom Finney had other ideas – perhaps he did not fancy another game against Ireland. Dashing down the wing in the final minute, he beat Pat Saward and Cantwell before floating a superb cross that cleared both Taylor and his marker Hurley. With every eye in the ground turning to see if there was anybody behind those two, John Atyeo ran in unopposed to head a vital equaliser.

"I remember it well. In the ninety-first minute. John Atyeo was behind me. I'm watching Tommy, the header went bump, bump, bump, just trickled into the net. After the match the referee revealed that he had added one and three-quarter minutes for stoppages," says Hurley.

Hardly a sound could be heard in the ground, save, of course, the England players who realised that they had qualified for the World Cup. Ireland had not made it, unlike Northern Ireland who joined Wales, Scotland and England in Sweden.

The referee's actions were very unusual for the time, most games ending within seconds of the ninety minutes. The *Daily Mirror* headline summed it up with "Referee's watch gives England a passport to World Cup Finals – SAVED IN EXTRA TIME SENSATION as the luck of the Irish was right out."

After the match Hurley's performance was lavishly praised, with the *Daily Mirror*'s report stating "...it was the Irish who produced a new great world-class footballer in centre half Charlie Hurley. Half the clubs in the First Division will soon be knocking on Millwall's door offering £25,000 for him."

Hurley recalls: "People say that Eire only had a good team under Jackie Charlton. I am not so sure; we had a very good team. For that match Dalymount Park was packed; they were sitting on the track round the pitch. I did OK, it was very early days for me – my very first cap. But it wasn't good enough for the press. How did they find this big young Irishman with a Cockney voice the star of the show? It set me up for forty caps. If it had been now I'd have had eighty as I played for over twelve years.

"The match was an insight for me into the best. Tommy Taylor played for Manchester United. Tom Finney? I'd say Tom Finney was one of the greatest players ever; he was just slightly before my day. I thought after the match, 'Well it's not beyond you, son'. As my father said, 'Always aim for the stars and if you drop down to the moon then you're not doing too badly'; a great philosophy for a guy who liked his pint.

"The game proved something for me. I always thought I could be good enough but there was nothing like being tested to the full by England! My father went over by boat. He would have rowed over if he'd had to. He told me that for two weeks he never had to do any work at Fords. All his mates did his work; all they wanted to do was to hear about what Charlie had done against England, and from my dad's angle it was fantastic. I let him have the cap. He took it, and he really did believe at the end of that fortnight that he'd played and not me!"

A little more than two months later, up in the north-east of England, Alan Brown became the first ever County Durham-born Sunderland manager. Writing in the *Sunderland Echo*, Argus reported that "Mr Brown has built up a powerful side at Burnley, and in the process has won a wide reputation as a disciplinarian and a forceful personality. The fact that he has founded Burnley's recent wave of success upon young locally developed players will be particularly attractive for the Sunderland board, since it is their avowed attention to concentrate more intensely than ever upon young players produced in the prolific Durham County 'nursing areas'."

Sunderland directors had seen how Matt Busby and Jimmy Murphy had revived Manchester United's fortunes by developing their own talent and were hoping to emulate their northern rivals.

Three years after he left Burnley, the Lancashire team Brown helped to develop went on to win the First Division and in the following season were unfortunate enough to compete against a brilliant double-winning Spurs team, finishing second and losing to Spurs in the FA Cup final. Of course, Burnley's days were already numbered by 1961 because with the abolition of the maximum wage they could not possibly hope to hold on to their star players. With much smaller gates than their rivals like Manchester United, Liverpool, Everton and Chelsea their income was considerably less. Higher wages drew players elsewhere.

The arrival of the new manager, joined by George Curtis as trainer/coach, did not bring immediate rewards, Sunderland kicking off the 1957–58 season by losing 1-0 to Arsenal in front of a Roker Park crowd of 56,493.

Days later Sunderland received the news that one of their greatest ever players, Len Shackleton was following specialist advice and retiring after nine and a half years of Roker Park wizardry that had baffled opponents and even some of his own teammates at times. Shackleton had made nearly 350 appearances for Sunderland, scoring 101 goals.

Hurley speaks highly of Len Shackleton, remembering seeing him on the television playing at Highbury. "He used to turn them inside out. Apparently in his early days he was turned down by Arsenal and he came back to haunt them. I saw his boots, big, heavy awkward-looking things, but he could do anything with the ball. When I went to Roker fans used to say 'give me ten minutes of Shack and that will be enough' so for me now to be regarded as one of Sunderland's great players, it is a great honour. He was a very skilful player, Shack."

Chapter Four

Seven and six, was he worth it? Hurley leaves London for Sunderland

For Millwall and Charlie Hurley the 1957–58 season in Division Three South started at home to Southampton. The *South London Press* reported that "Hurley was on the form that earned him his Eire cap – and that is certainly going to earn him a lot more. He completely dominated the centre of the field and the reports the talent scouts sent out must have set many a manager itching to get his hands on the cheque book."

The 2-1 defeat failed to knock Millwall, who followed up by recording four straight victories, the last 2-1 against Port Vale after which the *South London Press* match report stated: "Hurley so dominated the middle that Millwall were able to keep up a non-stop attack in a thrilling game."

In the sixth game, against Exeter City, Hurley and Anslow collided, resulting in a broken leg for the right back. Ten-man Millwall lost 2-0 and Anslow did not play again that season. Two weeks later Charlie Hurley left The Den.

Described by Hurley as the hardest full back he ever played alongside, Anslow has the following to say about the ex-Millwall centre half and football in general in the 1950s.

"Charlie Hurley's strengths were his ability to read the game and control the defence. His biggest weakness was his self-belief; at times he needed to be reassured that he was doing everything that was asked of him. He did play exceptionally well in some games. When the Millwall crowd take to you then you are on a winner. They certainly took to Charlie.

"In those days players had to be tough because of the conditions we played in. Playing in the mud with leather boots and a leather ball was not a doddle. Some of us lads at Millwall socialised after training, which gave us a close feeling as a team. It was the best time of my life and I wouldn't have changed a thing."

Hurley himself was in the wars at Home Park, injuring a toe as Plymouth Argyle triumphed 1-0, from where the *South London Press* reporter noted the home side's marked advantage in midfield but felt this could "not detract from the good work of Hurley."

The final game of Hurley's Millwall career took place in the derby at Loftus Road, won by Queens Park Rangers with three second-half goals against a flu-hit Lions. It was reported by the *South London Press* that "Charlie Hurley often came to the rescue and several times wandered up field to get his now disjointed attack going."

Until 1925 and a change in the offside law, centre halves had been attacking players. But then Herbert Chapman converted Herbie Roberts into a defensive player and the "stopper" centre half was born. That was the way it stayed until Stan Cullis, the Wolves and England centre half, who became manager of the Molineux side in 1949, leading to the Black Country club's finest period, decided the pivot of his team should be the man who started his own team's attacks as well as stopping the other team's. Cullis was convinced that an attractive team needed a good footballer at centre half. But it was rare for a centre half to wander over the halfway line.

Sunderland's season had started disastrously and when they lost 5-0 in the third match at Wolves, Argus reported that "the score would have been even greater but for wild shooting by the home team in the first half." A slight recovery was capped by the winning of the first Tyne–Wear derby of the season, a 2-0 Roker Park victory watched by only 45,718 on September 21st with Don Revie and left winger Colin Grainger scoring the goals. Grainger had been signed for £17,000 the previous season from Sheffield United, where he had won seven England caps. He went on to make 120 league appearances for Sunderland, scoring 14 times.

Despite the Newcastle victory, new manager Alan Brown, concerned about the heavy defeat at Molineux, was looking to bolster his defence. He had earmarked the Millwall youngster as the player he wanted at centre half. The Sunderland manager and his vice-chairman, Syd Collings, on holiday in London, attended the match at Loftus Road where they were given permission to speak to Hurley the following morning.

Hurley, with more than one hundred League appearances, not to mention his international debut, was not that impressed and was quoted in the *Sunderland Evening Echo* on September 25th: "I do not intend to leave my home in London. I am playing for a first team and I am on first team money. I am quite satisfied and I have already told the club that if I must be transferred then it's got to be to another London club. Why should I move? I am happy at Millwall."

Hurley's references to first team money are interesting in today's context. Players at all clubs were restricted from earning more than the agreed "maximum wage", which in 1957 was £17 per week during the season and £14 in the close season. It was Sunderland's breaking of these restrictions by making illegal payments that had put them in trouble during the summer of 1957. By moving, Hurley would not see his wages increased. Living at home with his parents and three brothers and three sisters was comfortable enough.

The *Echo* reported that "several clubs are known to be interested in Hurley" and that "no move has yet been made by Chelsea, but popular belief in London is that the player will end up at Stamford Bridge". Chelsea had won their first league championship only two years previously.

Bob Pennington, writing in the *Sunday Express*, urged the Pensioners to not delay, with the banner headline "DRAKE MUST BUY £20,000 HURLEY" accompanying a half-page article in which he stated "This supremely talented young Chelsea team needs only a player of Hurley's undisputed class to mature into Britain's greatest Soccer machine within five years."

Hurley was in such demand that he was asked to play for the South against the North in an exhibition six-a-side match at the White City, where, ironically, he lined up against Don Revie and Len Shackleton of Sunderland.

Meanwhile Millwall chairman Micky Purser said: "We have had

a chat with the boy and now the matter rests with him. We don't want to stand in his way if he wished to go into a better class of soccer." Millwall, however, needed the money and were lining up Ray Brand as Hurley's replacement.

Hurley refused to yield to Brown's persuasion and when the manager took the train to Leeds United for a midweek match that Sunderland lost 2-1 there appeared no prospect of Hurley changing his mind. Nevertheless Brown travelled back to London after the game to resume his appeal to the Millwall centre half.

On Friday September 27th 1957 the *Sunderland Echo* reported, alongside a Ritz Cinema advert for *The Prince and the Showgirl* featuring Laurence Olivier and Marilyn Monroe, that after Brown put his case to the family and "Mrs Hurley finally gave her parental approval (Hurley) had promptly made up his mind and signed on the spot."

In a series of radio interviews for the BBC years later Hurley admitted that in 1957 he "had no idea where Sunderland was and that my first reaction was 'no way' to going there. I really didn't want to go but Alan Brown was a charmer. He hardly spoke to me. He spoke to my mother, lovely family, lovely house, my what lovely kids... in all fairness they weren't that lovely, we'd had a tough old upbringing and a tough old life. My dad was a tough old cookie. The Bomber [Hurley's nickname for Brown] was using his charm and he melted my mother. My dad just wanted me to become a famous footballer, so there were no problems with Dad and in the end I said OK."

One factor which had weighed against Hurley signing for Sunderland was revealed by Bob Pennington, who wrote afterwards that "the reason for Hurley's indecision about leaving home was "a close knitted family where affection goes much deeper than family" with Hurley stating: "I'm one of the breadwinners here. It's not easy you know. Dad was ill for three months. I was here at home to help out. Mum needs all the help she can get. She's been wonderful to all of us."

When Hurley signed the contract he got £10 as a signing-on fee. He gave this to his dad to go out and celebrate with his mates. "He came back with £6 change – you've got to remember that he took an awful lot of people out. It was 10d [4p] a pint then, 10d a pint! Good beer as well."

By moving to Sunderland, Hurley joined a long list of Irish people who had migrated to the north-east. As long ago as 1851 the census showed there were 18,501 Irish by birth resident in County Durham.

It was reported that Hurley was signed by Sunderland for a fee of £18,000 plus an agreement for the club to play Millwall in a friendly game at The Den, the gate receipts of which were expected to add another £3,000 to the struggling club's coffers.

Comparisons with today's transfer fees are difficult but at the time the record fee for a player was £35,000, so the equivalent fee today might be around £15 million, and that for a centre half not yet twenty-one!

The Millwall fans knew just how good he was, because in 2007, in the run-up to the Dockers' Day events at the New Den, a poll was organised by the Supporters Association and the Millwall fanzine *The Lion Roars* to pick the best player to ever play for Millwall – the largest number of votes went to Charlie Hurley.

Following the transfer, Hurley was given time off to prepare for Ireland's World Cup qualifier against Denmark in Copenhagen the next Wednesday and so he missed Sunderland's 3-0 defeat of Luton Town on the Saturday, a result that moved the Roker Park club up to seventeenth.

In front of a very angry Copenhagen crowd, Ireland won with goals from George Cummins, in the fifty-third minute, and Dermot Curtis nine minutes later. Writing later in the *Sunderland Sports Echo*, Hurley stated that "Older hands assure me I shall never play in a rougher international and that there were times when the angry crowd looked like taking complete control. The police kept them off the pitch with difficulty. About a thousand excited people waited for us after the match, challenging us to 'come out'. We left the ground by a back entrance."

What appears to have caused particular fury was Ireland's decision to employ an offside trap.

Hurley could not know it but the journey north was to be the start of the most amazing period of his life. Sunderland remained a shipbuilding port, although the signs of decline were already there and in order to compete against foreign competition SP Austin had merged with William Pickersgill in 1954 to become Austin and Pickersgill, and in 1958 the company was to take on Ken Douglas as managing director. He immediately carried out a large-scale modernisation scheme at the Southwick yard, turning it over to welding construction, as opposed to riveting. Ships were built in one hundred and twenty days rather than fifty or sixty weeks.

Coal, too, continued to provide a rich source of fuel for the British economy, with thousands of miners from Durham and Northumberland drawing the black rock from the ground, often from seams under the North Sea. The nearby Wearmouth Colliery, over which the Stadium of Light now stands, had just celebrated one hundred and fifty years since the first pit shaft had been sunk to find coal beneath magnesium limestone previously thought to be impregnable.

Coal, however, had been transported down the River Wear for a good many years before the colliery had even been thought of. In fact in the rolls of Whitby Abbey for 1396, William Rede of Sunderland is mentioned with others as "bringing coal in ships to that monastery, at the rate of 3 shillings and 4d per chaldron." [17p] [Fordyce; *History of Durham Vol 2* p508]

If Hurley had the time to take a trip round Sunderland before signing he could not have failed to pick up that this was a place where hard work, skill, honesty and loyalty were important and valued qualities among a largely working class community.

He would have been able to visit the monastery of Wearmouth, one of the oldest in Britain having been dedicated to St Peter by Benedict Biscop ['Bede'] in AD 674. This stood on the banks of the River Wear looking down on busy shipyards that are long gone, having been replaced by a university drawing students from all over the world.

Religious as some of the inhabitants of Sunderland and the surrounding County Durham towns and villages were, the passion generated in the churches and chapels never reached anything like that witnessed in Roker Park, the stadium built in 1898 and later developed into one of the most imposing grounds in Britain.

Sunderland AFC was founded in 1879. James Allan, a Scotsman who arrived on Wearside from Glasgow University to work at Hendon Board School, had become a member of Sunderland Rovers Rugby club, but the game did not excite him anything like as much as the game being played in his own country whereby with the exception of one player on each team, a goalkeeper, the rest of the players were expected to largely rely on their skill in controlling and kicking the round ball with their feet.

When Allan had introduced the game to his colleagues interest was, like thousands of places around the world ever since, immediately aroused. 'The Sunderland and District Teachers' Association Football Club' which was formed in October 1879 soon found a ground and began to organise matches with local teams.

Sheffield was the birthplace of organised football in England with the world's oldest club, Sheffield FC, being formed to give cricketers a way to keep fit in the winter in 1857. In 1863 the Football Association was founded; it merged with the Sheffield FA and organised football began to spread with the FA Cup starting in 1871–72. Before this organised football was confined to south Yorkshire and Nottinghamshire and Derbyshire. Notts County were formed in 1862 to be followed by Nottingham Forest three years later. Sheffield Wednesday came into being in 1867, the same year as Chesterfield. Soon towns all over northern and midlands England were forming football clubs – Bolton Wanderers being formed in 1874, Birmingham City, or Small Heath as they were first known, in 1875, and Newton Heath, later to become Manchester United in 1878.

The period from 1860 onwards was one of unprecedented economic growth; workers were enjoying an annual increase in real wages, giving them more money to spend not only on essentials but also on activities they enjoyed participating in and watching.

There was also a reduction of the working week from six days to five and a half. With Saturday afternoons off, the fledgling football clubs in areas with large and growing populations soon realised that they could charge an entry fee for spectators keen to see games in the company of friends. With the money, the clubs could, after they had covered their expenses, start to pay players, managers and a training staff even if it meant obtaining them from outside their own localities and by 1885, despite initial objections from the FA, professionalism was legalised within the game of football in England.

The start of the Football League in 1888 meant guaranteed fixtures for the leading clubs and, depending upon how many entered the ground, a guaranteed income. By the beginning of the twentieth century a highly complex network of about two hundred mutually dependent business organisations supported by thousands of smaller amateur clubs was already in place – much as it is today in the twenty-first century.

When the Football League began it was agreed that at the end of each season the bottom four clubs would be required to retire and stand for re-election against teams from outside the league who wished to become members. The first team to lose its place in this way was Stoke City, replaced by Sunderland at the end of the second ever season in 1890.

Sunderland went on to be crowned champions on three occasions in their first five seasons and earn the accolade of "Team of All Talents". Large crowds for the time flocked to the home matches, then being played at their Newcastle Road ground, which had seen its first game on April 3rd 1886, but which had a capacity of only 18,000.

Local businessmen, recognising a good opportunity to strengthen their workforce's loyalty and also smelling the chance to earn a few bob by increasing attendances, had taken the gamble by starting the construction of an imposing venue called Roker Park.

Lord Londonderry opened this on September 10th 1898 in front of a 30,000 crowd for a match against Liverpool. There was a compact grandstand with 3,000 seats, in front of which was a small paddock, a covered stand for standing only and two open ends, then known as North and South.

Roker Park was located in the Monkwearmouth district of Sunderland and stood less than a mile from the banks of the River Wear and the North Sea.

Over the next one hundred years, on foggy days, the sea mist would roll in to cover the ground and the surrounding area and in the winter freezing gale-force winds would be something with which all footballers would have to contend if they were to perform at their peak.

The major problem with the ground even when it first opened was that it was too small; the club was losing out on additional revenues and there were also several pitch invasions over the years due to overcrowding on the terraces.

In February 1912 Sunderland had a crowd of 43,383 – 13,383 or nearly thirty per cent over capacity. People watching from the roof of the nearby Roker coal depot were injured when it gave way, with twenty of them taken off to hospital for treatment.

Something had to be done; otherwise what had happened at Ibrox ten years earlier when twenty-five spectators watching the Scotland v England game died after the south-western terrace simply opened up and they fell down on to the steel columns and concrete below, might be replicated at Roker Park.

Although it has never been confirmed, and records no longer exist, the Sunderland directors are believed, according to Simon Inglis, whose knowledge of British football grounds is second to none, to have employed Archibald Leitch's company, then based in Liverpool, to tackle the problem. Leitch had been the Glasgow Rangers chief engineer at the time of the Ibrox disaster and had been forced to learn from his mistakes.

The new developments got underway in 1913 and the new Roker End [previously the North Stand] was built on a web of reinforced concrete pillars, such that "there never was terracing like it, nor ever will be again," according to Simon Inglis. This raised the capacity by 25,000 and cost £6,000.

In 1925 the Fulwell End [South Stand] was expanded. Four years later the new Main Stand was opened at a cost of £25,000 that was a typical no-frills Leitch design and incorporated 5,875 seats with standing for 14,000 below.

The capacity leapt so much that 75,118 turned up on Wednesday March 8th 1933 for a sixth round FA Cup replay that kicked off in the middle of a working day. They saw an unsuccessful attempt by Sunderland to overcome Derby County.

Two years later the Clock Stand, named, hardly surprisingly, because of the clock on the roof, was re-built to allow 15,500 to stand in two sections and in 1952 floodlights arrived to enable matches to kick off on dark evenings.

By the time Hurley arrived Sunderland had won six League titles, a proud record then only surpassed by Arsenal. And despite the lack of post-war success, crowds of more than 50,000 were still common at Roker Park.

Scottish international Paddy Crerand, a Manchester United legend, recalls: "Roker Park? Fantastic – it had a great atmosphere. There were certain grounds you liked to go to, because the crowd were on top of you and Roker Park was one of them, Spurs was another. Everybody knew that fans in the north-east including at Newcastle loved their football. Also back then it was more of a working class sport. If you're playing at Sunderland that support is fantastic; that helps players, especially the home ones."

Terrifying as such numbers could be for opposing players it was still likely to be nerve-wracking for a relatively inexperienced player such as Hurley. As that brilliant writer Arthur Appleton, in his 1950s book, *Hotbed of Soccer*, remarked about Sunderland supporters, "their forbearance is soon exhausted", which he attributed to an intense desire to see the team do well.

Emotions among the Roker crowd could run high, and many a Sunderland player, both before and after Hurley's time, could expect to incur the crowd's wrath if they failed to produce the goods. Clearly a fine start was essential.

Which is precisely what did not happen on October 5th 1957 at Bloomfield Road, Blackpool, when Charlie Hurley replaced George Aitken at centre half for his debut game. Not all Sunderland supporters were happy about his inclusion and during the 1957–58 season a number wrote to the *Sunderland Sports Echo* to confirm this. Before the game, Argus had written that he fancied Sunderland to get a point. Buoyed by the signing of Hurley and the league debut of seventeen-year-old Alan Spence from Houghton-le-Spring in County Durham, not to mention the chance of a decent night out on the beer, a large number of fans travelled to the match. Argus reported that "there was a strong contingent of North-East supporters in the crowd", which was well above average.

Bloomfield Road, which in the twenty-first century has a limit of less than 10,000, had a near capacity crowd of 33,172 on the day. They saw the Seasiders equal their best ever league victory as, inspired by Stanley Matthews, they tore apart Sunderland, scoring in the first minute. Blackpool's team also included England full back, and now BBC radio summariser Jimmy Armfield and ex-Manchester United forward Ernie Taylor, later to join Sunderland.

At half-time it was 4-0, with Hurley's centre forward opponent Ray Charnley scoring twice. And, despite left winger Bill Perry being injured and virtually a spectator and Charnley off the pitch from the sixtieth minute, the home side scored another two to make it 6-0.

Then, with a minute to go, "Hurley in attempting to clear turned the ball against the underside of the bar and over the line" reported Argus, who commented that Hurley's introduction to the defence had "far from bringing about an improvement" thrown it into confusion.

Although it was a few weeks before most people, even in the USSR, knew about it, the day before Hurley's debut at Blackpool on October 4th 1957 the Soviet Union had successfully launched Sputnik I, the world's first artificial satellite. This hurtled into space and orbited the earth in little more than ninety minutes. Hurley, who celebrated his 21st birthday that day, would probably have found himself less confused had he been in space rather than in the middle of Sunderland's defence.

The two teams lined up that day as follows:

Blackpool – Farm, Armfield, Garrett, J Kelly, Gratrix, H Kelly, Matthews, Taylor, Charnley, Durie, Perry.

Sunderland – Fraser, Hedley, McDonald, Anderson, Hurley, Elliott, Hannigan, Revie, Spence, O'Neill, Grainger.

Although Spence was to play only four more times for Sunderland, he went on to enjoy a substantial career in the lower leagues and by the time he retired he had rattled home 120 goals in close to three hundred league appearances.

Things could only get better. They did, but only marginally when the following week Sunderland went back to Lancashire and lost 6-0 at Burnley. In goal manager Alan Brown, returning to his previous club for the first time, was forced by injuries to play Ronnie Routledge in only his second game. Unlike Hurley, who was to go on and make hundreds more appearances for the Wearsiders, Routledge never played again, moving on to Bradford Park Avenue.

"At Burnley Charlie put his foot on the ball and tried to go round somebody, lost it and it was in the back of the net; people thought 'Oh no, what have we bought here?'" recalls Stan Anderson.

And Hurley remembers his first game: "Goodness gracious, seven-nil. Someone said years later had I scored two own goals. I said I didn't score any but I did make four! Because I was a footballing centre half I could only play one way. Alan Brown signed me because he was once a centre half. But he was a cruncher, so he must always deep down have wanted to be a footballing centre half because otherwise you would never sign a guy like me. So anyway it got a lot better as it was Burnley away and we lost six-nil!

"Charlie Summerville, from the *Daily Mail*, came up to me and said, 'Charles, what are you going to do, you've been signed to improve the defence and it was seven-nil and six-nil' and I said to him, 'How many players improve so quickly? In about six games' time we could get to a clean sheet'. Charlie loved me after that... seven and six made thirteen. It could have been very unlucky for me.

"I was also lucky enough to go to Sunderland in 1957. I didn't like it when I first went there, plus the first time I went into a club you know and there was bingo on and the caller pulled out seventy-six and said 'seven and six' was Charlie worth it! I missed my family and loads of mates. I didn't know at the start what would happen, I just thought I'd be another footballer for Sunderland football club who'd play a few years and then move on. I didn't know I would still be remembered more than fifty years later for example. I didn't know that I was going to be as good as I was."

Hurley's arrival led to the departure of Ray Daniel, signed from Arsenal in June 1953 for the considerable sum of £27,500. Capped twenty-one times by Wales, he was highly thought of by the Roker Park crowd, not least for his willingness to go forward with the ball.

He made 136 league appearances for Sunderland, scoring six goals. A fee of £7,500 saw him return to Wales and Cardiff City. Billy Bingham, who when he left Sunderland in the summer of 1958 had already been capped thirty-three times by Northern Ireland, was disappointed to see Daniel leave.

Writing later in his book *Soccer with the Stars*, Bingham said that "Ray could still have given some useful service to Sunderland at a time when we needed all we could get. I couldn't understand why he was now relegated to being the second team's twelfth man, whose main duty was to carry the skip containing the team's gear. He was the kind of player who needed kidding along not slapping down. However it was obvious that Big Charlie was a player for the future. Almost as good a ball-player as Daniel himself, he made fewer mistakes and was brilliant in the air, both in defence and attack."

Charlie Hurley made his home debut on Saturday October 19th 1957 against Preston North End. The match ended goalless but that did not stop him being criticised by Argus who reported that "the defensive side of his work was distinctly shaky at times."

The Roker crowd, however, were prepared to be patient. Writing in the 1964 Promotion Souvenir Brochure, Hurley recalled his home debut: "You can imagine how I felt in my Roker Park debut... and if ever supporters stood by a player at a time when he needed it most then this was it. I shall always be indebted to you for that."

Hurley, in fact, took a big gamble playing against Preston. Tom Finney was due to turn out at centre forward and Hurley admits years later that he was nowhere near fit.

"I'd picked up an injury at Burnley. Alan Brown didn't want me to play but I said very firmly 'I'm playing, I have been crap up to now'. You see I had something to prove. But it was a relief to hear Tom, an absolutely brilliant footballer, wasn't playing."

According to Sunderland fanatic Brian Leng, who has followed the team for more than fifty years and who became a big fan of

Hurley, "Charlie looked out of his depth for quite some time when he first came to the club."

Apart from Bingham, Hurley's new teammates included Don Revie, bought from Manchester City in November 1956, Billy Elliott, signed from Burnley for £23,000 in August 1951 and who was capped five times by England, and a man who went on to make 402 league appearances for Sunderland, Stan Anderson. In goal, twice-capped for Scotland, was Australian-born Willie Fraser.

Sunderland were unlucky that a last-minute equaliser stopped them from winning at Sheffield Wednesday when George Aitken returned to the line-up alongside Hurley. In his after match report of the 3-3 draw John Bowman noted that "the biggest improvement of all came from Charlie Hurley. After a fluttery start, he really stood out, with his strong headers and smart passing." Hurley was on his way at Sunderland.

Supporters who travelled to Sheffield by train for the game would have left at 7.53am, arriving at Sheffield two hours and twenty-three minutes later at a cost of 17s and 6d [88p]. This would have represented a hefty outlay from the wages of, say, an assistant-cook where for a forty-six-hour week at the Sunderland Eye Infirmary the pay was £6 6s and 3d [£6.31]. The average wage was around £9. Hurley's wages were £17 a week or double the average, a not inconsiderable sum, but nothing like the gap there is today between a Premier League player, the equivalent of the First Division in Hurley's day, and those who follow them.

The players were at that time clearly right to be annoyed that despite large crowds they were failing to be properly rewarded. Perhaps as an indicator of changes to come, the Football Association decided in October to overturn the previous season's bans against Sunderland directors Stanley Ritson and Laurie Evans for making illegal payments to the players.

Mind you, according to Hurley, some of the players could have done a little more to earn their pay, revealing perhaps why Ray Daniel had been made twelfth man for the reserves. "Ray Daniel was a lovely guy who dressed immaculately. But he'd come in on the morning and stand in front of the mirror and say 'I don't know whether to take off my overcoat for training today'. On Fridays, some of the players would just walk round the pitch with their suits on, but the Bomber sorted them out."

Hurley had to wait until his sixth game before tasting victory in Sunderland's red and white stripes, a 3-2 win at Birmingham City with two goals from Revie and one from Bingham. Bryan Orritt hit the bar for Birmingham in the last few minutes; he was to get his revenge later in the season.

Making his debut for Sunderland that day was Ambrose Fogarty, who Hurley got to know rather well because he was sent to share a bed with his fellow Irishman at 33 Grindon Terrace in Sunderland.

As Hurley recalls: "The club put me up to lodge with Elsie Common and her husband Tom. Elsie was a lovely woman; Tom was a bit of a critic of mine. I was in a very small room, Amby Fogarty came and we were both sleeping in the same bed; thankfully it was at least a double one!"

Hurley's improved performances continued with his ninety minutes in a 2-2 home draw against Chelsea earning him praise from Argus, who stated: "It was a great day for the Irish, with Fogarty, Bingham and Hurley showing up well." He also played particularly well in a 2-0 defeat at Nottingham Forest in which Sunderland were outplayed but Argus reported that "Charlie Hurley took top honours for an excellent display."

Just before Christmas Hurley had a particularly fine game in a 1-1 home draw with Portsmouth, with Geoff Whitten writing below a "Hurley hits best form" headline that he "was especially sound in the air and also passed the ball well."

However, at the season's halfway point, after twenty-one games, only sixteen points were on the board – relegation loomed. When Sunderland failed to build on their 2-1 Boxing Day home defeat of Leeds United and lost to Wolverhampton Wanderers at home on December 28th there seemed little hope and it only got worse. Sunderland gained only two points from the following seven matches. Few would have bet against them avoiding relegation to the second tier of English football for the first time.

Hopes of an FA Cup run to dull the pain were ended by Everton, winners of a replay after a 2-2 draw at Roker Park from where

John Ross, writing in the *Newcastle Journal*, called Hurley "ice-cool" after he stopped the ball on the line and "waited until Fraser [the 'keeper] had regained his balance before rolling the ball to him." At that time, of course, back passes were still permitted. The Irishman could not, however, stop his immediate opponent Dave Hickson scoring twice as "even great centre halves cannot be everywhere," wrote Ross.

Hopes of revenge against Blackpool were dashed when Sunderland went down 4-1 at Roker Park on February 15th 1958. It gave them the record of being the largest single-league scorers in one season against Sunderland with eleven goals. Everton, in fact, hold the record for scoring the most goals in a single season against Sunderland with thirteen in the 1934–35 season, but seven of those came in two FA Cup ties, including the six that were needed to knock out a Sunderland team who themselves scored four in the replay.

On March 1st 1958 Sunderland were again well beaten by Preston by 3-0 at Deepdale. Hurley, suffering from a groin strain, missed the game. Preston's win took the home side within touching distance of Wolves at the top of the league. If they were to be relegated Sunderland would at least have the consolation of not having to play Preston at Deepdale the following season, having lost six and drawn one of their last seven games there, scoring just nine goals while conceding twenty-seven.

Two successive victories, away to Tottenham Hotspur, a single goal from Revie bringing home the points, and 2-0 at home to West Brom on a day when Sugar Ray Robinson regained the world middleweight title for the fifth time, beating holder Carmen Basilio in a gruelling Chicago Stadium brawl, raised supporters' hopes.

Hurley's injury meant he missed both matches, plus the goalless draw that followed away to Chelsea at which Argus reported that "Aitken was again the dominating figure in defence", and a 2-2 draw on Easter Friday at Old Trafford with a Manchester United side still to win a league game since February. United manager Matt Busby was still in his Munich hospital following the air disaster. Playing for the Red Devils that day were three players,

Bill Foulkes, Shay Brennan and Bobby Charlton, who were to go on to win European Cup winners' medals at Wembley ten years later.

Sunderland, again without Hurley, were then demolished 6-1 at home by a rampant Birmingham City side, Orritt scoring in the second minute as Birmingham romped to a four-goal lead within twenty minutes. Worse followed when Manchester United took home both points; the Red Devils' re-formed side having just clawed their way to an FA Cup final appearance against Bolton Wanderers. Their subsequent defeat did not obscure the courage of that makeshift team.

Off the field, the news in Easter 1958 was dominated by thousands of people walking from Trafalgar Square to Aldermaston, where a secret atomic weapons plant was found to be under construction. The Campaign for Nuclear Disarmament had only just come into existence after Britain had carried out its first H-bomb test on Christmas Island in the Pacific on May 15th 1957.

On April 12th 1958, Sunderland went to Manchester City's Maine Road and lost for the fifth consecutive season, this time 3-1. The returning Hurley had a fine game with Paul Chester in the *Sunday Sun* writing that "Hurley made a magnificent comeback at centre half and the Manchester crowd certainly appreciated his fine interceptions and thoughtful clearances."

In order to stand any chance of survival Sunderland knew that they had to win both their remaining games and hope that the sides around them failed.

Supporters writing to the *Sunderland Echo* criticised Alan Brown for persisting too long with a policy of blooding young players. Writing in the programme before the final home game of the season, against Nottingham Forest, the manager admitted that "It would seem, at the time of writing, that the chances of Sunderland staying in the First Division are very slender indeed" and the magical words "only club which has never played in any other than the First Division" which had appeared on the front of previous programmes for a number of seasons had vanished.

Perhaps realising that they had nothing to lose, Sunderland comfortably beat Forest with goals from Revie, Elliott and Don

Kichenbrand, a game in which Hurley was the best player on the pitch according to the match reports. Sunderland went into the final game of the season on April 26th away to Portsmouth knowing that if they won and Leicester failed to win at St Andrew's the club's proud record of never having been relegated could be maintained.

In opposition to Hurley that day was an emerging talent, Derek Dougan, who went on to play for Northern Ireland alongside George Best in the 1960s. Hurley, reported Argus, was "outstanding and had not played a better game for Sunderland" and was able to prevent Dougan from scoring. Kichenbrand's two goals proved enough to secure an away victory.

Could Sunderland dare celebrate? Sadly not, although this was an age when it took some time after the match to learn the results of other games. There was no instant news on the radio and Sunderland's players trooped off to find out that Leicester City, managed by former Sunderland centre forward Dave Halliday, had won by a single goal at Birmingham City, sending Sunderland down in twenty-first place alongside Sheffield Wednesday. Funnily enough the next time Sunderland were to be relegated from the top flight in 1970, Wednesday also joined them in dropping into Division Two.

Naturally, like all players should be, Sunderland's were devastated at being relegated, none more so than Stan Anderson who, Doug Weatherall later reported, had "wandered alone and heart-broken near Sunderland's hotel in London – and had to bear the sight of the return of promoted West Ham who were about to take Sunderland's place in the First Division."

"Sunderland are *my* team, and the fact that I'd played in a side that had got relegated for the first time was appalling, it was just horrible. Brown brought too many young players in too early. The experienced players couldn't help them as they were struggling themselves," says Anderson.

Meanwhile, despite relegation, Argus, or Bill Butterfield to give him his proper name, who did the job for thirty years from 1950, was convinced that Sunderland were following the correct course in trying to emulate Manchester United by producing their own players. He argued against those who had written to suggest the club would have done better to invest the money spent on Hurley on a forward, saying that he was "an excellent buy".

Nevertheless, after sixty-eight years of top-flight football, during which the championship had been won on six occasions and the FA Cup once, Sunderland had finally fallen from grace. Hurley had made twenty-two Sunderland appearances during this fatal season. Meanwhile back at Millwall, the Lions had slumped to twenty-third in Division Three South, ensuring they would start the following season in the new Fourth Division.

Hurley recalls events this way: "It was a funny year because Alan had all these players, Don Revie, Colin Grainger, Billy Bingham, he changed during that season. If Alan Brown ever did anything wrong in my opinion, it was that he didn't hang onto those experienced players, and let us younger ones gradually work our way in. You'll never really know, but if he'd done that I don't think Sunderland would have gone down that season.

"At Portsmouth we won 2-0 but Birmingham wanted Leicester to stay up more than Sunderland. It wasn't as sad a day for me as it was for Sunderland football club because they'd never been down. For me I'd hardly been in the First Division so it didn't hit me as much as the fans. It hit me a few years later about the record of never having been out of the First Division. My problem was proving to Sunderland that they had made a good buy."

Despite relegation, Brown never had any doubts that he had been correct to buy Charlie Hurley, remarking towards the end of the season that "...include Stan Cullis, Billy Wright, the lot, mark my words, this boy Hurley is going to be the greatest centre half of them all. He's got poise, balance." The latter was proved when Hurley, by far the biggest man at the club, had beaten the other players in a game of 'keepy up', notching 738 touches with feet, body and head before a ball touched the ground. And don't forget the balls were not exactly uniformly round in those days. Hurley's expertise was also shown when he used his feet to take a ball up a flight of a dozen steps and placed it into a large vase without the ball touching the ground. No one else managed the task.

Hurley was involved in two more internationals that year as Ireland went on an end of season tour of Austria and Poland, two other countries who had failed to make the World Cup finals.

There was disappointment at Prater Park in Vienna when, despite a goal from Dermot Curtis, the Republic lost 3-1. By playing in Katowice, the Republic became the first country from the west to play in Poland since the war and they were met with cheers of "bravo, bravo" when travelling to the ground where they received a hero's welcome. Things went slightly quieter when Curtis fired them into the lead, and again when George Cummins restored their advantage in the five minutes after half-time but at the end honours were even at 2-2 in a match watched by 100,000, a large number of whom had roared out Hurley's name.

WP Murphy, writing in the *Irish Independent*, was full of praise for Hurley, stating that "never – not forgetting Carey's famous last international match when he played against the Austrians at Dalymount Park in 1953 – have we seen as good a display of centre half work as that of Charlie Hurley. The Poles loved the big, handsome Irishman from Sunderland, who strolled through this game in majestic fashion, giving a display of coolness and confidence that was an inspiration."

Hurley admits that he had no idea that the Poles had been singing his name: "I didn't know they were shouting my name until afterwards. Charlie for them was different. It didn't sound clear to me. I had a hell of a game, I knew that. One of the selectors said they were calling my name and I was shocked; a great honour, mind."

Chapter Five

"You'll be seeing them"

The long summer following Sunderland's relegation meant that the attention of their followers turned in the direction of Sweden, where the sixth World Cup Finals were being held. Sixteen teams had qualified from the fifty-eight entrants, a record number. They included all four Home Nations, a feat that has not been seriously challenged since. No Sunderland player was good enough to get into an England squad weakened by the tragic loss of Duncan Edwards, Roger Byrne and Tommy Taylor in the Munich air disaster, but Billy Bingham played all five games at right-wing for an impressive Northern Ireland team who reached the quarter finals before, stricken by injury, they lost 4-0 to a fluent French team.

Not surprisingly some Irish papers could not help speculate what would have happened if an all-Ireland team had been assembled – a side drawn from Gregg [Manchester United], Keith [Newcastle], Cantwell [West Ham], Blanchflower [Spurs], Hurley [Sunderland], Cush [Leeds United], Fitzsimmons [Middlesbrough], Whelan [Manchester United], McIlroy [Burnley], McParland [Aston Villa] and Bingham [Sunderland] would have been very difficult for any team in the world to overcome.

Unlike their larger neighbours, Scotland and England, Wales had also raised their game to secure a place in the final eight and were desperately unlucky to go out to a single goal from the seventeen-year-old Pelé. Brazil went on to win the tournament for the first time after defeating the home side in the Stockholm final 5-2. Pelé's fifth goal, a header, was truly magnificent in a game where he and Vava were able to gorge themselves on a steady stream of crosses from Garrincha and Zagalo on each wing. Brazil's formation of 4-2-4 was in contrast to the traditional formation of the time of two full backs, three half backs and five forwards.

An important north-east 1958 summer event for Sunderland was the first Durham coast-boring for coal out at sea. A 230ft high tower had been constructed at West Hartlepool to operate in the deep waters of the North Sea and when it was located off Blackhall Colliery, nine miles south of Sunderland, a hole was drilled 2,100 feet below the sea bed. The aim was to discover the working reserves for pits along the coast. The results were good and the industry and the jobs within it were expected to have a long future.

According to Brian Leng: "When the Second Division fixtures were announced it really hit home just how far the club had fallen. It was a disaster. In the First Division you got to see all your boyhood heroes. You couldn't see them on the television of course. I used to look forward to the day when *Charles Buchan's Football Monthly* came out. I was football daft as a kid, and I'd never miss a home game after I went to the 1955 match at home to Spurs. At first it was the atmosphere that catches you; only later did I begin to appreciate the events on the field, especially watching Len Shackleton.

"In those days of course the shipyards were at work on the Saturday morning and the workers would pour out and go over to Roker Park in their working gear. I'd never seen men react in the excited way they do at football matches; to see them do all these strange things was magical. For years I used to stand under the number twelve sign in the Roker End, before it was partly knocked down at the start of the 1980s."

Less magical in 1958 was the immediate future of the local football club. It did not look that rosy when Sunderland lost their first ever Division Two match at Lincoln City by 3-1. Ron Harberstson scored for Lincoln in the thirteenth minute in a match in which "Sunderland were well beaten by a speedy Lincoln" said Argus in the *Sunderland Echo*. Sincil Bank had crammed in a crowd of 17,290.

In the weeks leading up to the start of the season the *Echo* ran a weekly series on "You'll be seeing them next season", most fans obviously hoping that it would be the only time they would see the likes of Lincoln, Scunthorpe, Rotherham and Barnsley. What ever were the famous Sunderland doing playing League games against that lot? Sadly, losing to them!

Hurley, who was suffering from strained knee ligaments, did not play at Lincoln or the next three games. These brought only two points [three points for a victory was not brought in until the 1981–82 season] from a 2-1 home victory against Liverpool in front of 36,168 spectators on an August Bank Holiday weekend dominated by news of riots in the Notting Hill area of London where Afro-Caribbeans, sickened of being terrorised by local racists and fascists, had finally fought back after gangs of Teddy Boys began to act increasingly aggressively. The Notting Hill Carnival was started the following year as a gesture of defiance and an assertion of community pride.

Hurley returned for the fifth game, against Stoke City, being joined by Don Revie, also making his first appearance of the season. But Billy Bingham was missing. He had moved on to Luton Town, the Hatters paying £15,000. A 3-1 victory pushed Sunderland up the table. Argus' match report praised Hurley, "whose cultured play was the outstanding feature of the match."

Revie had been dropped from the first team after requesting a transfer. His return showed how desperate Sunderland were. With such an inexperienced team, Sunderland manager Alan Brown was heavily reliant on established players such as Stan Anderson and Revie. Revie had joined Sunderland for £23,000 in November 1956 after coming to prominence during Leicester City's run to the FA Cup final in 1949 before playing twice for Manchester City in Wembley FA Cup finals in the mid 1950s.

A shrewd organiser, Revie had copied some of the tactics of the great Hungarian team which beat England 6-3 at Wembley in 1953 and 7-1 in Budapest a year later. In Revie's case this meant lining up at centre forward but then dropping behind the two inside forwards, a ploy used by Nándor Hidegkuti. This gave him the space to control the pace and direction of the play. Revie made 66 appearances for Sunderland, scoring 15 times before he left for Leeds at a fee of £14,000. Later, as manager, he built the famous Elland Road team which was beaten 1-0 by Sunderland in the 1973 FA Cup final.

Following his return, Hurley went on to miss only three further games that season, establishing himself as a regular Sunderland first team player alongside a growing band of youngsters.

At the Vetch Field, Sunderland received a lesson in attacking play from Welsh international Ivor Allchurch, whose four goals inspired his Swansea teammates to a five-goal demolition. Allchurch – "The Golden Boy of Welsh Football" – was playing one of his last games in his first period for Swansea as he was sold shortly afterwards to Newcastle United for £25,000. He later returned to Swansea to play from 1965 to 1968, ending up with 164 goals in 445 appearances. Swansea's finest also played 68 times for Wales, and he scored twice at the World Cup finals in Sweden.

However, speaking years later about this match, Len Ashurst, who had travelled to the Vetch Field as twelfth man after signing for Sunderland in the summer following a surprising release by his home town club Liverpool, remembers a moment of magic from Hurley that few players even today could repeat.

"We were beaten quite heavily – Allchurch scored the goals – but I remember Charlie getting the ball. I can't remember how it landed at his foot in the middle of the penalty box. He had a bit of space, another stopper would have hoofed it up the field, instead Charlie did one of those back flicks where he flicked the ball with his right foot behind the left one; it went out to the winger. You see Ronaldo do it now on occasions to flick the ball into the box, but for Charlie to do it in his own penalty area… I couldn't believe my eyes, but I was to discover that typified him. He always wanted to use the ball and generally speaking he was a constructive centre half with a trick up his sleeve, although occasionally it did go wrong such as at Old Trafford in 1964," says a man who played hundreds of times at left back alongside Hurley in the Sunderland defence during the late 1950s and 1960s.

Things got worse for Sunderland when six goals without reply were put into their net by a Sheffield Wednesday team that had come to terms with Division Two football much more quickly than the Wearside team.

Throwing caution to the wind, manager Alan Brown gave three new boys their debuts at home to Ipswich Town. Len Ashurst and Cecil Irwin came in at full back and Jimmy McNab at half back. Little good it did, as two awful back passes, the first from Alan O'Neill, who was told off by Hurley, presented Jimmy Leadbetter with an easy goal before Hurley himself repeated the feat and Leadbetter crashed home the second. At the end Hurley trudged off dejectedly.

Argus reported that the "club's fortunes were at their lowest ebb ever." He also attacked those in the Roker crowd who had made Alan O'Neill a target for their displeasure. Burley, a letter writer from Red House, also criticised those who had mocked O'Neill and suggested that perhaps "Mr Brown might try Hurley at centre forward – I think he has the ability of [John] Charles."

O'Neill was to make 76 first team appearances for Sunderland, scoring 28 goals. Transferred in October 1960, he scored on his Aston Villa debut against Birmingham City after twenty-five seconds, which could be a record for a debutant.

Hurley was in his usual position at Eastville, where he once again had a brilliant match, the *Sunday Mirror* stating "in 90 minutes he never put a foot wrong" for a Sunderland side that it was suggested might just be heading out of Division Two into the league below after Bristol Rovers won 2-1.

So it was with some relief that Sunderland were able to prise a point out of a tough battle at Ayresome Park, where Len Shackleton reported that "Hurley puts a stop to Clough's capers" although this did not stop the now *Daily Express* reporter suggesting at the end of his following week's report on a 3-0 victory for Charlton Athletic at Roker Park that Alan Brown should consider trying "Charlie Hurley at inside forward. His extraordinary ability is wasted at centre half. Sunderland only need a spark to set them alight. Hurley in the forward line might be the ignition."

Hurley was aware of the Clown Prince's view, saying "Shack always said I should have been a centre forward, and when he was asked 'Where should Charlie play?' he would say 'Up front.' I wish Shack had come along a lot earlier as I would have been up front; a goalscorer is worth his weight in gold."

The month of September 1958 had seen the Football League agree that Wolves could kick off their October 4th Saturday match against Manchester United in the evening. This was of little use to the West Midlands side as the League then refused to allow television coverage of the game, arguing that "it would interfere with the family's night out together and so attendances would suffer."

However, the entertainment on offer at the Sunderland Empire may have prompted many to look for an alternative; one of the shows of the time was the bizarre *Girls in Cellophane*, which boasted naked women, primitive clingfilm and comedian Bill Waddington, who later found fame as Coronation Street's Percy Sugden. The Empire was to close as a privately-run venue in May 1959, but was rescued by Sunderland Corporation in a deal unique for the time.

Of course TV was here to stay. And as a demonstration of that fact, Tyne Brand brought out its first ready meals so that those determined not to miss a minute's action on the small screen could cook "a good hot meal in five minutes." Football on TV and fast food: it would never catch on!

These days it is rare for a home crowd to applaud a visiting player, no matter how good their play or the goal they've scored. Not so back in the 1950s and even though Sunderland were easily beaten 4-1 at Bristol City with John Atyeo again scoring, Argus reported that "Hurley was the outstanding figure in the Sunderland side and the City supporters left no doubt in anyone's mind that they appreciated the quality of his play." Grainger had given Sunderland hope after he beat three defenders before thrashing the ball past Cook from fifteen yards to make it 1-1 in the thirteenth minute.

Supporters were one thing, football reporters and critics another and some were not unafraid to be highly critical of Hurley's determination to play the game with style. Malcolm Usher in the *Newcastle Journal* wrote after a 2-2 draw with Barnsley that he "was disturbed by his continued temptation to take too many risks in the penalty area" and that "his first job is to block the middle". Shackleton put it even more bluntly with "Hurley is not a good centre half. Apart from unnecessary chances he takes he cannot tackle."

In the *Daily Express* Bill Fryer, however, was having none of it. "How a player like Shack can prefer a stopper centre half I'll never fathom. Hurley is class. What sort of a team would Sunderland be with youngsters round a basher?"

Hurley himself was clear about his role and defended himself, saying, "Many people just can't get used to the idea of a centre half playing football. They think his whole aim should be to boot the ball as hard as he can first-time and in any direction as long as it is away from his own goal. I always try to be constructive in everything I do, and I shall continue to play the game my way. The truth is it is easy to be a basher, but I have always preferred to play football."

Hurley had a difficult time against the Huddersfield centre forward Derek Hawksworth in the away game in which an emerging talent, one Denis Law, showed his class. The *Newcastle Journal*'s Malcolm Usher reported that "this Sunderland team has a lot of flaws which perhaps is understandable in view of the sudden upsurge of youth to its ranks."

Meanwhile it was reported that Arsenal were on the verge of bidding £20,000 to take Charlie Hurley 'home' to London, where he was due to marry his fiancée Joan Gale. News of their engagement had become known only three months after he had popped the question to the ex-typist who had won a part in the *Jubilee Show* on Associated-Rediffusion, appearing alongside Shirley Eaton, after her mother had sent her picture to the TV company. She captured one of only eight places from among five hundred entrants and she appeared in all eight shows in 1958.

When Joan first met Charlie Hurley she had no idea he had taken such a fancy to her, and she also had no knowledge of professional football. "It's not like today where footballers have their photographs in all the papers. I didn't know that people played football professionally when I met Charles, which is my name for him and I've always called him that. I had never been to a game until I moved up to Sunderland. I didn't know till much later that he'd been trying to get to speak to me before we met, but I did like him, he had a great personality," says Joan Hurley.

Ironically, Charlie Hurley had realised he was in love only after he had taken the decision to sign for Sunderland and his wife to be had sent him a good wishes telegram after they had been out together on a couple of occasions.

The couple's engagement was even mentioned by one of the first celebrity gossip columnists, William Hickey, of the *Daily Express*, who described the clearly overjoyed young woman as "looking remarkably like 'My Fair Lady' Julie Andrews".

Unfortunately, the love of Hurley's life showed she did not have quite the ability of her future husband to tiptoe her way out of difficult situations when she put her foot right in it by declaring that "Charles and I plan to marry next June. But Sunderland is so drab Charles wants to get back down south as soon as he can."

Sympathy for the young couple came from an unlikely source, Newcastle's Jimmy Scoular using his *Sunderland Sports Echo* column to declare that "the south has much to offer that the north cannot match, but it cannot offer the friendship, sportsmanship or the welcome such as is to be found among the folk of the North-East." Scoular had moved to St James' Park from Portsmouth in 1953.

One man definitely on the move was Don Revie, whose final Sunderland match was a four goals victory away at Rotherham, during which Kichenbrand grabbed a hat-trick. The win still left the Wearsiders in serious trouble with only fourteen points from eighteen games. Worse followed with another three defeats out of four. Crowds, while still respectable, were naturally well down on previous seasons with only 20,178 turning up at Roker Park for the return match with Lincoln City that Sunderland won just before a Christmas that witnessed the "hula hoop" craze which captured the imagination of youngsters up and down the land. Originally produced as a sideline to autographed "Stanley Matthews" footballs, they far outsold the plastic items with which many a kid destroyed his parents' front windows.

The ex-Liverpool man Len Ashurst returned to Anfield for the first time on January 3rd 1959, a day on which Alaska became the forty-ninth US state. Three days later Fidel Castro arrived in the Cuban capital Havana to assume control. This followed the overthrow, after a two-year guerrilla struggle by members of the 26th of July Movement, of the dictator General Fulgencio Batista.

Shortly after came the tragic news that Mike Hawthorn, Britain's first ever motor-racing world champion, had died in, what else, an automobile accident. Hawthorn had won the title the previous year, benefiting from Stirling Moss's sportsmanship; Moss intervened to ensure his countryman retained his second place at the Portuguese Grand Prix despite breaking the rules by pushing his car. Hawthorn went on to win the title by just a single point; Moss never won it but remains well loved by the British public for his actions.

Fears that Sunderland might fall into the newly organised Division Three were allayed by the three straight victories during which Gateshead-born John Goodchild scored both goals at Ipswich to push Sunderland eight points clear of the bottom two. An ex-miner, Goodchild was to score a more than respectable 21 goals in 44 league appearances before moving to Brighton and Hove Albion.

When Sunderland kicked off their home match the following Saturday against Bristol Rovers they were joined by perhaps the first group of away fans to travel to Roker Park by aeroplane, the Pirates' supporters chartering one to depart at 10.30am from Bristol which arrived at Newcastle airport two hours later. Arthur Ellis, later better known as one of the judges on the 1970s TV programme *It's a Knockout*, was the referee, for a game the home side won 2-0. Sunderland also beat Rovers' local rivals Bristol City at Roker Park, this time by 3-1, but guess who scored for the away side? Yes, that man John Atyeo!

Hurley suffered his own "knockout" at Derby when an opponent's head crashed into his face. Carried off, he returned to finish the match in considerable pain as Sunderland lost 2-0 before a hospital visit confirmed he had suffered a broken nose.

The largest Roker Park crowd of the season was just 45,594 for a goalless draw against near neighbours Middlesbrough, with Hurley again blocking out Brian Clough. The following Saturday Sunderland beat Barnsley 2-0 at Oakwell. This was the only time Hurley ever played at Barnsley, who finished bottom of the Second Division that season, but he clearly made a big impression on the watching public, including Michael Parkinson, the chat show host and journalist, who wrote:

"Remember Charlie Hurley of Sunderland? He could play a bit. He used to give his supporters and teammates palpitations by dribbling the ball out of the tightest situations. I saw him at Barnsley beat three attackers in his own penalty area and then float a perfect pass out of defence, but not before he first flicked the ball onto his head and down onto his instep as if he was centre stage at the London Palladium."

Perhaps because he was now so used to Hurley's mastery of the ball, even in a struggling side, Argus reporting on the match does not even mention this incident.

One of the scorers that day was Northern Ireland-born John Fraser, a winger Sunderland were hoping would take over from the much missed Bingham who was leading Luton Town to Wembley in the FA Cup, although they were beaten 2-1 by Nottingham Forest. One of Forest's scorers, carried off with a broken leg, was Roy Dwight, better known now as the uncle of Elton John.

Immediately after the game at Oakwell Hurley rushed off to play the following day for Ireland against Czechoslovakia in Dublin. Getting there meant a train journey to Liverpool, followed by a boat trip to Dublin, arriving in the early hours of the morning, before dashing to his hotel and unsuccessfully attempting to catch a few hours' sleep.

Despite this Ireland won 2-0 with Liam Touhy, later to become manager of the national team, timing his run perfectly to head home Shamrock Rovers teammate Tommy Hamilton's cross in the twenty-first minute and when a penalty was awarded just before half-time Noel Cantwell strolled forward to score the second. This was a fine result, but the home team missed opportunties in the second half which meant the Czechs still had a chance when the second leg took place a month later.

Sunderland closed the season by hammering Brighton and Hove Albion 4-1 in front of just 12,024 at Roker Park, Kichenbrand ending the season in style with a hat-trick, his second of the campaign, to take his total to twenty-one. Signed from Scottish League champions Glasgow Rangers in 1956 the South African-born centre forward was aggressive, very quick and had a powerful shot. He is certainly the only player nicknamed 'rhino' to turn out for Sunderland. He earned it for his willingness to batter down defenders.

According to Brian Leng: "Brown had been heavily criticised for taking Sunderland down, but people forget that the previous season, 1956–57 we'd only stopped up in twentieth place. The turning point came when he started to blood the kids, but it was to take some time for them to gel. Brown must have known that would be the case and that until that happened he could expect to get stick from some supporters."

Sunderland finished fifteenth with forty points from forty-two matches. Meanwhile Sheffield Wednesday jumped straight back up as Division Two champions with sixty-two points. In the First Division, Wolves, led by Billy Wright, who had become the first man to win one hundred caps, became champions for the second consecutive season. While in a repeat of the first ever European Cup Final of 1956, Real Madrid once again beat the French side Stade de Reims, only this time 2-0.

Hurley and his Republic of Ireland teammates suffered a major disappointment in his final match of the season when in the Teheine Pole Stadium in Bratislava Czechoslovakia were simply too good in the second leg of the European Championship qualifier. Goals from Stacho [a penalty], Bubernik, Pavolic and Dolinsky saw Ireland knocked out 4-2 on aggregate. The failure to take their chances in the first leg ultimately counted against them.

Hurley's season, in which he had made some outstanding man of the match performances, thus ended with another defeat. It had not been the best of times for either club or country. Surely things would improve in the next?

Chapter Six

Tying the knot and having his best season

On Saturday June 20th 1959 at the Church of St Joseph and the Immaculate Conception in Waltham Cross, east London, Charles John Hurley was married to Miss Joan Eileen Gale. Charlie Hurley's best man was Walter Emmitt and the bride was given away by her father Samuel in a ceremony officiated by Father J McEntee. Also at their wedding were Joan's mother Marie and Charles Hurley's parents.

The photographs that appeared in the newspapers over the following days show a handsome smiling couple; Joan resplendent in her bridal gown and Charlie a picture of happiness in a new suit and tie.

"It was a lovely day. We've had a good marriage and I am glad we met when we did," says Hertfordshire-born Joan.

Meanwhile, one of Charlie's Sunderland teammates was also keeping busy during the summer. As well as a talented footballer, Colin Grainger was a fine singer as he proved by topping the bill with Max Miller at the Metropolitan Theatre in London for a number of weeks.

Although none of Grainger's songs was taken up by football fans, a new generation of supporters had not missed what had happened during England's televised international friendly against World Cup holders Brazil in Rio de Janeiro on May 13th 1959. The home fans had repetitively chanted "Bra-sil, cha-cha-cha! Bra-sil, cha-cha-cha!". When the following season got underway, supporters across England simply replaced "Bra-sil" with the name of their own team. Terrace chants were up and running.

There was good news eight miles south of Sunderland at the new town of Peterlee. This was named after the Durham Miners' leader during the 1926 General Strike, and constructed after the Second World War to provide better housing and facilities for those used to living in poor housing in colliery villages, where inside toilets and bathrooms were still something of a novelty.

It came with the announcement by Peterlee Development Corporation on August 8th 1959 that at a cost to the taxpayers of £250,000 they were to construct their fourth factory, which when it opened would produce crisps on behalf of Tudor Food Products Limited. One of the north-east's best-known products of the 1960s and '70s was shortly to be born. Many a good Sunderland supporter has made his or her way to the match from the factory that still stands today, only now it is owned by Walker's Crisps. They include the author of this book, who worked there in the 1970s and '80s as a labourer and later semi-skilled machine operator.

When the squad details were released that season Kichenbrand at 6ft was the second tallest, Hurley topping him by half an inch. But when it came to weight Hurley was considerably heavier than the South African at 14st and 3lbs. No one else was even close; Hurley was now an imposing centre back and still only twenty-two years of age.

The *Sunderland Echo*'s previous close-season feature – "You'll be seeing them next season" – was not repeated. Instead supporters were treated to "Great Games recalled" and they hoped it was not too long before they saw some. But the first game of the season would not feature in any future list. Sunderland lost 3-1 at Stoke City, although Graham Fisher reported in the *Daily Express* that Alan Brown could at least take some "consolation from the performance of his defence, or rather Charlie Hurley, whose personality spilled from his boots all over Sunderland's half of the field."

Results quickly improved. By the time Sheffield United were crushed 5-1 in the eighth game hopes had risen as with four wins and just two defeats ten points were on the board. The previous season it had taken Sunderland nearly twice that number of games to reach double figures. In the game against Sheffield United

Sunderland-born Ernie Taylor, signed from Manchester United in December the previous year, scored twice.

Hurley was injured for the ninth game, in which Sunderland crashed 6-1 at Portman Road against an emerging Ipswich Town shortly to go on to greater things.

Up front Kichenbrand had lost his place to Ian Lawther, whom Sunderland persuaded to join them from Belfast Crusaders. He had been playing there after returning to Northern Ireland from Manchester United where he had been homesick. Two years later Manchester United were to suffer the same fate with another Belfast boy. But unlike with Lawther, Matt Busby was able to persuade him to return to Old Trafford where he went on to be one of the greatest players ever seen, the inimitable George Best.

Lawther was not of the calibre of Best – who was? – but he was to prove a prolific scorer in the two seasons he was at Roker Park, hitting 41 league goals in 75 games, almost a third of Sunderland's 127 for the period.

When Sunderland travelled the short distance to Ayresome Park on October 10th they took with them a considerable following. So many that those present were informed they could not transfer ends at half-time, a habit that lasted at many grounds until well into the 1960s.

The 47,047 present saw Ambrose Fogarty, later in the season to join Charlie Hurley in his dash over the Irish Sea to play for the Republic of Ireland, equalise an Edwin Holliday goal for a 'Boro side most reporters felt would have won the game easily had it not been for Hurley. "Clough in shackles of Charlie Hurley" and "Hurley was the hoodoo" were typical headlines with one reporter asking "Where was Brian Clough? He was trying to escape the shackles of Charlie Hurley, surely one of the most complete centre halves in the game." In goal for 'Boro was Peter Taylor, later to form such an important managerial partnership with Clough.

Two days previously a General Election had returned the Conservatives to power with a much-increased majority. Among the new batch of MPs was one Margaret Hilda Thatcher. In Sunderland itself little changed, although the majorities of the two sitting MPs, Tory Paul Williams in the south seat and Labour's Fred Willey in the north, were both cut. An amazing, certainly in comparison to today, eighty per cent of people registered to vote did so. Others, particularly the young and female, had had much more exciting things to do the same evening when a young singer called Cliff Richard was in town, where his appearance at the Odeon was reported as creating hysteria.

Unlike the government, Sunderland AFC were still in transition. Eight games had yielded ten points, the next eight only seven. But Martin Harvey, only just turned eighteen, was blooded at Home Park, Plymouth, and his display pleased the watching Argus from the *Sunderland Echo* who reported, "Harvey promises to develop into a wing half of the finest class."

Unfortunately for Harvey he was to find his opportunities restricted for many years by the fine form of Stan Anderson, scorer of Sunderland's only goal at The Valley on November 7th. But Charlton Athletic scored three, meaning the north-east team had only seventeen points from those first sixteen matches. This was the only match Charlie Hurley's mother Christina saw in his professional career, and it also happened on the day the author of this book was born.

Hurley's mother saw her son play a decent game. Writing in the *Sunday Mirror* under a banner headline of "Charlie is Britain's best", Ken Jones waxed lyrical, stating that "the 'whispering giant' strolled through the game with the grace of the complete artist. Dominating in the air, he has harnessed his strength to ball control that is phenomenal for such a big man. And around him manager Alan Brown is assembling a defence that is lifting the shadows from Roker Park."

In a sign of the times, the week preceding the match had marked the opening of the first motorway in Britain when the M1, between what is now junctions eight to fifteen – St Albans to Northampton – gave car owners an opportunity to dash from place to place. And my goodness they took it! Normally placid individuals became little more than lunatics when given the chance to 'hit the road'. Ernest Marples, the Transport Minister and a man with close connections to the road-building industry, opened the road and became the first to drive on it. He subsequently watched in horror, remarking that he "was appalled at the speed at which some cars were travelling" and that drivers "were ignoring the rules and regulations". No doubt he expected drivers' behaviour would improve over time!

Hurley played his seventh game for the Republic of Ireland on November 1st 1959 in Dublin. This was on a Sunday, the Catholic Church taking the view that as long as people attended Mass beforehand then there was nothing wrong with watching or playing in a match in the afternoon. That was unlike their northern counterparts who debated long and hard about sending the Northern Ireland team to the World Cup in Sweden the previous year because they might have to play on a Sunday. They went and reached the quarter-finals.

It was Sweden who were Ireland's opponents in Dublin. As World Cup runners-up, the Swedes represented a formidable challenge although only four of the team which lost to Brazil in the 1958 final played at Dalymount Park. One was centre forward Agne Simonsson, in direct competition with Hurley.

Today many international friendly matches are seen as little more than a distraction, including by some players. In the 1950s this was certainly not the case. There were far fewer internationals – Hurley would have had close to a hundred caps were he playing today – and Sweden arrived in Dublin fresh from a Wembley victory known to have damaged relations between the England manager Walter Winterbottom and the selectors after he'd fielded a young side.

The match at Dalymount Park was thrilling, producing a great 3-2 win for Ireland. The result was particularly gratifying because after twelve minutes the Republic were 2-0 down, the unfortunate Mick McGrath gifting the away side the lead with a seventh-minute own goal.

But Johnny Giles, then of Manchester United and making his debut, was determined not to go down without a fight and a magnificent thirty-yard volley on sixteen minutes brought the 40,000 crowd and the game to life. With Hurley now dominating Simonsson, Ireland were level in the twenty-fourth minute when Dermot Curtis was on the end of Joe Haverty's cross. And the

Ipswich player scored his second just after half-time when his chip dipped over the Swedish 'keeper Brent Nyholm and, as the crowd waited to explode, dropped into the back of the net for a truly sensational winner. The ground was to erupt again when the referee blew the final whistle on what was at the time one of Ireland's finest ever results.

Hurley remembers the game fondly, stating: "Sweden had gone to Wembley and won 3-2 before they came to us. Dalymount Park was a bit of a fortress; it was very small with the crowd right on top of you. Very Irish, they'd laugh at the other team's mistakes. Our draw with England was a travesty; we should have beaten them. I loved Dalymount Park although not as much as Roker Park. We were nearly always the underdogs. I often wondered if the pitch was kept deliberately bumpy.

"I remember that when Johnny Giles put his strip on he looked like a shirt and shorts stuck on a peg. Our strips had buttoned-up collars and buttoned-up cuffs – they must have bought a great big block of these things which we carried on wearing until they wore out. The shorts were either big or bigger. Johnny stood there, he was very small and you couldn't see any flesh. He had the collar up and he said 'I'm not going out looking like this'. I said to him 'You're lucky you haven't got the big shorts!' He had to roll over the shorts, and they were starched! At the end of the day we all brought our own shorts from our clubs.

"When we were quickly two-nil down big Noel Cantwell said to me, 'It's not looking too good, Chas'. Anyway Gilesy hit this purler which screamed into the top corner and then the Swedes disappeared."

Hurley, like the rest of his teammates, had played the previous day. He had to dash off the Roker Park pitch after a 1-1 draw with Liverpool to travel by car to the railway station to catch a train to meet up with the overnight boat at Holyhead.

Considering this 'preparation', Hurley's 'Man of the Match' display against Sweden was all the more remarkable. Simonsson was asked after the match if he had injured his foot, as he was so uninvolved in the match. Replying honestly he said: "It was not my foot hampering me, it was my shadow." One of the greatest centre forwards of the time had paid Hurley one of the biggest compliments imaginable.

"Hurley threw a shadow over the Swedes yesterday by paralysing the centre of their attack," WP Murphy, *Irish Independent*.

"My match star for blotting out wonder man Simonsson," Desmond Hackett, *Daily Express*.

Ireland's victory raised hopes that the FAI's request to be included in the Home Championships would be taken seriously. Manager Johnny Carey said: "This was a great day for us. We hope it is the beginning of a new era in Eire's football history."

Some reporters could not help speculate what might have happened had Hurley been born seven months later than October 4th 1936, because by then, of course, his family were settled in England. Ken Jones declared in the *Sunday Mirror*: "Charlie Hurley would step into any Great Britain side". Bill Fryer, in the *Daily Express*, followed the same theme by stating that if Charlie had been born in March 1937 "he would be turning out for England now!"

Back in the north-east a 3-2 victory on November 14th at home to Bristol City in front of just 21,025 spectators did little to lift the gloom among the dwindling band of Sunderland followers. This was followed by one of the most depressing runs ever by those running out in the red and white stripes. There were six successive defeats, four of them at home – to Rotherham, Hull, Stoke and Lincoln respectively.

Prior to the match against Hull, Argus had bemoaned the fact that "each of Sunderland's last three defeats has been due to their failure to accept goalscoring chances" and when Hull won 3-1 he reported that they had done so because they "knew how to take their chances."

Despite the poor results Charlie Hurley was producing some tremendous performances. Take for example this from Argus on his play at Ninian Park, where Sunderland lost 2-1 to Cardiff: "The one department in which Sunderland clearly outshone City was at halfback. And the outstanding player was Hurley who was very much the dominating centre half in every respect. There was real power in his challenge and he was so on top of centre forward

Moore, the Welsh international 'wonder boy', that there was little real menace from this quarter. At one corner kick he also forced himself through to make one header which would have beaten many goalkeepers."

It would take up far too much space but there are similar reports from other matches by Argus, and other reporters, on the Irishman's outstanding form during these desperate times for Sunderland.

Sunderland's gates had, of course, fallen because they were failing to produce either winning results or entertaining football, but gates generally were on the decline. Ten years earlier seventeen clubs had averaged more than 35,000 a game and another six more than 30,000. In the 1959–60 season only eight teams – Spurs, Arsenal, the two Manchester clubs, Everton, Wolves, Newcastle and Chelsea – averaged more than 35,000 and only four others averaged more than 30,000.

Football clubs were being forced to compete against newer forms of entertainment and leisure opportunities. In July 1957 the new Prime Minister Harold Macmillan had declared that most people "had never had it so good". The tightening of belts that had marked the years after the war had given way to a booming economy and with it a guaranteed job and a steady income.

Between 1955 and 1960 average weekly earnings, which included overtime payments, had risen by a third, comfortably more than the rise in the cost of living. With the NHS providing improved medical care and a system of benefits to assist the really needy, most people in Britain were healthier and more prosperous than ever before.

Alongside this relative affluence there arose new forms of entertainment that included – please don't laugh – going shopping with the wife and the kids to seek out a bargain among the explosion in consumer goods, consumption being necessary to maintain and extend production.

Fashion, refrigerators, TV sets and records became regarded as essentials, eating out was no longer seen as a luxury, takeaway restaurants and nightclubs were slowly being opened and then there was the increasing opportunity to buy a car and travel to places once out of reach. By 1960 almost thirty-three per cent of households owned a car, a figure that jumped to forty-nine per cent by 1966.

People bought many of them on credit, or 'tick' in everyday language, which Sunderland comic Bobby Thompson quickly incorporated into his stage act with his immortal gag "There's plenty of money around here: look at the amount we owe." Another was: "If everyone here took off their catalogue stuff we'd be in a nudist colony."

Hurley may have been king on the football park in Sunderland but Thompson was the main man off it when it came to live entertainment.

The club's performances, and particularly the results, had led some Sunderland supporters to argue that they needed to spend heavily in the transfer market. That was what the club had done before when they were in trouble. Argus was dead against this as he felt that with crowds down, and Sunderland apparently in considerable debt, it would be foolish to risk their long-term future. "The impatient ones who want results now must be prepared to bear their disappointments for a while yet," he wrote just before Christmas 1959.

Events at Sunderland were overshadowed by those off the pitch at Newcastle United, where in December 1959 inside forward George Eastham had refused to sign a new contract and asked to be allowed to move to another club. Newcastle, under the "retain-and-transfer system" operating then, refused to allow him to go and kept his registration.

The Professional Footballers Association [PFA] chairman Jimmy Hill explained what this meant in his autobiography: "When a player signed a contract with a club, that club controlled his whole future playing career. Under the standard terms of the contract, he could not leave to join another club without his original club's consent. Even when the contract ended, the club still had the option to prevent the player moving elsewhere. If he didn't want to re-sign, the club could retain his registration and were not obliged to pay him anything at all. The club could, however, transfer the player to another club whenever they wanted. If he refused to go, again they were not obliged to pay him anything at all."

The PFA, which until 1958 had been known as the Players' Union, embraced Eastham's case and with their assistance the player took the club to the High Court, arguing that it was an unfair restraint of trade or in rather more emotive terms "a modern form of slavery". Newcastle relented later that season and allowed Eastham to move to Arsenal but the PFA were not prepared to drop the legal action, seeing it as a test case between themselves and the Football League.

It was not until 1963, two years after the maximum wage had been lifted, that Mr Justice Wilberforce, one of the descendants of the great anti-slave campaigner Sir William Wilberforce, ruled that the retain-and-transfer system was in restraint of the footballer's trade and was therefore unlawful. Players could now hope to be better paid for their efforts and if they did not like the club at which they were playing they could seek different pastures.

Adam Faith's record *What Do You Want?* was at the top of the UK Charts as Christmas approached. Most Sunderland fans would have been glad of two points from a Boxing Day match with Lincoln City but the Imps took both in a 4-2 victory. Hurley was missing through injury. Back in the side two days later, he was the star in a goalless draw in the return fixture at Sincil Bank, with the headline writers competing for superlatives to match his performance – "Hurley takes all the honours" and "Three Cheers for Hurley" were typical.

In recognition of his performances throughout 1959, Hurley found himself voted Ireland's top player of the year as chosen by the sports editors of the Republic's ten major papers. Ironically the Caltex Trophy was to be the only award he was to win during his playing career, although plenty have followed since.

At the start of 1960 Sunderland were in real danger of being relegated to the Third Division, especially as on January 2nd 1960 they were beaten 2-1 by Brighton at the Goldstone Ground. Lawther gave the away side a shock lead late in a first half during which Argus reported: "In the first half it seemed that Hurley was playing Brighton on his own." Sunderland travelled home with only twenty points from twenty-five games.

In the circumstances it was a very decent sized crowd of 34,129 that turned out for the visit of First Division Blackburn Rovers in the FA Cup. Lawther again scored but it was only enough to force a replay. Bryan Douglas, who played that day for Rovers, and who represented England thirty-six times, appearing in the World Cups of 1958 and 1962, speaks warmly about Roker Park: "I remember it very well; Sunderland were a big club. It always has been. It wasn't far from the docks and it was a nice place to go. We used to stay overnight not far from the ground on the seafront.

"They're mad up there. At both Newcastle and Sunderland, the supporters are very, very passionate. Every team claims that their supporters are passionate, but Sunderland and Newcastle are probably the most passionate of them all. Sunderland isn't that big a place, but they get good crowds."

Today a replayed FA Cup game would take place ten or eleven days later on police advice but in 1960 it took place just four days after the first match and Sunderland went out 4-1.

Blackburn went on to reach the FA Cup final that year, during which they were to deny local rivals Burnley a possible "double" when in the FA Cup 6th round at Turf Moor, watched by more than 51,000, they came back from three down to force a replay, which they won 2-0. Blackburn lost badly at Wembley to Wolverhampton Wanderers, going down 3-0, having sold star player Roy Vernon to Everton in the run-up to the final, a move that still rankles with older Rovers supporters.

Blackburn veteran Ronnie Clayton, who played thirty-five times for England, including five in which he was captain, recalls Hurley as "a strapping centre half, fierce in the tackle. I think I must have kicked him a good few times when I played against him. He had a tremendous game for Ireland in 1957 when we qualified to play in Sweden. He was a very good player, Charlie Hurley."

Only 13,501 were at Roker Park for the match with Swansea Town but they were treated to a marvellous centre forward display by Lawther, who rattled up a hat-trick as the Welsh team were beaten 4-0, revenge for the previous season's thrashing at Vetch Field.

There was disappointment, however, in the following home match when Ipswich Town won 1-0. Heading his Monday column

"Sunderland tumble nearer to relegation", Argus reported that "This was a shattering defeat. Apart from Hurley, who had a great game, and Anderson, the rest of the side played so far below their individual standards that there could not be a scrap of confidence in any of them." With just twenty-three points from thirty games Sunderland remained in trouble. Brown's young side relied heavily on Hurley and Anderson to pull them out of the danger zone.

Twenty-seven years later, of course, Sunderland did eventually sink into the Third Division, but by then they had played a number of seasons in the Second; in 1959–60 it was only their second ever.

Sunderland's largest crowd of the 1959–60 season was only 37,059 for a thrilling derby with Middlesbrough which finished 2-2 and in which Hurley had another fine game. The *Sunday Pictorial* reporter Vince Wilson wrote that his opponent Clough "never had a chance. It's a long, long time since a Sunderland player got the cheers Hurley deserved coming into the tunnel at the final whistle."

The following week "Burly Hurley keeps them out" was the banner headline in the *Daily Mirror* after the Irishman produced an inspired display at the Baseball Ground where a single Ian Lawther goal gave Sunderland a priceless 1-0 victory against Derby County. It was their first away victory in six months.

When victory followed at home to Plymouth Argyle, Sunderland fans could breathe a little more easily. But three straight defeats followed, including one at Ashton Gate where a single goal from John Atyeo helped Bristol City win 1-0, and it was not until after consecutive home victories against Scunthorpe and Portsmouth that the threat of relegation was finally lifted.

Hurley played his eighth international on March 30th 1960, a friendly against Chile. This was a bad-tempered affair, easily forgotten except perhaps for those who played in it and particularly the two goalscorers for Ireland, Noel Cantwell with a penalty and Dermot Curtis.

Sunderland finished the 1959–60 season as they started it – losing, this time away to Liverpool by 3-0. Charlie Hurley, however, maintained his form as this snippet from Jim Beecroft in the *Daily*

Mirror reveals: "Liverpool captured third place in Division Two for the third time in five years by beating a magnificent footballer and ten others. The footballer supreme was Charlie Hurley, the bastion on which Sunderland's defence is built. What a classy player this big tall centre half is. And what a pity for England he was born in Cork."

Sunderland, with thirty-six points, ended the campaign only six points clear of relegated Hull City, with Bristol City a further three points below. Going in the opposite direction were champions Aston Villa, relegated the previous season, and runners-up Cardiff City who replaced Leeds United and Luton Town respectively.

Interviewed years afterwards, left back Len Ashurst is full of praise for Charlie Hurley's play during a difficult season, saying simply: "Charlie was at his best that season I feel. He held the team together and it was when he gained his great reputation as a leader."

Sunderland fans were naturally disappointed, hopes that the club would bounce back at the first attempt had proven wildly optimistic and the second season in Division Two had resulted in the club's lowest ever league position – sixteenth. Average gates had been much reduced to 23,344.

Meanwhile in a thrilling finish in Division One, Burnley, managed by Harry Potts, born in Hetton-le-Hole and who had taken charge of the club after a short spell by William Dougall following the loss of Alan Brown to Sunderland three years previously, beat Wolves by a single point to capture the Division One trophy. This stopped the Black Country side from becoming the first team to win three consecutive titles since Arsenal in the mid 1930s.

During the 1950s and 1960s Burnley were particularly successful in finding and developing what appeared to be an endless stream of football talent from the north-east. It was an era when it was said you "could shout down a mine" in the region and "up would pop a footballer."

On May 18th 1960 Glasgow's Hampden Park was the scene of one of the greatest games ever played, Real Madrid beating West German champions Eintracht Frankfurt 7-3 in a European Cup final watched by 127,000. At the heart of the Madrid side was the simply superb partnership between Ferenc Puskas, destroyer of the England team at Wembley in 1953, and Alfredo Di Stefano. On the day Puskas scored four and his partner three, Eintracht even had the temerity to score first!

In Malmö in Sweden on the same night Hurley was making his tenth appearance for his national team – the ninth had come nine days earlier when Ireland defeated West Germany in Düsseldorf with a Fionan Fagan goal on thirty minutes.

Writing in the *Irish Independent*, WP Murphy reported that this "was a success gained by Irish courage, pluck and a little luck, of which they had their share in the early stages." Praising new Irish captain Pat Saward for his fine display, he also reported that "co-starring was Hurley at centre half, who was the Irish rock against which waves of German attacks lapped and ebbed without making any impression. He ruled his area with head and feet, deadly in the tackle when danger threatened, and shrewdly masterful in possession as he stroked and pushed the ball to his advantage."

Hurley recalls the match as follows: "It was like Torquay going to Old Trafford and winning. We just didn't have the squad; Haller played, and these guys were different class to us. They pounded us for ninety minutes. I don't think I ever took such a pounding, but you get used to it and it can become a good habit. You get to a stage where you feel the other side isn't going to score, a point where you think you're going to sneak a draw. Then we broke away and won 1-0. I am glad there were no guns around, as the Germans would have shot the lot of us. They never expected Ireland to go there and win in Germany. It was great".

Goalkeeper Noel Dwyer had been injured in the Germany game, and although he was declared fit he did not look it when the game got underway in Stockholm. In the circumstances it was hardly surprising that Ireland could not repeat their famous victory. They were three goals down at half-time before Dwyer was replaced by Drumconda's Maurice Swan. Fagan did pull a goal back but Borjesson scored in the eighty-ninth minute to make it 4-1.

According to WP Murphy, the defeat might have been even heavier but for Charlie Hurley, who "rose to new heights, with a defensive display of the first magnitude. Even though pitted against the great Simonsson, Hurley was never in the least flurried and was easily the outstanding Irish player."

Hurley thus ended the season as he started it, in fine form. It was a year in which he'd shown a single-minded determination to keep Sunderland in the Second Division and he had taken his magnificent performances for the Wearsiders onto the international stage. This and the reduced attendances meant that there was speculation that Sunderland might be forced to sell their prized asset, with chairman Stanley Ritson admitting to Charlie Summerbell in the *Daily Mirror*: "Hurley represents a valuable cash asset and in a sense he is better than we need. He is of First Division calibre. We have to face the fact that gates are inadequate to meet our expenses."

Chapter Seven

Fatherhood but no promotion

Charlie Hurley, who had become a father for the first time when his daughter Tracy was born on June 7th, started the 1960–61 season in good form as Sunderland opened their third year in Division Two with a 2-1 victory over Swansea Town, their first opening day victory for six years. Argus commented that "none did better than Hurley for his ice-cool control and mastery in the air" and, remarking on a feature of the defender's play for which he was to become famous during his time at Sunderland, stating "there is nothing quite so emphatic as the headed clearance by Hurley which sends the ball practically to the half-way line."

Younger readers may be unaware of how difficult such a feat was at the time. The ball used was rock hard and when it got wet it became a very heavy object indeed. A leather 'food', Dubbin, best described as thick yellow axle-grease, was often applied to the ball to "soften it up". In fact it was waterproof and did nothing of the sort.

There are many former footballers who suffered in later life after repeatedly heading those footballs, including former Sunderland manager Bob Stokoe. The classic 1960s West Bromwich Albion centre forward Jeff Astle's death was ascribed to this after the coroner found that the repeated minor trauma of heading the ball had been the cause of death by industrial injury. Astle scored the winning goal in the 1968 FA Cup Final and was top scorer with twenty-five goals in Division One in 1969–70. Duels between him and Hurley were fierce competitive battles with no quarter given.

Some of today's footballers would certainly regard the balls of the 1960s as unsuitable and they would definitely destroy a manicured hairdo or two. To head such a ball the distances Hurley managed demonstrated perfect timing, balance and power, not to

91

mention an awareness of players around you and a determination to get to the ball first. Hurley was a master at all this. Of course it helped to be over six feet tall and fourteen stone, but this should not obscure his talent in this respect.

Football boots, of course, were very different. A new pair of leather boots had to be "broken in" and studs, which had to be rounded and no longer than half an inch [1.25cm], had to be hammered into the soles of the boots, which were heavier than today's and offered much greater ankle protection. Players often had several pairs of boots with different length studs as only later did moulded and screw-in studs appear. Club apprentices were given the job of keeping the boots of senior players clean and dry in between games.

Strips, numbered one to eleven, could be guaranteed to collect the rain and mud along the way. Many was the time when spectators were unable to tell who had passed the ball as the player's number was covered with mud. On particularly dark and dismal winter days it was often a problem to make out which team was which. The shirts were also advert free and remained that way until the 1974–75 season when England signed a commercial deal with Admiral that saw the players wear shirts with the manufacturer's logo on them.

Then, in 1979, Liverpool become the first side to run out with a sponsor's name on their shirts, in this case Hitachi.

When two away draws were followed by a 4-0 home win over Stoke City, in which Anderson was outstanding before a very disappointing attendance of 19,007, it seemed that Sunderland might finally be coming to terms with life in Division Two.

That proved to be wrong and, starting in mid-September, the side from Roker Park lost five consecutive matches. They included one against Middlesbrough at Ayresome Park where Brian Clough scored the only goal which, according to Argus, "was all he did do in the game, for once again he came under the spell of Charlie Hurley." The attendance on the day was 20,000 less than the same fixture in the previous season. Sunderland were left with just nine points from thirteen games – another long troubled season stretched ahead of them.

Since the start of the 1956–57 season Sunderland had played 181 League games, winning only 52 and drawing 45, a total of just 153 points. It was the worst record in the Football League.

Hurley was in the Ireland team on September 28th when they hosted their first match against Wales. With an eight-match unbeaten home record to defend, Ireland were favourites, but they reckoned without two men who were instrumental in Spurs' success that season, wingers Terry Medwin and Cliff Jones.

Goalkeeper Phil Kelly, making his debut for Ireland, was sent one way and then another by Jones and although Fagan managed to equalise, Jones scored a second and West Ham's Phil Woosnam a third, before a late penalty by Fagan gave Ireland a little consolation. Most reporters afterwards agreed that Hurley was Ireland's best performer as press speculation about a move nearer London continued to mount.

It was Lawther who rescued Sunderland by scoring in five consecutive League matches, six in all games as he scored the team's first when Sunderland went down 4-3 away to Brentford in their first ever League Cup match. The 1-1 draw with Rotherham almost produced Hurley's first goal for Sunderland when, down to just nine men due to injuries, he raced forty yards to meet Hooper's corner and force a magnificent save from Roy Ironside in the Rotherham goal.

Outside right Harry Hooper had been signed from Birmingham City the previous September. Exceptionally quick with a strong shot, he made 80 first team appearances for Sunderland, scoring 19 times.

Hurley played his twelfth match for Ireland when Norway's largely amateur team provided little opposition in a game won 3-1 by the home side. Fagan scored again while Peter Fitzgerald grabbed two.

With the PFA continuing to mount a vigorous campaign for improved pay and an end to the retain-and-transfer system, Alan Hardaker, the Football League secretary, had been putting forward proposals to try and break the deadlock. By suggesting that the future should include retaining the maximum wage he could not expect to obtain PFA approval even if the clubs had agreed that they would pay the additional bonuses and signing-on fees he was proposing.

Players wanted the freedom to earn as much as an employer was prepared to pay, although writing many years later, Jimmy Hill believed that, despite a series of meetings which had approved strike action, the players would probably have settled for a maximum wage of £30 a week and some reasonable adjustments to the retain-and-transfer system. But many of the clubs were determined not to budge.

Charlie Hurley's first goal for Sunderland should have come when Ipswich were beaten 2-0 at Roker Park at the start of December because, reported Argus, Ipswich goalkeeper Roy Bailey "admitted that Hurley's header from a corner from Jack Overfield had crossed the line but the referee didn't see it."

The Suffolk team were lying third behind Sheffield United and Liverpool but two goals from Willie McPheat, who had only just got into the team after signing for Sunderland the previous year, put Sunderland's fortunes on the up. So Hurley's opening goal for Sunderland would have to wait – but not for long.

The decision to send Hurley up for corners was revolutionary when Sunderland tried it towards the end of 1960. Since Herbert Chapman's decision to make the centre half a stopper they had remained firmly on the halfway line at set pieces no matter how good they were in the air.

It was this tactic which helped make Hurley so popular with Sunderland fans. After a while no corner at Roker Park would be complete without the cry of "Charlie, Charlie, Charlie" as the crowd roared the big man to get up into the opponents' box to cause as many problems as possible.

"I was always good in the air. It was Stan Anderson's idea. So I went up for a corner and although I didn't score it caused a lot of problems. The fact that I attacked the ball meant I got an awful lot of goals because we had some good crossers of the ball and Harry Hooper, George Mulhall and Nicky 'the nicker' Sharkey got on the end of some of my knock-downs."

Anderson's foresight changed the face of English football forever – now every team sends at least one of their centre backs forward for set pieces. Anderson says: "I thought that it was a natural thing for Charlie to do. He was a big fella, brilliant in the air. What else were we supposed to do with him? It was logic. It meant when he came up the other side had to say 'Whoa, we'd better mark him, look at the size of him'. Normally the centre half marked the centre forward but when you had Charlie up there standing at the far post the centre half didn't fancy going out there. The number of goals that Charlie scored, and the number of knock-downs that he allowed others to score was a very decent return.

"He was a magnificent header of the ball. It doesn't take rocket science to think what I thought. Brownie never said a word against it. In fact Brownie rarely spoke to me, except when he played hell with all of us. I said to Charlie at his seventieth birthday party that Brownie thought the world of him and to be fair Charlie was his best buy ever, so he should have."

Charlie Hurley's first goal for Sunderland was a belated Christmas present, delayed by just a day. It came on Boxing Day 1960 in a 1-1 draw with Sheffield United watched by 46,099 spectators. It was the first goal by a Sunderland centre half since Ray Daniel had scored at home to Sheffield Wednesday back on February 16th 1957. Daniel's goal came from the penalty spot.

There was only a five-day wait for the next Hurley goal as he scored in the 7-1 win over Luton Town at Roker Park on December 31st.

Luton manager Sam Bartram, once a great goalkeeper who thus knew a thing or two about playing behind a centre half, wondered afterwards: "If John Charles is worth £60,000, how much is he worth? He's the greatest in the business. I wish we had Hurley."

The genial Irishman remembers: "I used to get more knackered going up for corners than playing back in defence. If we had ten or twelve corners in a game I had to get up and then get back. But the crowd wouldn't have it any other way because if I stayed back you'd hear 'Charlie, Charlie' and up I went... it was the number one thing that the fans loved."

It was in the report of the Luton match that Charlie Hurley earned the nickname "King" for the first time. It was written by Vince Wilson in the *Sunday Pictorial* on New Year's Day 1961. And it stuck.

The FA Cup draw had brought a home tie against Arsenal and there was genuine excitement among supporters for the first time in many years. Roker Park was packed with 58,765, including four Arsenal fans from West Hartlepool who were mocked as "traitors" by Argus in the following Monday's *Echo*. He could not understand how anyone from the north-east could support a Cockney team. Clearly this was well before television got its hands on impressionable youngsters to ensure that today, wherever they live, they must support fashionable and successful teams even if they are never likely to see them play live.

Arsenal proved to be the better team for the first thirty minutes with David Herd putting them ahead after just five minutes. But with Anderson at his very best, Sunderland equalised and then won the match with his second goal of the game. Ashurst made a last-ditch tackle to prevent an equaliser from George Eastham, who had signed for the Gunners after his refusal to play for Newcastle.

Recalls Hurley: "Stan Anderson was brilliant against Arsenal. He was one of the greatest wing players that I ever saw. People say he lacked a bit defensively, but you can't have it all. He had flair, and tremendous vision; one sad thing was that he wasn't there when we got promotion."

Monday's *Echo* brought the news that Sunderland had drawn Liverpool away in the fourth round, along with new peace proposals from Alan Hardaker to try and prevent a players' strike. This time he suggested increasing minimum wages to £12 a week for lower league players, £14 for those in Division Two and £15 for Division One. These were actually below the then increasing average wage in some areas of the country. He also proposed, however, to end the maximum wage system after the following season but not to end the retain-and-transfer system.

Jimmy Hill felt that this might be good enough for the better-off players to abandon the PFA's campaign; it meant one of the two major demands had been met and the opportunity of earning considerably more was within the grasp of players from Divisions One and Two. However, they stood overwhelmingly with their less fortunate colleagues and at a players' meeting in Manchester 344 players invited the press to witness them voting for strike action.

On Wednesday January 18th 1961, the PFA and the Football League finally appeared to have resolved their differences when it was agreed that any player whose contract had come to an end and who had not been transferred by August 31st would be able to depend on "the management committee of the Football League to deal with the matter." The players took this to mean that the committee would help the player to get a move. They were delighted; it meant the end of the maximum wage and the retain-and-transfer system.

In fact the clubs dug in their heels and while the players were now free to negotiate wages it was left to the PFA to mount a successful legal challenge, using George Eastham's case, before the transfer system was completely overhauled. Nevertheless it marked the beginning of the end for the clubs in their fight to keep players' wages and conditions under their strict control and Hurley has no doubts who to thank:

"All the players who played during my era and those since should always say a prayer for Jimmy Hill before they go to sleep. He went in to get a maximum wage scrapped and he managed to do so. If I ever saw Jimmy I would walk up to him and say 'I'd have stayed on £20 a week for all my career if it hadn't been for you'. The clubs might have moved it up a bit but not by much. Mind, some players today are getting paid far too much: if Sky pulls out tomorrow the clubs will be bankrupt and fans will be regarded as sacrosanct once again."

The *Liverpool Echo* was looking forward to Sunderland and Charlie Hurley's appearance at Anfield. Before the cup tie Sunderland enjoyed two impressive performances, beating Lincoln 2-1 away, where Lawther was one of the scorers, and winning 4-1 at home to Portsmouth, when Lawther scored twice to make it fourteen league goals in fourteen league games.

A cup tie special train at a cost of 35 shillings [£1.75] took some of the mass support to Liverpool. Those travelling could be sure of the chance to enjoy a good drink afterwards as the return did not leave Lime Street until 11.30pm. How football fans would enjoy such departure times these days!

The *Liverpool Echo* reporter was in no doubt who was likely to be Sunderland's key player, reporting that "the king-pin and king-sized centre half Hurley is one of the keys to their success. Liverpool have no comparable personality."

Argus had warned that Sunderland would have to be at their very best to beat not only a decent Liverpool side but also the Liverpool Spion Kop, which "there is nothing to compare with anywhere in the country". This area of the ground behind one of the goals was named in honour of the battle between the Boer and British Armies in January 1900 along the Tugela River, Natal, in South Africa.

Liverpool were not then the force they were to later become. Like Sunderland, they were in the Second Division, having slid out of the top flight after a long spell, but they were to go up as champions the following year so a victory at Anfield was no mean feat. And that's what Sunderland achieved with goals from Harry Hooper and Lawther sending them into the fifth round. Off the field, and not for the last time, the travelling Sunderland fans humbled the famous Kop.

Sunderland's young team had finally come of age and one player particularly pleased at the result was Liverpool-born Len Ashurst, who had been released by his home-town club at nineteen after being on their books for three years. "I enjoyed the FA Cup match, but I always enjoyed playing at Anfield as my parents and relatives were all Liverpudlians but also because they gave me a free transfer, which I think was a mistake," he remembers.

As Hurley recalls: "We were two-nil up in twenty minutes. We had to defend the Kop in the second half and the longer it went on the more they lobbed the ball in. It was like manna from heaven. It was easy. To play in front of the Kop and get a standing ovation, which we got after that game, is something to remember because the Kop were great fans. They were very fair. If you played well they clapped you off the park. It was a fabulous day. I was chosen as 'Man of the Match' for that game, I was given a lighter. I gave it to my dad and he lost it – that was my dad – or perhaps he flogged it!

"Yes, my dad was a character. But what I got from him was a determination to win. Even today if I play tennis or snooker or darts I want to win. You never hear of the player who comes second, no matter how many times he does it. One good win is worth much more. I came second to Bobby Moore in the 1964 Player of the Year awards and no one remembers. I think I was a born winner and I got that from my father. I'll give you an example. I used to be a very good athlete as a kid and Ford works used to have an annual garden fete, with athletics for under-fives, under-tens and under-fifteens. You got seven shillings and sixpence [37p] for winning, five bob [25p] for second and two and six [13p] for third. It was a lot of money. One year it was raining and there could only be one race and the older ones were naturally put at the back.

"Halfway up the field were the little five-year-olds. On your marks, get set go and with me wearing spikes I was off like a shot. I was nearly there but this little five-year-old beat me – he was nearly at the tape to start with. I go to my dad with the money still puffing and panting and he said 'fancy letting a five-year-old beat you'. I never forget that. It instilled into me that you've got to win. Winners are not necessarily nice people when they're actually competing, but you put on a different hat. You just feel different, quite frightening.

"Now my mother had a massive heart, all my brothers and sisters are still very close; I think we got the strength from my dad but the feeling and affection from my mother. I have never got pleasure from seeing people getting hurt during life. My father used to say 'Always be honest, boy, then you don't have to have a good memory'. When I look back it wasn't a bad principle to be brought up with."

Two weeks after the Anfield match more than 53,000 packed Roker Park to see Sunderland defeat Middlesbrough 2-0, Brian Clough again missing out. Some Sunderland supporters thought he was not as good as reported or as good as he thought he was!

Sunderland drew Norwich City away in the next round of the FA Cup and not for the first time a player and team were motivated by mind games from the opposition. Charlie Hurley recalls: "I will always remember Norwich because I remember reading the headlines the day before the match. I don't know if it was a wind-up or not but it said 'Hurley, the weakness' so I couldn't fathom that one out. It put my back up anyway. We took a bit of a battering and then we had a good spell in the first half where we could have got something. Then we got one corner with about ten minutes to go, which Harry Hooper took.

"He was the type of guy who'd say 'Which way do you want the lace Charlie?' He always curled the corner away from the 'keeper, beautiful for someone good in the air. One corner, and bop and in the back of the net, halfway up the iron stanchion. Before I could even get off the floor there was a mass of players on my back. I was carrying six when I went over to shake hands with Harry Hooper.

"Then we took a pounding for ten minutes, and won 1-0. Those types of games will always stick in your mind. An awful lot of Sunderland fans from those days who I talk to pick that game out. It was packed at Norwich that day; in those days fans and players were one, there were no prima donnas. OK, we were earning a lot more than the fans even in those days but our players loved the fans."

Stan Anderson rates Hurley's performance at Norwich as the best he saw from him in a Sunderland shirt. "He was brilliant. It is a shame that TV in those days wasn't as good as it is now because if they'd looked at that goal from all the angles that they do now – it was such a bullet-like header from twelve to fifteen yards out. I remember it coming over my head and just turning to look and I've never seen anything like it in my life.

"He must have hit it flush on the head and if it had hit the crossbar it would probably have broken it. It just absolutely flashed into the net. The goal won us the match. I bet we were under the cosh for eighty-five per cent of the time but Norwich never looked like scoring. I remember one of the Norwich players asking 'How the bloody hell have we lost this match?'"

The goal arrived with eleven minutes remaining and Argus described it as: "From a Hooper corner-kick Hurley beat Keenan with a magnificently placed header which was a goal all the way."

"Hurley could be the rage of the Continent in a classy side like Real Madrid," wrote Charlie Summerbell in the *Daily Mirror* the following week. Madrid were, of course, the best side in the world at the time having won the first five European Cups between 1956 and 1960.

When the sixth round draw was made it meant Tottenham Hotspur, the best team in England and looking to become the first since Aston Villa in 1896–97 to record the 'double' of League and FA Cup in the same season, would be making the long journey to Roker. It was swiftly announced that the tie would be a 63,000 all-ticket affair and even though Spurs returned around 10,000 from their allocation of 15,750 on the Thursday before the game they were soon sold. The atmosphere was electric. Younger readers should think of Manchester City in the FA Cup at Roker in 1973 and Newcastle at home at the Stadium of Light in 2001, when Sunderland came from two down to grab a draw.

Sunderland won both matches between the draw and the tie, maintaining good form for the biggest game of their lives for some of the players involved. The 4-2 defeat of Leeds United included a hat-trick from Johnny Goodchild, playing his only game of the season and the last of his 44 games for Sunderland.

The Spurs side included Danny Blanchflower and Dave Mackay, the Scot having been signed by Bill Nicholson from Hearts six months after Nicholson had taken over as manager in October 1958. It was the away team who took the lead on nine minutes when Welshman Cliff Jones headed past an unsighted Peter Wakeham. It stayed that way until ten minutes into the second half, when Hurley went forward for another corner.

He remembers: "I dived and got a header in. Bill Brown pushed it out and Willie McPheat drove it home. I've got a big picture at home of the crowd of 63,000."

Dave Hillam, a long-time Sunderland fan, did not have a ticket, "so for want of anything better to do I ended up on Tunstall Hill with some mates and we heard an incredible noise from the ground. It transfixed us. I can still remember hearing a great roar coming over the river and us all standing there listening to it."

According to Argus "there was no Roker Park precedent for the scenes which followed" as supporters invaded the pitch in celebration of the equaliser, holding up the match for two minutes.

It was suggested that this intervention assisted a shaky Spurs team, giving them time to regroup among the mayhem. That is certainly how Danny Blanchflower recalled events in the *Sunday*

Express when a week after Sunderland's Wembley victory against Leeds United in 1973 he wrote: "Hundreds of fans jumped over the fence and on to the field. They were like a mad religious sect waving their hands to the glory of the equaliser. 'Let them come,' I said, 'let them get it all out of their system. The worst is over. This is the climax … keep your heads. Let's start going for their goal. We don't want them near ours. Not with that crowd."

Blanchflower claimed that Spurs then "pressed the game for a spell and then it faded into a midfield struggle."

Yet this is not what journalists reported. For example, Alan Hoby, also in the *Sunday Express*, wrote: "Spurs shocked and shaken by the tremendous fervour of the Roker fans could never click back into their classic pattern. Indeed for five minutes the Division One leaders were forced to kick anywhere … conceding three corners as they somehow survived the blitz."

Hurley remembers "Danny Blanchflower kicking the ball over to Stan Anderson. Now Danny never ever hit a ball more than twenty yards, but the crowd that day was going berserk, the panic button was being pressed. But we just couldn't get the goal although in the last minute John Dillon was very, very unlucky not to pinch the winner."

Argus reported that "Mackay was forced to boot the ball away and the famous Lilywhites so riled Hurley by their tactics used against him that he came near to losing his temper."

In the days following the game Blanchflower said that "nothing I have ever heard equalled the intensity of that wild roar at Roker Park last week when Sunderland drew level with Tottenham."

The Irishman retained his affection for Sunderland fans the rest of his life, writing in his *Sunday Express* post-1973 FA Cup final piece that seeing them at Wembley "had pleased me. It brought back old times for me. In some ways this was better than the last time. They had won the Cup. They had beaten the best team of their day and that did not bother me at all this time."

Spurs had been lucky but four days later they showed no mercy as they thumped Sunderland 5-0 in front of a White Hart Lane crowd of nearly 65,000 which contained a large number from the north-east, including some supporters who travelled by boat!

"The sea-going supporters are the crews of at least six North-East colliers, which will be moored in the Thames today" reported the *Newcastle Journal*.

Argus felt that the scoreline was a little harsh: "It was still a great game to watch and not nearly so one-sided as the scoreline indicates. But Spurs did everything a little better and a little quicker and that was the basic difference between the sides."

He was probably being a little generous. My dad, Noble Metcalf, was one of the Sunderland supporters who travelled that day, and he told me years later: "They hammered us, but they were a great team, especially Danny Blanchflower."

They were only weeks away from establishing their own legacy and one wonders what might have happened if the pre-Munich Manchester United side had not been so tragically destroyed. Spurs against Manchester United in 1960–61 would have been some game.

Hurley recalls that "Jimmy McNab missed the return match. He was a good defender. I used to call Jimmy 'Mac the knife' as he knocked guys over, but he rarely got booked. He'd knock the guy over, pick him up, say nothing and walk away, always smile. Don't forget referees have got their own problems. If you don't give them too much trouble then you could get away with three or four challenges.

"Lennie 'the Lion' Ashurst and Mac were the two best defenders I played with. They were rock solid. In the Second Division they got known as the flank to be wary of. The blend Alan Brown got was very good and don't forget a good number came through the youth side, including Cec Irwin who was a solid, no nonsense defender. Lovely lad also.

"Underdogs against the very best rarely get a second chance and we didn't at Tottenham. For about twenty minutes we played really well, as good as them. Ian Lawther had two good chances. Even if he'd got one of them it wouldn't have helped. They had a fantastic side, and once they went one up we showed our inexperience and ended up losing by five.

"But it was an experience. There were thirty thousand locked out. Word had gone out that this young Sunderland side were going to cause an upset. For twenty minutes we did, but that's not what counts."

Stan Anderson says: "I didn't think we were going to win the cup: we weren't good enough. You need luck as well. If we were going to win it we had to beat Tottenham at Roker Park. We could have done it but John Dillon fluffed it in the last few minutes. He still cries about it even now. He's a lovely lad is John. He comes for the players' reunion dinners and we rib him, saying 'You were through against Tottenham' and he throws his hands up and moans 'Oh no!'"

The cup defeat did not seem to affect the team too much. There was a 0-0 draw at Rotherham and a 2-1 victory against visitors Brighton and Hove Albion. This put Sunderland on forty points from thirty-three games. They were still some way behind Ipswich Town and Sheffield United but they were in sensational form and had gained seventeen points from ten games.

But promotion was not to be. In the very next match at Eastville, Hurley was injured early. Although he limped through the game it would probably have been better had he gone off as it meant he would miss the following games, and Sunderland lost by 1-0 to Bristol Rovers anyway.

The defeat knocked the stuffing out of the still young Sunderland side. Hurley missed the next seven games, in which Sunderland lost four times. Still, sixth was a lot better than the previous two seasons. These days it would get you into the play-offs and offer a back-door route to promotion but they were not introduced until 1987.

One of the defeats occurred in Sunderland's final away game of the season when Ipswich Town scored four goals without reply. The following week the East Anglian club were crowned Division Two Champions with fifty-nine points, pipping Sheffield United by a point. With thirty-nine league goals Ray Crawford had knocked Middlesbrough's goalscoring machine Brian Clough off his perch as top scorer in Division Two for the first time in four seasons.

With no previous experience of top-flight football, the Portman Road side were expected to struggle the following season. In fact they went on to confound everybody by winning the First Division title under the guidance of manager Alf Ramsey. Ramsey had been appointed in 1955 when the club were in the Third Division South and led them to promotion two seasons later. Ramsey himself had won back-to-back Second and First Division titles as a player with Tottenham Hotspur in 1950 and 1951.

Since then only one team has repeated the feat, Brian Clough's Nottingham Forest capturing the First Division title in 1978 only a year after winning promotion. It is unlikely to be repeated.

Spurs went on to beat Leicester City in the final, thus adding the FA Cup to the First Division title they won by finishing eight points clear of Sheffield Wednesday. The then famous 'double' had been achieved only twice previously when Preston North End won both competitions in the first ever season of league football, 1888–89, and then Aston Villa in 1896–97.

There was no beach for Charlie Hurley that summer. Ireland had been drawn with Scotland and Czechoslovakia in World Cup qualifying group eight with the winners going forward to play in Chile the following summer. The Scotland games took place over a four-day period at the end of the season, the first at Hampden Park and the return at Dalymount Park.

It was very much unlucky thirteen for Hurley in Glasgow. Ireland awarded a first cap to Andy McEvoy of Blackburn Rovers, but at right half, not in his usual position of inside forward, and Ireland were behind in the fourteenth minute when Hurley made a poor clearance and Rangers forward, and later Sunderland teammate, Ralph Brand was on hand to score an easy goal. When he scored his second just before half-time it looked all over but Haverty did pull a goal back before David Herd added two for the home side to make it 4-1.

Four days later Herd was missing, his place taken by Alex Young of Everton. Mick Meagan made his debut for Ireland at left half.

The 36,000 crowd were treated to a magnificent display, sadly not from their own team. Jim Baxter, Paddy Crerand, who had made his debut in the first match, and Celtic's Billy McNeill, later to become the first skipper of a British team to lift the European

Cup, ran the show. After four minutes Young scored the first, twelve minutes later Brand got the second and Young got his second and Scotland's third two minutes before the referee's final whistle brought a chastened Ireland's misery to an end.

Had the game taken place under today's rules there is little doubt that one player at least on the Scotland side would have been playing in the green of Ireland. Paddy Crerand had been brought up in the Gorbals area of Glasgow, traditionally home to thousands of immigrants from Ireland and often referred to throughout the '50s, '60s and '70s as the most dangerous place in Britain as street gangs were rife. Crerand, in his own words was "totally Irish, my parents were Irish, all my pals were Irish. We kept ourselves to ourselves because everyone from outside of it hated you.

"I remember when I left school in 1955 there were adverts in the papers, 'No Irish or RC [Roman Catholics] may apply.' It was only later on that they allowed people to play for the country of their parents; the first player ever to play for Ireland not born there was my United teammate Shay Brennan. If that law was there in 1961 I would have played for Ireland. I stopped playing for Scotland because of the bigotry. It also didn't help that I played in England but to be fair I never looked at myself as Scottish anyway."[2]

Chapter Eight

The arrival of Brian Clough

Charlie Hurley would not have to face one regular opponent during the 1961–62 season, Sunderland having decided to spend £45,000 on Brian Clough. It was a statement of intent that they were determined to win back their place in the First Division. At least two matches would give Sunderland the flavour of the big time as there were derby matches against Newcastle United to look forward to after the Magpies had suffered the indignity of relegation.

Clough had asked for a transfer and then gone on a two-week cruise on the *QEII* from Southampton. He was unaware of the negotiations until he arrived back in Southampton to be met by Alan Brown, who had cut short his holiday in Cornwall.

Unlike Hurley in 1957, Clough quickly agreed to sign for Sunderland and "expressed himself as delighted with the housing accommodation offered" by the Roker Park club. Clough also said some years later that he was "well aware of my new gaffer's strict, straight and honest reputation."

The move, a club record for both clubs, brought back memories of another famous transfer between the clubs in 1903–04 when Alf Common moved in the opposite direction at a cost of £1,000, the first four-figure transfer, which astonished many who predicted the figure would never be broken. Part of the Clough fee was offset by the sale of Ian Lawther to Blackburn Rovers for £18,000. Lawther went on to score a total of 178 league goals in his career.

There were plenty who said it was ridiculous that a football club should be spending £45,000 on one player, particularly as, according to Labour Party leader Hugh Gaitskell, speaking before the quarter of a million assembled at the Durham Miners' Gala, that same weekend: "It was now evident that Britain was drifting into a major economic crisis."

Clough had scored an amazing 204 goals in 222 matches for his hometown club but it was not entirely a surprise that they were prepared to let him go. Such was his status in the Ayresome Park dressing room that nine fellow professionals signed a petition demanding his removal as captain. But he was a proven goalscorer joining a young team which had started to show great potential.

Hurley remembers the man who later managed Nottingham Forest to European glory in 1979 and 1980: "I played against Cloughie a few times. He was a very, very good goalscorer. Brian Clough's aim was to score goals; he cared about nothing else. He didn't think about having a good game, leading the line. He was not interested. 'I'd rather score one goal off my shin,' he'd say rather than be a good spreader of the ball around. It's greed, but a great striker is always greedy and Brian was a very good signing for Sunderland football club. I used to change my game when I played against him. In the papers it was always Clough versus Hurley, who's going to win? Not being big-headed, I knew at the end of those games that I was going to win because I looked at Cloughie and I forgot about playing all the football and the clever stuff and just concentrated on him.

"He was the main man at Middlesbrough. I kicked him an awful lot of times. He wasn't that good in the air, but you couldn't give him an inch. I think it was as good a signing as we ever made. Mind you, Brown did take a risk because even then Clough was very outspoken."

The fee only just broke Sunderland's record transfer fee at the time as they had spent £42,500 on George Herd at the end of the previous season, the Scotsman making his debut in the final match, at home to Liverpool. He was bought from Clyde and had played in the side that had won the Scottish Cup for the third and final time in 1958.

Herd had played five times for Scotland. By the time he moved south he was twenty-five years old and he was in peak form at inside right. As Hurley recalls: "George Herd was a very skilful player, also very honest and a very, very nice guy."

Argus reported that "the fresh wave of enthusiasm which has hit Wearside is just as evident among the players and staff as it is among the public. While the players are raring to go in what they are convinced will be their promotion season, supporters are piling up season ticket receipts far beyond the all-time record."

Amid all the excitement it was therefore extremely disappointing when the campaign got underway with two defeats, Sunderland losing out in a seven-goal thriller at Fellows Park to Walsall, who were playing their first game in Division Two after winning promotion the previous season. Harry Hooper had given Sunderland the lead at 3-2 with a penalty but a Tony Richards hat-trick marked a wonderful debut for the West Midlands team.

Liverpool's easy 3-0 victory at Anfield in Sunderland's second match came after Hurley was carried from the pitch following a clash of heads with Kevin Lewis at 0-0. Although he returned to play at centre forward his loss at the back was a big blow.

The big Irishman had to miss the following two home games, one of which saw Liverpool complete the double with a 4-1 win. The Liverpool front man Roger Hunt, later to star in England's 1966 World Cup final victory, remembers that this was a vital match: "Like us, Sunderland were fancied for promotion but after twenty-six minutes we scored when Alan A'Court fired in a shot at Wakeham which he could only parry and the ball dropped at my feet for an easy goal. The Sunderland fans gave Liverpool a great reception and many of them told us afterwards we would get promotion at the end of the season."

Herd had been missing after suffering an injury during the match at Walsall, but his return galvanised Sunderland and he scored two in a 4-0 thrashing of Scunthorpe at Roker Park, before Clough grabbed his first hat-trick of the season as Sunderland took revenge in a 3-0 defeat of Bury. More than 74,000 attended the two matches.

Hurley had regained fitness in time to make his fifteenth appearance for his country in a very disappointing game at Dalymount Park, a World Cup qualifier against Czechoslovakia. Although Johnny Giles equalised for the Republic of Ireland, a couple of goals from Andrej Kvasnak and one from Adolf Scherer set them up for the return fixture on October 29th. With three straight defeats Ireland would not be going to Chile the following summer.

Hurley had travelled from Derby to Ireland, his second game in two days, buoyed by his second goal of the season for Sunderland. Bill Curry had given 'the Rams' the lead on seventy-one minutes but Hurley rescued a point in the last minute, starting his run from outside the penalty area and meeting Hooper's inch-perfect inswinger at the far post to head well wide of the 'keeper Ken Oxford.

Hurley's first goal had come the previous Saturday at the Goldstone Ground when from another Hooper corner kick he had been left unmarked and punished Brighton by powering his header past Baker for the equaliser. It was trademark Hooper and Hurley.

The Irishman then grabbed his third goal in four matches. This proved to be the only goal of the match at the home of Preston North End, the one thousand Sunderland fans at the game delighted that the club's long run of defeats at Deepdale had come to an end. The goal came from "another powerful header from a Jack Overfield corner from the left" in a match in which Hurley was outstanding. Sunderland now had sixteen points from fourteen games.

Signed from Leeds United, Overfield played 65 league games for Sunderland, grabbing five goals from outside left before moving on to Peterborough in 1963.

Ireland's return with Czechoslovakia was at the Stanhove Stadium in Prague on October 29th 1961 and Hurley was joined in the side by clubmate Ambrose Fogarty. It proved to be a terrible day. Ireland were destroyed by a Czechoslovakian side which hit seven with Andrej Kvasnak and Scherer both grabbing a couple, against which there was only a single goal from Fogarty. To make matters worse the second half was beamed back live to Ireland. At 4-1 Hurley decided that "the only way I was going to get noticed was to do a bit of fancy work, so I was doing a bit on the ball, flicks and all that. I was told afterwards the commentator remarked that if it hadn't been for Hurley it would have been ten."

The Czech newspapers themselves were also full of praise for the Sunderland centre half with *Svobodne Slovo* stating that Hurley was Ireland's only decent player, calling him "a player of striking elegance and assurance", while *Prace* said "the only one standing out in the Irish side was Hurley."

The result remains Ireland's heaviest World Cup defeat and it meant they failed to clear the first hurdle, having played and lost all four games, scoring just three goals and conceding seventeen.

The Czechs, who needed to beat Scotland in a play-off to get to Sweden, went on to great things at the World Cup. One of the scorers in Prague, left half Josef Masopust of Dukla Prague, was to be named European Football of the Year that year after his inspiring performances in those seventh World Cup finals, helping his country to the final where they lost 3-1 to a magnificent Brazilian side who retained the trophy.

According to Ambrose Fogarty, "Hurley was a terrific player for Ireland. He thoroughly deserved to get into the Irish Hall of Fame. He often played half-injured as well."

The eagerly anticipated first local derby of the season with Newcastle took place on December 2nd. It proved an exhilarating occasion with three pitch invasions at St James' Park adding to the tension. Len White rushed Newcastle into a seventeenth-minute lead, but when Clough equalised in the sixty-sixth minute Sunderland fans danced on the pitch. Two minutes later Johnny McGuigan shot Newcastle back into the lead, provoking an invasion from home fans. When Clough then struck his second equaliser five minutes from time the police were forced to prevent the Sunderland players from being mobbed by the ecstatic away support. In the final minute a Hooper drive flashed inches past Dave Hollins's right-hand post. At the end both sets of fans applauded the teams as they left the pitch.

An injury forced Hurley out of Sunderland's two away games over Christmas; both were lost, which as it transpired proved crucial at the season's end.

Says Stan Anderson: "Charlie did miss a few games because of his knee. It was a shame because you want to turn out your best team every time. When Charlie was missing there was something lacking. He was an inspirational character. If things went across you from the left you had a feeling that he was going to win the ball and that was a nice comforting thought. He was also a strong tackler. I think he got quite a few of his injuries from his last-ditch tackles."

It was now that another Sunderland legend stepped into the limelight. Jim Montgomery, who made a record 623 appearances in goal for the club, made his debut in the 5-2 League Cup defeat of Walsall at Roker Park on October 4th but he had to wait another five months before his League debut. It is likely he would have replaced Peter Wakeham sooner but politics played their part. Captain Stan Anderson advised Alan Brown to make the switch but Brown did not want to be seen to be taking advice and it was not until the game with Derby County at Roker Park on February 24th 1962 that Montgomery finally got into the League team.

Montgomery recalls: "Alan didn't pick me because it would have looked like someone else was taking the key decisions, so he waited and then it looked like he was the man making the choices. Stan always had a mind of his own, which was fine as he was the captain, but Alan Brown didn't always take too kindly to Stan's advice."

Wakeham was to make only one further appearance for Sunderland as Montgomery went on to make the number one position his own for the next decade and a half. Wakeham left in the summer of 1962, having made over 151 appearances for Sunderland, during which time he had acted as understudy to Fulham's Tony Macedo during an England tour of Italy and West Germany, although he never got to play. Ironically Wakeham was a lot closer to being capped than his successor, who proved to be a much better 'keeper as he showed when he finally ran out at Wembley on May 5th 1973.

Montgomery's problem was that he was born too early. In an age when English football was probably best known for its 'keepers, the top man was Gordon Banks, who was replaced by Peter Shilton. Today there is little doubt Montgomery would have more than fifty caps. No current English 'keeper comes anywhere near him in terms of talent although when pressed in an interview for this book he preferred not to comment, saying simply, "That's up to other people to decide. For some reason England just seem to have stopped producing 'keepers."

Against Derby, Hurley scored again but this time not with his head. He shot home in the thirteenth minute from the edge of the penalty area after an Anderson free kick had been forced out. Herd got the second as Sunderland won 2-1.

Although they were playing well, the Christmas defeats meant that when Sunderland ran out at Ayresome Park at the end of March they remained promotion outsiders. Liverpool were a long way out in front and Leyton Orient seemed set to snatch second place. Clough, who the previous weekend had hit another hat-trick at home to Huddersfield, stole the winner at his former club and a victory over Southampton racheted up the tension.

For Charlie Hurley the push for promotion was interrupted by his seventeenth international appearance. It was a friendly against Austria on April 8th in Dublin and despite the disappointment of losing 3-2 it was one of the happiest days of his life as he captained Ireland for the first time. It was 2-2 with goals from Noel Cantwell and Liam Tuohy before Erich Hof scored the Austrian winner in the 64th minute.

Making his debut was Tony Dunne of Manchester United, who in 1968 won a European Cup winners' medal at Wembley and who remembers that it was "a little frightening. I knew all my mates would be there watching me, so I was nervous. I can't remember how I got on."

Match reports show he had a fine game alongside Charlie Hurley, again the man of the match. Derek Jones, writing in the *Daily Mirror*, said "and what a performance from Hurley. He was master of the middle even though he had only had one hour's sleep after performing for Sunderland on Saturday."

Hurley was captain for twenty of the remaining twenty-three games he played in the green of his country. He may have moved to London when he was less than a year old and spoke with a southern accent but he remained a proud Irishman while also being grateful to the country he'd settled in for providing him with a chance to play football for a living.

A slight injury picked up against Austria meant Hurley missed the victory over Luton at Kenilworth Road but he was back on Easter Saturday when 57,666 saw Sunderland beat Newcastle 3-0 with Herd knocking in two and McPheat the other. Bragging rights were firmly with the supporters in red and white.

McPheat's goal was one of nineteen league goals he scored for Sunderland.

One reporter, David Haigh, wrote that "Sunderland packed themselves round the world-class Hurley like Indian blood-brothers... everywhere in the penalty area, his curly head and lightning boots got there first – and that is where Newcastle died."

Two days later, as the hour mark approached and Sunderland were struggling to hold on to a 1-0 lead at home to Rotherham, the strain was beginning to tell but a Hurley header from an Overfield corner doubled the lead and a much more relaxed side went on to win 4-0.

Charlie's sixth goal of the season followed the next day when Sunderland won the return 3-0, which set the scene perfectly for the final match at Swansea. Promotion could be gained if Sunderland won. If they drew and Leyton Orient won at home against Bury then the Londoners would go up instead. So many fans wanted to go that there were not enough coaches to take them and two flights from Newcastle to Swansea had to be arranged.

Things looked rosy when Brian Clough's twenty-ninth league goal of the season put Sunderland in front against a team fighting for survival. Swansea were level on points with Bristol Rovers, but had played a game less and were due to play Division Two champions Liverpool the following Friday. If Rovers won away at Luton Town, Swansea would need at least two points to make sure of staying up. As it happened Bristol lost 2-0; but Swansea were not to know that until after the match.

Half the crowd of 18,071 had began to dream of return trips to Old Trafford, White Hart Lane and Goodison Park, only for Swansea to equalise in the sixty-fifth minute. It produced a frenetic finish as Sunderland piled forward and with nine minutes left McNab "went in to make a 'suicide' header eight yards from goal and received a blow in the face which fractured his nose. He was carried behind the goal and out of the game and had to be physically restrained from going back to join in those last desperate few minutes," wrote Argus in the following Monday's *Sunderland Echo*.

The match finished all square, leaving the players and fans to await the result from Brisbane Road. It was bad news: Orient had

(top left) Charlie and sister Sheila at their confirmation. (top right) Charlie's grandparents Daniel and Julia. (bottom) Charlie and his brothers and sisters. top row: Charlie, Sheila, Danny. front row: Arthur, Christy, Iris and Phylis.

(top) Lining up with Sutton School – Charlie is holding the ball. (bottom) the Hurley family.

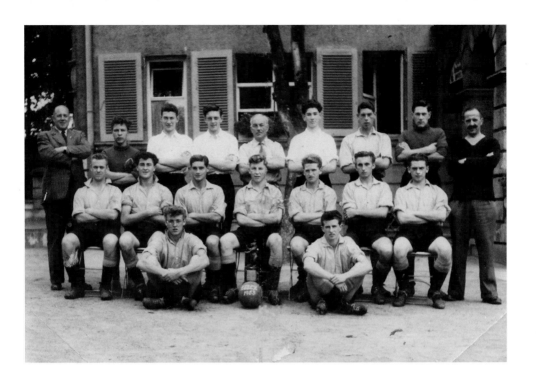

(top) Essex Schools. Charlie is second left on the middle row. (bottom) Millwall 14th October 1954 Back Row: John Short, Joe Heydon, Stan Anslow, Malcolm Finlayson, Pat Saward, Charlie Hurley; Front Row: Johnny Johnson, Denis Pacey, Alex Jardine (captain), Johnny Summers, Gordon Prior

(top) During National Service. Charlie is far right on the bottom row. The man in the middle of the top row is Gerry North who went on to be an international athlete and win the English cross country title. (bottom left) Millwall's new signing. (right) Lance Corporal Hurley, no. 23113593

Malcolm Finlayson and Charlie go up to baulk Jimmy Rodgers, Bristol City's centre forward, in a match Millwall lost 3-1 at The Den on September 4th 1954.

Charlie's first match for the Republic against England in Dublin. (top) The teams line up before the match. Charlie is fifth from the left. (bottom) Goalkeeper Tommy Godwin clings on to the ball as England press for an equaliser to take them to Sweden, Noel Cantwell and Charlie Hurley are the other Irish players.

Alf Ringstead [third from left] forcing the Republic into a fourth minute lead against England, others in the picture are Billy Wright (no 5), Roger Byrne [no 3], goalkeeper Alan Hodgkinson and Ronnie Clayton.

The Irish team for the match against Czechoslovakia at home in 1961 which Ireland lost 3-1. (back row left to right) Fitzgerald, Nolan, Hurley, Dwyer, Cantwell and McGrath (front row) Haverty, O'Neill, Giles, Fogarty and Kelly.

At 8.10 pm Charlie agrees to join Sunderland by shaking hands with manager Alan Brown.

Leaving the Ford motor company and signing for Millwall.

Alan Brown – 'The Bomber' – in jocular mood. (Sunderland Echo)

George Hardwick took over from Brown as manager but did not last long.
(Sunderland Echo)

Ian McColl was Charlie's third manager at Sunderland. They did not get on. (Sunderland Echo)

Len Ashurst, Sunderland left back and a long-time member of the defence with Charlie. No one has made more outfield performances for Sunderland. (Sunderland Echo)

George Mulhall. His corners provided many of Charlie's goals. (Sunderland Echo)

Jimmy Montgomery, Sunderland goalkeeper, who played 623 games for Sunderland, the most appearances for the club and a record unlikely to be beaten. (Sunderland Echo)

Sunderland chairman Syd Collings (Sunderland Echo)

won 2-0. It meant Sunderland remained in Division Two. Argus reported that Sunderland players "had slumped dejectedly on the dressing room benches."

As such it was left to manager Alan Brown to roar defiantly that "there'll be another year. Never mind, lads, your time will come, don't worry." And despite the financial implications of losing out, chairman Syd Collings said he was "proud of the boys."

Recalling the events at Vetch Field forty-six years later it was the attitude of Alan Brown that stuck in Hurley's memory. "It's a long way from Sunderland to Swansea. We had a lot of fans down. We were desperate but the fans even more so. They'd have done anything. Over the years the loyalty of Roker fans has been superb. It was terribly sad. We got a result away from home, but we needed a win. The one great thing about all this was that the Bomber always took it very well. I nicknamed him the Bomber because he used to bomb in here and bomb in there. He frightened a few, and I am not just talking about the players.

"Alan Brown was a hard man. In life you get bastards, but an honest one is pretty good to work for. He doesn't do anything behind your back. He tells you to your face what he thinks. I put the Bomber down as an honest bastard and I still think he was very good for Sunderland Football Club."

Ironically for Hurley it was an ex-Republic of Ireland man who had inspired Orient to promotion to the top flight for the first and only time in their history. Johnny Carey had won the Footballer of the Year award in 1949 and as Orient manager he was rightly lauded for taking a club whose average gate in 1961–62 was only 14,751 to the highest level in English football. For Sunderland the final day results proved not to be the last time they were to be denied at the finishing hurdle.

While also disappointed, Stan Anderson remembers 1961–62 as one of his favourite seasons during his twelve-year period as a first team player. He says: "We had a lot of young players coming into the side. That year we were playing as good football as anything we would have played in the First Division. It had just started a little bit too late in the season to guarantee promotion. There was a good bit of comradeship between the players. We were playing catch-up but doing it with some style."

It would have been of little consolation to Hurley but at The Den his first professional team Millwall had managed to drag themselves to the top of Division Four to pip Colchester United by a point. Fourteen years after dropping down into Division Three South, Millwall were on their way back up the Football League.

Chapter Nine

Pipped at the post

Charlie Hurley and Sunderland began the 1962–63 season in the style they had finished the previous one. On the opening day more than 48,000 passed through the Roker Park turnstiles to witness a 3-1 defeat of Middlesbrough with 'Boro old-boy Brian Clough rattling home two and Hurley the other.

The first away game of the season was against another northern team who were on the hard march back to the top division, although like Sunderland, Leeds were not to reach the promised land until the following season. The way they did it was uncompromising in the extreme and they made many enemies. Sunderland were one and it was at this game that the hostilities started. They have never really gone away.

The flash point was an horrendous thigh-high tackle by Bobby Collins which resulted in Willie McPheat being carried off with a broken leg. Never recovering properly, the Scotsman did not play again for Sunderland. He moved back to Scotland to join Airdrie.

Although the Yorkshire club won 1-0, Hurley at least had the satisfaction of winning his personal duel with Welsh legend John Charles, who had returned to Elland Road from Juventus after five years in Turin.

"The man the Soccer World is talking about as the chief rival to United's John Charles and Stoke's Stanley Matthews as the personality of the Second Division is Eire international centre half Charlie Hurley." Match programme from Leeds United versus Sunderland on Saturday 25th August 1962.

Sunderland fan Brian Leng, who was lucky enough to see virtually all of Hurley's matches, feels that he was at his peak in 1962. "Nobody could beat Charlie in the air. Yes, he would give a headache to supporters and journalists brought up on centre halves booting the ball away when under pressure but he was so skilful on the ball that he rarely got caught. He may not have been the captain at that time but he used to run things at the back. When Montgomery got in the side he was very, very young and if anybody tried to rough him up then Charlie was there making sure the player knew he'd have to deal with him first."

Despite Hurley's star status, left back Len Ashurst states: "Charlie was popular in the dressing room. There was very little resentment towards him – there were one or two players who felt that Charlie hogged the limelight but as an excellent player and later captain of his team most felt he was entitled to do that. He was full of character, full of charisma. He was a good captain because he was a good encourager of all the players."

Len Ashurst had a magnificent career at Sunderland. Never one to shirk a tackle, he made 452 starting appearances for the club over a twelve-year period – a record number for an outfield player. He later managed a number of clubs and led Sunderland to the Milk [League] Cup Final against Norwich in 1985.

There were 38,172 at Roker when Swansea visited and lost 3-1, with Clough again grabbing a couple, but Hurley was missing. He was needed for his second international match of the season. This was against Iceland at the Laugardalsvollur Stadium in Reykjavik in the second leg of a European Championship qualifying match, the first leg on August 12th having resulted in a 4-2 victory for Ireland.

With Hurley again captaining the team, the second leg proved more difficult than expected against the mostly amateur Icelanders. Tuohy put Ireland ahead before Arnason's goal gave the home crowd something to shout about, even though their team went out of the competition by five goals to three on aggregate.

Sunderland took maximum points from the first four home games of the campaign but Alan Brown still felt the team needed strengthening so he spent £23,000 on outside left George Mulhall from Aberdeen. At that considerable fee Sunderland fans were hoping Mulhall would be able to provide even more chances for Brian Clough.

The Scotsman is still convinced he did the right thing by moving south. "I couldn't have picked a better place to go than Sunderland, but my first morning provided a shock. Charlie Ferguson had brought us down in his car. It was 11.30 at night and I had been asleep. We got booked into the hotel and when I woke up in the morning all I could hear was this noise. I honestly thought I was on a ship. I looked out of the window and all I could see was the sea battering against the walls. The hotel [the Roker Hotel] was right on the seafront. I didn't even realise Sunderland was on the sea. I saw all the beach and I thought that's great. I had a fantastic time at Sunderland, no complaints at all. Roker Park could be frightening though. It was all standing of course. We were getting 40,000, unbelievable the noise, the Roker end, oh dear, incredible." Mulhall's move saw his wages jump from £22 a week to £38.

Mulhall made a fine home debut against Luton Town with Clough again scoring two in a 3-1 victory. Settling in for Mulhall was helped by the large number of fellow Scotsmen at the club. Throughout the 1960s the first team usually had three or four Scots in the side, not that everyone approved. The dissenters included the team manager of the successful Fulwell Christian and Youth Society, who saw six of his players from the previous season go for trials with Newcastle United. Using language which some may describe as not exactly Christian, Reg Watson said: "It seems that you have to be Irish or Scottish to get into Roker Park these days."

Despite Hurley's excellence Sunderland were having problems away from Roker Park, with only two victories in their first twelve matches on the road. But at least they avoided defeat at St James' Park on October 13th. The derby attracted 62,321 but Hurley was recovering from knee ligament damage and Dickie Rooks, later to sign for Middlesbrough, played alongside Anderson and McNab in the halfback line. Clough scored the opening goal in the thirtieth minute, which brought younger Sunderland fans dancing on to the St James' Park pitch. Newcastle forced an equaliser when Anderson put though his own net seconds before half-time in a match that flowed from end to end.

Hurley returned at Carrow Road and put Sunderland into a 2-1 lead but three goals in the last twenty minutes gave Norwich victory. Meanwhile at home nothing could stop Sunderland. Brian Clough scored his second hat-trick of the season in a 6-2 victory over Grimsby Town watched by 43,087. This was new signing Johnny Crossan's debut and although it appeared from results such as that at Carrow Road that Sunderland needed a stronger defence, Crossan was, of course, an inside-forward. He was another Irishman, from the north, and was returning to play in Britain, after a life ban for taking a payment while he was still officially an amateur had been overturned. The suspension had forced him to earn his living on the European continent, where he had played for Standard Liege in the previous season's European Cup semi-final against the mighty Real Madrid which the Belgians lost 6-0 on aggregate.

The hope was that he would form a partnership with Mulhall that would terrorise the right side of opposing teams. The fee of £27,000 took manager Alan Brown's spending in just over a year on his inside right, centre forward, and inside and outside left to £138,000. Based on the Retail Price Index this would be worth more than £2m in 2008, which shows how transfer fees have spiralled.

In the *Sports Echo* Argus said Crossan made "an assured though unspectacular debut." Despite his hat-trick, Clough was overshadowed by the sight of Herd who, after scoring his first of the season, "celebrated with two somersaults before his colleagues pounced to shower him with congratulations."

Hurley scored his third goal of the season against Preston North End as Sunderland again won at home, making it nineteen points out of twenty. The goal came when "Hurley met a cross from Mulhall and from the inside right position hit a tremendous right foot drive which glanced off a defender on the way into the net," reported Argus.

Brian Clough again scored against his old team when Sunderland travelled down the north-east coast to play in a six-goal thriller just before Christmas. Sunderland had McNab stretchered off in the twenty-fifth minute, by which time they were three up, and his absence in no small way contributed to the loss of a point in a match described by the *Newcastle Journal*'s Alf Greenley as "a great game by any standards."

Jimmy McNab's career at Sunderland included two broken legs and two broken noses. Despite this he still played more than 320 games between 1958 and 1967. After he left he made more than two hundred appearances for Preston and thirty for Stockport County.

The Irish international inside forward Ambrose Fogarty made one of his 174 Sunderland appearances, during which he notched an impressive 44 goals, that day. In October 2007 he made a special trip across Ireland to catch an early flight to join up with some of his ex-teammates at the Stadium of Light, who along with an audience of around three hundred fans, turned out to mark the occasion of the fiftieth anniversary of Charlie Hurley signing for Sunderland.

"I have travelled a long way because I have a tremendous affection for Charlie, who was a terrific player. For me personally he was just a lovely fella. He was never bumptious; confident yes, but never bumptious. He was one of the lads and you could ask him to do anything and he'd do it. We shared digs together. The fella who owned the digs was strange but the food was good.

"Charlie would have a laugh, sometimes out of me, especially out of the fact he was much bigger than me. Humour was and is an important part of a footballer's life. You need to be able to have a laugh and enjoy yourself. Mickey-taking on the training ground was great, but it wasn't nasty. There was a good atmosphere and we were a good group of friends.

"Charlie was the king of the mickey-takers, and he'd use humour to inspire you. When Jimmy McNab got hurt at Middlesbrough it was from my tackle he got taken off. Charlie looked at me and said 'You little bastard, get back here' – that type of humour. I played for Sunderland in every emergency position you could think of because of Charlie's fist.

"He had fantastic feet; he would pull down the ball and play it off. Brilliant in the air. I can still see him as the ball came out of the middle of the field, he'd let on he was going to head it forward and then he'd glide it back twenty or thirty yards to the 'keeper. It was unheard of then. The audacity was amazing.

"He had so many good games, Charlie was the 'Roker Roar'. It took six people to mark him at times from corners and he ploughed through the lot of them. Clough and I got a hat-trick each against Swansea Town in 1961 in a 7-2 victory. Charlie was getting up and knocking them down to three foot from the line and all you had to do was 'get in'.

"It was very exciting to play at Roker Park. You've heard of the Roker Roar; well you wouldn't be able to hear a single thing. You'd be running around with this noise in your head thinking 'bloody hell'. You couldn't get it out of your brain."

The return match with Leeds came three days before Christmas and although Brian Clough failed to score – surprising because he'd notched 24 from just 23 games – Hurley did. It was the winning goal in a 2-1 victory – "[he] had time to bring the ball under control before hammering it left-footed wide of Gary Sprake."

Again according to Argus: "Hurley had caused trouble with his presence in the box and Leeds had delegated two men to watch him including Jack Charlton but he scored with his feet from a corner after Ambrose challenged for the ball."

The goal was one of Hurley's sweetest of his career. The Sunderland team were still bitter about the challenge on McPheat at Elland Road. The man responsible, Bobby Collins, had been in fine form for Leeds and had played in the Yorkshire side's previous game, a 3-1 victory at home to Stoke. But he was not playing that day.

He had appeared on the pitch before the game but according to the *Yorkshire Post* report on the Monday following the game "Collins, the inside-left, missed the match because of a strained calf muscle." It suggested that had he played the away side might have pulled off "a notable victory in a match where Sunderland were inspired by the 'Roker Roar' from a crowd of 40,282." The game was the only one in the league Collins missed for Leeds in the 1962–63 season.

It appears he might have missed a few more had he played that day and you have to wonder if he was left out for reasons other than injury.

Hurley remembers the day, and the man, well: "Bobby Collins – he broke Willie McPheat's leg with a very bad tackle and if there was one player I was going to get on a football pitch it was him. I said to Len Ashurst and Jimmy McNab that Willie McPheat's career could be finished and sadly I was right, his thighbone was broken. I said to them 'I am a hard player but today I am going to be a dirty player'.

"Before the match all the Leeds players were on the pitch including Collins. I said to him 'Bobby, you'd better be careful because there are twenty-two legs out here ready to kick you all over the place.' When they came back out for the match he wasn't picked. I think it would have been a tough time for Bobby if he'd played that day. Leeds and Don Revie, they had a fine side, but they could never really dominate us."

Collins, voted Footballer of the Year in 1965, continued to captain Leeds until 1966, when ironically he suffered a broken thighbone in a Fairs Cup tie against Torino.

The significance of injuries on the careers of players in those days was rammed home on Boxing Day when Sunderland met a Bury team led by Bob Stokoe. In those days Stokoe was known to Sunderland fans only as a man who had spent ten years as a centre half with Newcastle. Ten years later, of course, his skipping run across the Wembley turf to embrace the inspirational Jimmy Montgomery following Sunderland's FA Cup final victory over Leeds would enter football folklore, inspiring the statue outside the Stadium of Light. On December 26th 1962 he was centre half, captain and player/manager of Bury.

There were some who said at the time that the match should never have been played because of the icy conditions. Clough himself later described it as "one of those grey, biting, forbidding days that only the north-east can produce."

The straw that Sunderland had paid for back in 1957 may have done its job [it always did as from Christmas Day 1925 until December 30th 1961 Sunderland never had a single game postponed] and ensured the game went ahead although the pitch was still as hard as tarmac. But it did little good for Brian Clough.

Charlie Hurley still wonders if a penalty he missed changed the course of the match and whether Clough would have suffered what he did had it gone in. Beforehand, after leaving out Harry Hooper,

Alan Brown had asked who would take the penalties. "Everyone turned their backs so muggins here said 'I'll get that sorted out at half-time', thinking we wouldn't get a penalty in the first half. Sod's law we got one. So up I went to take it. I didn't place it or blaze it, I walked up and pushed it a couple of feet wide, disgraceful really. Cloughie was still on the field. Had I scored it would have changed the whole context of the match. Shortly afterwards his cruciate ligament was done. He was on for fifty goals that season."

In those days a cruciate ligament injury often spelled the end of a career and thus it was with Brian Clough. Argus described the awful moment – Clough was "stretching out for a ball which was beating him into the goalkeeper's [Harker] arms, Clough went down in agony after a sharp clash."

As Clough said: "His shoulder crunched into my right knee." Agony.

Stokoe was so convinced that Clough was faking that he shouted "get up, get up" and told the referee "come on, he's only codding [kidding]." The referee was not convinced, replying "not this lad."

Stokoe ought to have known better; this was the early 1960s when to try and con a referee and the other team was regarded as "not part of the game". Clough received onfield attention from Sunderland's' club physiotherapist John Watters and trainer Arthur Wright before being carried off on a stretcher. Furious at Stokoe, he never spoke to him again unless he had to.

Clough later said: "Neither Alan Brown nor Johnny Watters said anything, but both must have realised that there was no earthly chance of my ever being the same player again."

With no substitutes, Sunderland played on with ten men but lost for the first time at home that season, their first defeat at Roker in thirty-two matches. The single goal was scored from twenty-five yards in the sixtieth minute by Turner. The following day's *Echo* headlines summed it up when it reported "Home Defeat Was Only A Minor Tragedy – Clough Could Be Out For Rest Of Season."

Three days later, after it had been confirmed that Clough would not play again that season, Nick Sharkey lined up at centre forward in the return game at Gigg Lane, his first match of the season. Sunderland played poorly and lost 3-0.

Sharkey did, however, get two as Preston were easily beaten 4-1 on another heavily frozen pitch at Deepdale in the third round of the FA Cup. With many other games postponed the BBC rushed cameras to the ground to record Preston taking the lead through Doug Holden on four minutes, but viewers watching the highlights on Saturday night then witnessed a fine Sunderland performance on a treacherous pitch.

Sharkey was in the team which ran out at Roker Park the following Saturday when Sunderland played the first leg of the League Cup semi-final against Aston Villa from Division One. It transpired that this was the nearest Charlie Hurley got to grabbing a medal during his long career. Sunderland had progressed to the last four by beating Oldham Athletic 7-1 at home in the second round, knocking out Scunthorpe 2-0 in the third, winning a replayed tie at home to Portsmouth and then defeating Blackburn Rovers by a single goal in a five-goal thriller.

After sixty-one minutes against Villa, a minute after Jim Montgomery was led from the pitch with concussion, Sharkey equalised for Sunderland. However, the Birmingham side took the honours, winning 3-1 on a snow-covered pitch.

Hurley had faced Derek Dougan, and George Forster from the Supporters Association, now in his eighties, recalls that he had been given a far from easy time: "Dougan was different from other centre forwards at that time who generally stayed in the centre of the park. Dougan would drag Charlie out of his normal position as he would play anywhere on the park. He did this in the League Cup semi-final and Dougan in my view had the better of Charlie on that day."

This view is echoed by Brian Leng, who feels that "Dougan was more skilful than the average centre forward. He could also handle the physical side of the game; games involving him and Hurley were mammoth tussles and Charlie didn't always win out."

George Forster is, however, a big fan of the Irish centre half, stating: "Hurley had tremendous stature; he got better over the seasons he played. He was very good in the air; he could head a ball into the other half of the field; only Dave Watson could also do it for Sunderland. I liked Hurley's calmness in the box: he tried to dribble the ball in the box. Usually it came off, but nothing comes off every time, mind."

Sunderland's chances in the second leg, held nearly three months later, were slim and so it proved when they drew 0-0. Only 21,500 were at Villa Park. Unlike the FA Cup, the League Cup failed to attract the public's attention. Some supporters, not to mention the managers of the more successful clubs who did not enter at the start, argued that there was already too much football, and that fans didn't have the money to watch extra matches.

It was not until the Football League decided the final would be played at Wembley and that the winners would be granted a place in the Inter-City Fairs and later the UEFA Cup that the competition succeeded. The larger teams took notice and began to take the competition seriously. It was therefore ironic that the very first Wembley winners were Third Division Queens Park Rangers in 1967 when they defeated West Bromwich Albion 3-2 in a marvellous game in which Rodney Marsh was outstanding.

Villa's victory brought them up against local rivals Birmingham City in the final, but they lost 3-1 on aggregate.

The big freeze meant there were no frost-free nights in Britain from December 22nd 1962 to March 5th 1963, which had a huge effect on football. Sunderland, for instance, were unable to play a single league game in January and only one in February, a 2-2 draw at Derby on the 23rd.

Finally on March 2nd, after an absence of more than two months, league football returned to Roker Park and although the visitors were Newcastle there was little for Sunderland fans to shout about. Newcastle were clearly intent on a point and were grateful to their 'keeper Dave Hollins, who saved Stan Anderson's thirty-eighth-minute penalty. The game's most notable feature was the crowd of 62,240 – the last ever 60,000 plus league gate at Roker Park.

The enforced break certainly did Sunderland's forwards a power of good. Johnny Crossan hit a hat-trick at Walsall but was overshadowed in the next game by Nick Sharkey, who hit five as Norwich were crushed 7-1. Sharkey became the third and to date last Sunderland player to score five in a match, equalling Charlie Buchan's feat against Liverpool in 1912 and that by Bobby Gurney in 1935 against Bolton. Coincidentally the first two were both achieved on December 7th.

Not surprisingly Hurley remembers the Norwich game, although Sharkey's five goals are secondary. The club's directors had drawn up a bonus scheme they felt would inspire the players to put behind them the previous season's failure, and gain promotion. It was quite simple. If Sunderland were in the top two after ten games the players got £300; if they were not they could make it up and earn another £300 if they were in the top two after twenty games, and another £300 after thirty games and another £300 at the end of the season. If the team were never at any time in the top two until the final game of the season the players still got £1,200 each. What the directors had not banked on was the players being in the top two after thirty games, banking £900 each and then still failing to gain promotion. Which is exactly what happened.

"After ten games we weren't in the top two so we didn't get the first £300 and that was the case after twenty games. The twenty-ninth game was against Norwich and if we won we were sure to be in the top two. So if we won we got £900 and for that you could buy a little terraced house in those days. I went round to see every player. They didn't need an awful lot of encouragement. Nicky Sharkey's five won him the match ball and we got £900 each – a fortune," recalls the big Irishman with a smile.

Although he was never going to match Sharkey, Charlie Hurley at least had the satisfaction of scoring his fifth goal of the season, against Grimsby Town at Blundell Park. He forced home a corner with only minutes remaining to give Sunderland a 2-1 victory.

Two days later, however, there was major disappointment when Sunderland crashed out of the fifth round of the FA Cup away to Third Division Coventry City, now managed by ex-PFA chairman Jimmy Hill. Jim Montgomery made two mistakes in the last eight minutes to turn victory into defeat. First he punched Dietmar Bruck's cross into his own net, leading to a pitch invasion by Coventry fans, and on eighty-six minutes he came too far for a cross from John Sillett and George Curtis headed it over him into the net, which sparked another invasion. At the end, when the crowd spilled onto the pitch for a third time, both sets of players were forced to fight their way to the dressing rooms. Despite the disappointment Alan Brown offered no complaints, stating: "Coventry deserved to win."

The attendance at Highfield Road, 40,487, was a record, though several entrances were broken and there were believed to be more than 50,000 inside the ground.

Off the pitch, Sunderland fans who had got used to travelling to matches from places such as Easington, Horden and Blackhall Colliery by train were going to have to find alternative modes of transport when Dr Beeching's report was released, calling for massive cuts in the UK's rail network. In the north-east ninety-five stations were closed, destroying for ever a comprehensive rail system that linked small towns and even villages across the region.

Stan Anderson remembers the trains for some unusual reasons: "I'd go through to the game on the train from Horden, I'd play the match and then go back on the train, which was usually packed. You'd hear some people saying we were lucky and that I'd played rubbish. They didn't know me from Adam and my dad would get angry at their comments."

According to Brian Leng: "Stan's dad should have got angry. Stan was an exceptionally talented player. When he was on his game he was phenomenal, a driving midfield player and you had to admire everything about him. He had skill, he could tackle and he had this cross-field ball that he could drive from right half to left wing to the winger's feet."

The cup defeat sparked a disastrous run. Clearly not convinced that Sharkey was the man to lead Sunderland to the promised land, Alan Brown went back over the border to spend £11,000 on Andy Kerr from Kilmarnock at the beginning of April 1963.

Kerr was a good player – he had proved it by playing in five major Scottish Cup finals although he had been on the losing side in each of them – but he was no Brian Clough and it was doubtful he was better than Sharkey. Put straight into the side, he scored just twice in the following seven league games; ironically they came in the two Sunderland lost. And with only one win in seven, promotion seemed unlikely, although in a tight league in which teams had the capacity to beat each other, wins in the final four matches might have been enough.

The Roker Park crowd were not convinced, particularly after the draw with Huddersfield, another team with an outside chance of promotion. With the season stretching into May, fewer than 35,000 turned out to watch the match against Southampton. This was 27,000 fewer than had packed the ground a month earlier for the first of two Easter battles in four days with Stoke City.

The Potters' fortunes had been revived after Stanley Matthews returned in 1962 following a fifteen-year spell with Blackpool. Unfortunately Matthews was missing when Stoke arrived at Roker Park but even without him they were good enough to grind out a goalless draw. The return seemed certain to end in anther draw, after Kerr replied for Sunderland following a Dennis Viollet opener. According to the great Stanley Matthews, in his autobiography, "we were awarded a penalty late in the game. Put it this way, I'd seen penalties not given for such challenges, but up stepped Dennis Viollet and coolly tucked it away to give us the points. Sunderland had had strong appeals for a penalty turned down earlier and probably came off feeling a little hard done by, but that's football."

Sunderland easily defeated Southampton with Crossan snatching three, his second hat-trick of the season, and he was also the hero the following weekend at the Vetch Field, heading home the match winner with ten minutes left, but injuring himself in the process. This was a magnificent game in which Swansea appeared to have ruined Sunderland's chances by coming from 3-1 down to equalise.

The two points put Sunderland in the driving seat as they travelled to play Luton Town, where Sharkey scored a near-post header on twenty-one minutes. Anderson made it two with six minutes left and then Sharkey scored a second. This left Sunderland facing their promotion rivals Chelsea at Roker Park in the final match of the season. The equation was simple. Sunderland needed to get a point; Chelsea needed two and to win their game in hand. The odds were in Sunderland's favour.

As might be expected, the game itself was not the greatest; the tension among the spectators, which included a good number from Stamford Bridge, clearly got to the players. The size of the crowd was also a surprise, at only 47,955. Some fans had stayed away after the newspapers had expressed fears of overcrowding. The Saturday lunchtime *Sunderland Echo* had also reported that fans had been queuing overnight, saying there was bound to be a 60,000 plus crowd.

Before the match Argus had described it as "Sunderland's Match of the Century" and represented all fans when he hoped it "will be Sunderland's last game in 2nd Division football." He confidently predicted that "with the magnificent 'Roker Roar' to keep them on the right track the team should not fail again" while a Tyne–Tees television programme the day before had, in the view of some, celebrated promotion prematurely. Stan Anderson says: "We did this programme before the match on 'our promotion' which I was dead against. It was the biggest bloody joke of all time. I said to George Mulhall that we hadn't even played the game yet."

Montgomery was unoccupied for much of the match as Sunderland pushed forward from the start and he could only watch as Peter Bonetti, later to act as understudy to Gordon Banks and thus keep the Sunderland man out of the England squad at the 1970 World Cup finals in Mexico, was outstanding. Then, on twenty-five minutes Chelsea won their first corner and Bobby Tambling's inswinger confused both the home defence and his own teammates. But the ball hit the unmarked Tommy Harmer and went in at the back post. First blood to the Londoners.

Sunderland once again piled forward with Crossan, Sharkey and Mulhall all missing glorious chances. The second half was little different but Bonetti and his teammates, who included Terry Venables and hard-man Ron 'Chopper' Harris, refused to wilt. Argus praised the team for their efforts but reserved a special mention for Hurley "for a tremendous performance in the dual role of defender and striker for set positions."

Charlie Hurley recalls: "We had a better team than Chelsea. We had an excellent squad of players, no matter who was out. If I was missing we had Dickie Rooks and he was a very, very good player, legs like tree trunks. If he whacked you you knew about it. He was a different type of player from me, a local lad, lovely bloke. The Doc [Chelsea manager Tommy Docherty] just banged out Frank Upton up front to upset me. It did. I started kicking chunks out of him. Now, when I think of it, it was a very intelligent thing to do by the Doc. He had a plan and he got a very, very fortunate goal, off Harmer's midriff.

"That match was my biggest disappointment in football. The Doc came out after the game saying 'I've watched you for years, you're a great player, if there's any tiny little feeling I have it's for you on not getting promoted'. I said to him 'Well, we should definitely have got a result' and he said 'Charlie, that's football'. Tommy – bloody – Harmer, a little dwarf. He walked through my legs once and never touched me.

"Chelsea still had to beat Portsmouth and I phoned their captain to say 'Come on you've got to do your best, you don't want Chelsea to go up, they're a London side, rivalry and all that'. 'Oh we'll do out best,' he says. Anyway I was listening to the result on the radio. It was Chelsea two Portsmouth nil and they'd only played ten minutes. It went three, four, five, six, seven... it was a terrible day. I felt sad, more for the fans than myself."

So Sunderland had finished third, falling at the final hurdle once again and they could only stand and applaud as Chelsea joined Stoke City in Division One. Matthews won his second Football Writers' Player of the Season award – his first had come fifteen years before.

Stoke's gates, never the biggest, had averaged just 9,252 in the 1960–61 season; in 1962–63 they had leaped to 25,426. No wonder they gave Matthews the key to the city. Sunderland had averaged 40,883, easily the highest in Division Two and the fourth highest overall behind First Division champions Everton, who for the only time in their history recorded an average gate of over 50,000 – 51,603 in fact.

"It was a great feeling to play in front of a large Roker crowd. I was fortunate in that I did well at the start and they took to me. But there were times when I didn't do well and they were still encouraging me to do my best," remembers Jim Montgomery.

Hurley, at least, had the pleasure of captaining his country when they defeated Scotland in Dublin on June 9th with Noel Cantwell scoring the only goal on six minutes. Jim Baxter, Denis Law and Billy McNeill were all kept quiet on the day. No mean feat. It was little compensation – it was now over nine years since Hurley had made his debut for Millwall in the Third Division and despite some superb performances at centre half for the Lions and Sunderland he was due to kick off his tenth season in professional football in the second tier of English football, having played only twenty-two league games in Division One.

There are those who have suggested that Hurley played too much of his football in the lower leagues to earn the accolade of Sunderland's finest footballer but not Stan Anderson. "I've heard that argument. No, it was fate. You're landed with something and you've got to get on with it. He gave everything he had, he did his absolute best. The shame of it was that when they got to the First Division there was a change of manager and it didn't work in his favour.

"I've heard lots of stories about what was going on and that wouldn't have suited Charlie at all. Charlie wanted everything straight. All good players have an arrogance about them and Charlie was an arrogant player. He knew how good he was. He could beat a player. But it wasn't arrogant to the point where you can't stand a bloke, none of that. All good players have arrogance – look at Wayne Rooney now. If someone takes the ball off him he looks like he wants to crack someone. If Charlie had been English there's no doubt he would have been playing at centre half for England. What might have counted against him is that the England side was often picked from the sides that are successful.

"In present day football Charlie would have been transferred up to the top flight fairly early on in his career, £25 million to Man United or someone else. He was very good on the ball. People might say he didn't play all his football in the First Division and you can't really argue with that but in those days there wasn't the vast difference there is now between the clubs at the top and those in the second league. These days all the good players are in the Premiership because the clubs have the money to buy them. That wasn't the case in the early 1960s."

Chapter Ten

Back where they belong

Stan Anderson's assertion that the differences between the divisions were not as pronounced in the 1960s as they are today was borne out as Sunderland started their sixth season in Division Two. They were in tremendous form, winning six and losing just once.

Then they came up against Cardiff City, who had Ivor Allchurch, the one-time Swansea hero who had scored four at the Vetch Field back in September 1958 when Sunderland limped off beaten 5-0, and John Charles in their team. This time Allchurch scored three times in sixteen minutes as they overturned a two-goal deficit before being pegged back when Charlie Hurley scored Sunderland's equalising goal after sixty-four minutes, out-jumping Charles.

Don Murray, a Cardiff player that day, described the struggle between Charles and Hurley as "a clash of giants. Like John, Charlie was tremendous in the air. That was some battle. The corner came in from the left and Charlie jumped above John and sent a header screaming into the net. To beat John in the air took some doing but Hurley could do it on his day."

Hurley is a big fan of John Charles, stating: "John Charles was the cleanest giant you've ever seen. He was built like a brick shithouse and he was a cracking player and even to be compared to him was and is a privilege."

The feelings were clearly mutual, with Vince Wilson in the *Sunday Mirror* reporting that Charles had told him before the game: "Hurley's the best centre half in Great Britain and a world class player."

Interestingly Charlie Hurley's opinion of the Welshman is borne out by a story from Italy when Charles was starring for Juventus. In time-honoured Italian fashion he was being kicked so badly by opposing defenders in one game that he lost his temper. He turned to his inside forward, Argentinian Omar Sivori, to say he couldn't kick them back and could Sivori do it for him. Sivori was 5ft 7ins tall, Charles was 6ft 2ins!

Charlie Hurley had an outstanding game at the County Ground against newly promoted Swindon Town, with Argus reporting that "the man of the match by any standard was undoubtedly Hurley, whose immaculate play won cheers from even such a partisan crowd as Swindon's." However, he had been powerless to prevent Jack Smith heading a winner for the new boys.

Next he was captain of an Irish team which recorded a useful 0-0 draw in the first leg of their second round European Championship tie with Austria at Prater Park, Vienna.

The Irish centre half then scored for the third season in four at Carrow Road – Norwich really did suffer for suggesting that he might be the weak link before the FA Cup game back in February 1961! His goal was Sunderland's first in a game in which they scored twice in the last eleven minutes to win 3-2 because a by now terrified home defence were so intent on preventing the big centre half reaching the ball that they left gaps for Jimmy McNab and Johnny Crossan to head home two George Mulhall free kicks. The result was a big boost for the "match of the season" against Newcastle on the Saturday.

That game saw full back Len Ashurst score his first goal, one of only four in his long career, at Roker Park. Unlike today, full backs were not expected to overlap and some rarely crossed the halfway line. Their job was to stop the opposing team's winger getting beyond them and crossing the ball.

Things had looked bleak for the home side when, after Newcastle had taken the lead, Hurley had been forced from the field with his eye split open.

He remembers: "Oh dear me, there were no subs in those days. Stan Ritson was the old surgeon, brilliant in his day, but he was eighty by then. So I wasn't too happy about this. He was going to sew my eye up. He's got, what do you call it, 'the gut', and he was coming towards my eye with a very shaky hand and I said to Johnny Watters 'For bloody Christ's sake would you just hold his hand while he's sewing'.

"The things you did in those days. I was sewn without any injection and it was sewn with a cock-eye. When I saw what he'd done afterwards! I put a plaster over it and out I went. I got a great cheer when I ran on to the field. While I was off we equalised. I asked who'd scored and someone said Len Ashurst and I said 'He's never scored in his life' but he had and we went on to win 2-1. In those days we were on twenty pounds a point. I went off and we were losing one-nil, came back on and we won 2-1 and we collected forty quid. The incentive to win was very, very high in those days. We could earn over £100 a week in the early sixties, so it was vital to get out there. It wasn't being brave. It was practical. With no subs, if you were injured you went on the wing."

George Herd scored the winner in front of a crowd of 56,903, firing home a Mulhall pass from the edge of the area.

Buoyed by the result, Hurley travelled to Dublin for the second leg of the Austria tie on October 13th. It was to be a famous night. Making the journey with him was Ambrose Fogarty, by this time finding it difficult to get a first team game for Sunderland because of Herd's form. Shortly afterwards Fogarty was sold to Hartlepools United [as they were then known, the 's' being dropped in 1968] where he played 127 League games, scoring 22 goals. He also made one further international appearance while at the Victoria Ground, making him 'Pools' only international so far.

Austria took the lead through Walter Koleznik before Cantwell equalised and then Karl Koller deflected Fogarty's header into his own net, sparking a pitch invasion from excited home supporters that even threatened to see the game called off. The Austrians then threw a dampener on these premature celebrations by equalising through Rudolf Flogel with eight minutes left.

In the very last minute, however, Thor Poulsen, the referee, awarded Hurley's men a penalty. It took three minutes to clear the pitch of the already celebrating crowd before Cantwell brought them back on by driving home the spot-kick to take Ireland through by a single goal.

The celebrations went on long into the night around Dublin. At the time it was arguably the best ever result achieved by a Republic of Ireland football side because the famous victories of 2-0 against

England in 1949 and 3-2 against Sweden in 1959 had come in friendlies.

Hurley's week was complete when Sunderland beat Derby 3-0 away on the Saturday. Things got even better the following weekend when, in another man of the match performance, he scored his third goal of the season to help beat Plymouth Argyle 1-0 at home. It came from another powerful header, this time from a Brian Usher corner. "Heads – King Hurley Strikes Again" was the headline in the *Sunday Mirror* the following day.

Sunderland had twenty-three points from fifteen games, easily the best start they had made in the six seasons since relegation. Genuine hopes of promotion filled the hearts of Sunderland fans, who were still in a state of shock after manager Alan Brown decided to break up the established half back line-up of Anderson–Hurley–McNab.

Stan Anderson had made 402 League appearances, 34 in the FA Cup and 11 in the Football League Cup, not to mention England caps at schoolboy, under-23, B, and full levels – in fact Anderson was the only Sunderland player capped by England during the 1960s. Yet Horden Colliery's favourite son left to join Newcastle United! Not many had done that before; not many have done it since. Anderson did return shortly after for one further appearance in Sunderland's colours. It was a testimonial he'd earned after playing for more than ten years at Roker Park.

In spite of the fee of £19,000, there were many who felt Alan Brown was making a mistake. But in Martin Harvey the manager had a younger man with international experience with Northern Ireland who could not be expected to hang around playing reserve team football at the age of twenty-two. The end justified the means. Harvey went on to make more than three hundred league appearances for Sunderland, and would have played much longer but for an injury which ended his career when he was just thirty. But the loss of such a fine player, not to mention captain, as Anderson was something to worry the fans.

Anderson had assumed the captaincy after Don Revie gave up the position when Sunderland were relegated, but not before it had been awarded to Charlie Hurley. When the latter was injured and out of the team, Anderson was asked to fill in. When he did well Hurley suggested he should keep the post. It was typical Hurley.

Anderson and Brown never hit it off. Speaking years later, Anderson had the following to say about their relationship: "Was Alan Brown a difficult man? That was like asking if the sun was hot? He was the *boss* and he wouldn't have any truck with anyone challenging his authority. I used to want to go up on a Monday morning to discuss the match with him because you'd get players moaning and groaning and saying 'We should have done this, or that' and as captain I thought I should relay that to the manager. I think Alan Brown believed all of the comments were mine and not those of the players in general. But I couldn't go to the manager and say 'Brian Clough says this'. When I left I had no problems – Martin Harvey was a young lad coming through – but the way it was done annoyed me.

"It got to the point where the formation of the side was totally wrong. When the younger lads like Cec Irwin, Len Ashurst and Jimmy McNab were brought in they were right as players but we should have played 4-2-4 and the only time Brown did that was at Preston in the FA Cup in '63. There was ice on the ground and we beat them 4-1. We played absolutely perfectly that day but the following week it was back to normal. Alan Brown and I had this conflict of ideas; he thought I was too big for my own boots. I wasn't trying to take his job off him, I was quite prepared to work with him, I just didn't get on well with him.

"The delight of going to Newcastle and working under Joe Harvey as manager was like a breath of fresh air. He was a class man and we met every Monday and he was prepared to listen. Brownie wasn't. The players who are on the field get a feel of what's going wrong. A manager in the stand isn't right all the time, and some managers aren't prepared to listen. And if players want to discuss problems then that's a difficulty."

With Anderson transferred, Hurley was free to assume the captain's role. He says: "A good captain has to have the respect of the players. That doesn't necessarily mean you're the best player. You've got to be the guy who makes decisions on the pitch. I was fortunate that a lot of those lads came through from the youth team at a period when I was gradually gaining ground as a good player. I loved being a captain. Brown had this plan when he first signed me that I was going to be the captain. £18,000 was a fantastic amount of money in those days; he knew all about me before he signed me. He said I'd become a better player under him as a manager and he was right."

Sunderland suffered a set back when Middlesbrough beat Sunderland 2-0 at Ayresome Park, the first Tees–Wear derby victory since Clough made the trip between the two towns, but this was soon forgotten as Sunderland claimed seven points from the next eight, during which Hurley scored his fourth and fifth goals of the season. These came at home against managerless Leyton Orient [Johnny Carey having departed to Nottingham Forest in the close season] and Swansea City.

Orient's First Division experience had lasted just one season, during which they gained just twenty-one points and finished bottom. It was Hurley who gave Sunderland the lead in the fifth minute, meeting a Mulhall free kick to head it beyond the 'keeper for the first of the home side's four goals. Alf Greenley in the *Journal* reported that "Hurley, as ever, was a commanding figure and seemingly revelling in his new authority as skipper."

Attending his first match at Roker Park was nine-year-old George Davis from Station Town. His recollections give a flavour of the time and of Hurley's status as the Sunderland star player among the County Durham mining community. "Station Town was a typical small community of the time where everyone knew everyone. Fathers worked down the mines and front and back doors were left open as people could trust each other.

"There wasn't a lot of money but we were always well fed and clothed. It was a happy childhood with the main sport being football. I played from the age of five or six in the back street. We played gatie, you defended your own, and we'd be out for hours. Windows did get broken, balls went into people's yards and you had the odd person who wouldn't give it back.

"My first game, Sunderland won 4-1, Charlie scored. We got Roberts coaches to the match. I was in the Clock Stand Paddock, it was 2.00pm, there was still a few people around even at that time. The Fulwell End had no roof and the Roker End was massive. I remember the record of *Secret Love* by Kathy Kirby being played before the match. The players came out to the *Z Cars* theme. I saw this big fella, tall and handsome and I said to my dad, 'Who's that?' And he said 'That's King Charlie.' 'Charlie, Charlie, Charlie' was the cry but I can't remember anything about the game," recalls Davis, who at the time of writing was the chairman of the Wingate SAFC Supporters Branch.

Two days before the Orient game, Sunderland had the great experience of playing a friendly against Benfica, the Portuguese champions and European Cup winners of 1961 and 1962. With both teams playing an attacking formation the crowd was treated to an eight-goal spectacular, all of which came in the second half with Sunderland winning 5-3.

Eusebio was one of the world's greatest players and had scored twice in Benfica's 5-3 victory over Real Madrid in the 1962 European Cup final. Realising he could not beat Hurley in the air or by dribbling around him, he dropped deep to avoid the Irishman and showed his class by scoring twice. Alf Greenley, of the *Journal*, reported that there had been "nothing half-hearted about Benfica's efforts" but "as it turned out they were soundly beaten by a better footballing side" on the night.

Benfica's arrival had failed to overshadow the launching of *The Borgsten*, an 86,500-ton-870-feet long Norwegian tanker in November 1963. Fifteen thousand Wearsiders turned out on a foggy day to see the launch and the police were called to maintain order, particularly among the youngsters who skipped school to witness the event.

Hurley's goal at the Vetch Field, along with one from Sharkey, had helped Sunderland win 2-1. Thomas had given the Welsh side the lead with only twenty-three minutes left, and despite an injury that was hampering him, Hurley provided the equaliser when he hurled his huge frame to get on the end of a McNab free kick and bring the scores level in the eighty-first minute.

It was the winning goal, however, which had fans talking after the match. A minute after scoring, Hurley breasted down a centre in the Sunderland goalmouth, raced upfield over the halfway line before slipping a neat pass to Usher, whose cross was whipped into the net by Sharkey. It was a goal worthy of winning any game of football.

Football, and virtually everything else, was overshadowed by the news from Dallas that weekend that American President John F Kennedy had been assassinated. Two days later his alleged assassin Lee Harvey Oswald was mortally shot by Jack Ruby in Dallas on live television.

The day after Kennedy's death the BBC had decided to ignore the problems then affecting the world and explore what might happen in the distant future with the first series of *Doctor Who* being broadcast on November 23rd. Critics slammed it and said it would never last.

With Hurley missing, as it turned out, his one game of the season, Sunderland slumped to their second home defeat, losing 2-1 to Southampton. The Cork-born man was back in the side for the visit to Charlton Athletic and after a game which finished goalless Greenley reported that "the personal duel between Charlie Hurley and Eddie Firmani, who since his return from Italy a couple of months ago had hit ten goals in nine matches, ended with the honours clearly in favour of the Sunderland captain."

Sunderland fans suffered a shock when the team travelled to the County Ground in Northampton, the home team recording the 'double' over their illustrious visitors. Northampton had used basketball-type shoes that left Sunderland to slide and slip to a crushing 5-1 defeat. Hurley was Sunderland's best player with Greenley remarking in his report that he "was a law unto himself as despite his bulk, his nimble footwork got Sunderland out of trouble time and again."

The heavy defeat was soon forgotten with the mouth-watering prospect of two games against promotion rivals, Leeds United. Don Revie's team had started the 1963–64 season in fine form and they and Sunderland were in a battle for top spot.

The first was a Boxing Day special at Elland Road, where Sunderland were backed by 10,000 travelling supporters in a crowd of 41,167 and they were delighted when Sunderland snatched the lead after Hurley's long free kick was dropped by

Gary Sprake to allow Mulhall to slam it home. Leeds' goal was controversial. In the eighty-fourth minute Don Weston appeared to barge Jim Montgomery off the ball to leave Ian Lawson with a simple tap-in.

The size of the crowd was something of a disappointment. Leeds had decided to make the match all-ticket and restrict numbers to 50,000. It backfired on them because it meant many Sunderland fans without a ticket did not bother to travel, even though there were 10,000 who did. The Leeds programme extended "a very warm welcome indeed to Sunderland and all the good folk of Wearside and County Durham" but there was an indication that the hooliganism that was to plague and later almost destroy English football was becoming a problem because the programme editor found it necessary to appeal to fans of both clubs to "check any throwing of anything, any running on the pitch and too fierce arguments."

Two days later Leeds made the return trip to Roker Park, arriving on Wearside at the top of the Division having lost only one of their twenty-four games. This was the team which would become the most hated in Britain in the 1960s and '70s, receiving endless criticism for their style of football which was hard and ruthless. Neither were they, with Johnny Giles and Billy Bremner at the forefront, prepared to allow the referee to control the game. They became the first English team to constantly question the referee, although not, of course, the decisions that went for them!

The Roker crowd was totally incensed by Leeds that day with Argus saying the crowd had never been as angry with an away team "for many years", possibly not since the fateful day in 1936 when Chelsea roughed up goalkeeper Jimmy Thorpe, which undoubtedly contributed to his death a few days later.

Leeds' tactics, in fact, did them little good as Nick Sharkey put Sunderland in the lead after he beat Freddie Goodwin to an Ashurst free kick and drove home. Then Herd scored the second for a 2-0 victory.

Hurley recalls: "All our games with Leeds over a number of years were kicking matches. They were the hardest team in the game, and they took a very fine line in tackling. At home in 1963 I remember

Lawson went in and looked like he had kicked Monty in the head. I went over and grabbed him and pulled him, I was really going to thump him one but fortunately he hadn't kicked him in the head, Monty was all right. Every time I see Lawson when I am in the north-east he says 'Do you remember, Charlie, when you lifted me up? I was frightened to death that day'."

On January 4th 1964 Sunderland gained some measure of revenge over Northampton Town when before a crowd of 40,683 they knocked them out of the FA Cup with goals from Crossan and Mulhall. With a fourth round draw at home to third division Bristol City to follow at the end of the month, fans' thoughts turned once again to the twin towers of Wembley that Sunderland had last visited before the war, twenty-seven years previously.

Even with John Atyeo, previously Charlie Hurley's nemesis, at centre forward, Bristol City proved no match for a strong Sunderland side growing in confidence with each match. In fact it was Hurley who gained a measure of revenge over Atyeo by scoring his first FA Cup goal since his winner at Norwich in 1961. It was one of six against which the Robins managed only a single goal from Peter Hooper. Hurley's goal came when the Irishman ran on to a squared free kick and blasted home a tremendous drive which Mike Gibson, the 'keeper, saw late but would not have saved in any case.

Atyeo was a magnificent player for Bristol City during the 1950s and '60s, scoring 315 goals in 596 matches. This was a particularly outstanding record considering that for much of the time he was only part-time as he was training to become a teacher, a career he pursued when he finished playing. He also scored five goals in just six appearances for England and was unlucky not to play for his country at the 1958 World Cup finals in Sweden.

With Crossan in great form – he'd scored twice for the fourth game in a row, a feat which only David Halliday (1925–26) among Sunderland players has managed – Sunderland were top of the league. Victory against Cardiff at Ninian Park made it forty-four points from thirty matches and promotion was definitely on. Before then there was the little matter of the fifth round FA Cup match with defending Division One champions Everton.

The fifth round FA Cup tie with Everton on February 15th attracted what is officially Sunderland's last ever 60,000 plus home crowd, with 62,817 passing through the turnstiles, a quarter of them from Liverpool.

At the time the Sunderland team used to run out of the tunnel to the music from the popular TV police series *Z Cars*. It was intended to inspire the team, but as Everton also used the same tune at Goodison Park it was decided to drop it for the game. The replacement was *Charlie is m'Darling*, but he was not to be for the Everton forwards.

The Merseysiders were well beaten by a rampant Sunderland side skippered by an inspirational Hurley, who had the joy of watching his charges scored three in the first thirty-two minutes. Hurley's partner Jimmy McNab got the first in the third minute in front of the Fulwell End; Hurley headed the second from a corner and then in the twenty-sixth minute "after a corner, which West missed, the ball bounced off Usher to Hurley who hit it first time and it deflected off Harris over the line," reported the *Liverpool Echo*. Brian Harris did score a beauty for Everton, heading home a free kick from Alex Scott but Sunderland ran out worthy winners 3-1.

Hurley was simply sublime. It was one of his finest ever performances in a Sunderland strip and in his Monday match report, the *Liverpool Echo* reporter remarked that Jimmy Gabriel, normally a wing-half but standing in at centre forward, missed an eighth-minute chance, "the only time Gabriel was able to escape the magnificent Hurley, the best centre half I've ever seen since TG Jones." Welsh international Jones is an Everton legend who made more than 400 appearances in the 1950s.

Hurley remembers the match well: "They stuck Jimmy Gabriel up front. He was a midfield player who'd been doing well. I thought 'Well Jimmy, it's going to be a different game today, son'. I scored and Jimmy Mac scored and our third was an own goal from Mick Meagan, another wing half... all the goals were scored by half backs. It was as good a display as we had when I was at Sunderland. It was a tremendous day, and the fans went crazy."

The Sunderland team had taken to visiting Wetheralls, the first nightclub in the north-east, after Hurley had found out about it.

"Oh yes. Wetheralls was a very pokey little place. My wife and I have always loved going out; we love socialising. We always dig out these places, and I found out about this one. It was a membership place so I got all the players free memberships because we were very popular.

"The club became very successful. After the Everton match I remember the manager phoned my house to see if we were going in on the night. They'd been inundated by calls from members asking if the players were coming in and he said if we did then there'd be a meal and free champagne. So all the lads went – we had dinner, champagne all night. Tom Jones was on, the place was packed and we were all sitting together, signing autographs. It wasn't fans and players, we were all part of the same club. The '60s were a good time to be around and the players at Sunderland got on well with each other. We also had Crossan and Mulhall at the time, who were a great comedy duo!

"It would be nice if players today had more contact with the fans. I think they're missing out today. After all, these players have to realise that if the supporters don't come in then there would be no £10,000 or £20,000 a week in wages. I think fans are now being priced away from the game and the danger is that the game will kill itself.

"You might end up with a Premier League but a lot of the smaller clubs will go out of business. I think that the players have lost their way. I read their comments in the papers about financial matters; it just seems football has turned into a pound note, multi-pound notes, no great camaraderie between the fans and the players. You've got to remember that without the fans you've got nothing."

The win over Everton took Sunderland within touching distance of Wembley. Just two wins would do. Standing in their way were the holders Manchester United. Matt Busby had forged a formidable side following the 1958 tragedy which destroyed a young team certain to go on to great things.

A crowd of 61,700 jammed Old Trafford for the eagerly awaited tie and it was to be a thrilling game; perhaps not as good as the one that took place between the two teams in November 1974 and rated by BBC viewers as the best match shown on *Match of the Day* in the 1970s, but a game definitely worth remembering.

Sunderland took 16,000 tickets for the match and after 6,700 had gone to season ticket holders the rest went on open sale, which caused overnight queues. The *Echo* reported that one supporter had gone to the trouble of painting his car red and white from bumper to bumper and quoted a pessimist saying: "He'll look funny crawling back to Sunderland if they lose."

Hurley remembers the Alan Brown team talk beforehand. "When I asked who was going to stop Bobby Charlton, Denis Law and Georgie Best he put his hand on his chin and walked around for a bit giving it some thought and said 'I don't think you'll be able to do it on your own, Charlie' ha, ha, ha... This broke the ice among the players, because, don't forget, we were still a young team. We went out there as a swashbuckling squad."

The Second Division side made a thrilling start and George Mulhall's goal, headed from a narrow angle after a Brian Usher cross had eluded 'keeper Dave Gaskell, had Sunderland fans going mental. When Johnny Crossan scored the second most were already dreaming of Wembley. Then disaster struck and Hurley, a rock until then, was responsible when, under no pressure, he headed the ball back towards Jim Montgomery. However, the young 'keeper had advanced out of his goal and on fifty-five minutes Manchester United had been handed a lifeline.

Len Ashurst recalls that "most times Charlie's tricks came off and he looked brilliant. When they didn't come off it wasn't so good and that match at Man United was one of them. Charlie tried a bit of cleverness and found Monty was shaking hands with him as his header sailed into the goal. It wasn't the best thing to do."

Five minutes later no one cared as Crossan scored his second, this time from the penalty spot. Did he always score in twos? As the seconds and minutes dragged on it seemed that despite United's pressure Sunderland would not be overcome.

With less than two minutes remaining, however, a very rare headed goal from Bobby Charlton gave Matt Busby's team a glimmer of hope and Sunderland were stunned when just fifty seconds later

George Best drove the ball through a crowd of players to tie the game up at 3-3.

According to Charlie Hurley: "One player scored an o.g. playing for Sunderland... I think his name was Charlie something. I used to have this trick, the crowd used to love it. I used to go to hammer the ball away and then just flick it back. I really don't know who shouted because there were about 64,000 there and I've just done a little flick on. I turned round and there's Monty right up my backside. Don't forget it was early days in Monty's days and he wasn't used to what I would do. He knew after that.

"It was maybe Johnny Crossan's greatest game for us, he was magnificent. Then Denis Law whacks Monty in the face when he went for a cross and Monty went down. At 3-1 up a 'keeper would stay down, put on all the agonies and roll around, waste a bit of time. Monty was asked by [the referee] Arthur Ellis 'Are you all right?' 'Not really,' he says. 'Can you get up?' 'Not really, Charlie's got his foot on me arm.' Monty got up. If he'd stayed down for maybe another two or three minutes it could have made a bit of a difference. He wasn't quite ready. They scored from a corner and they equalised in the last minute."

Despite the obvious disappointment Sunderland still had a second chance. Argus wrote: "I would like to go on record that the famous 'Roker Roar' will need to pull out something special if it is to be classed with the wonderful work of the 16,000 gathered at Old Trafford on Saturday. They were terrific and the day finished with the team and their supporters proud of each other."

The replay was just four days later, making it impossible for Sunderland to ensure that apart from the 5,700 seats the ground would be all-ticket. With the whole town and surrounding areas at fever pitch, it was obvious that anyone turning up after half-past five for a seven-thirty kick-off was unlikely to see the match.

The semi-final draw had been made, and although the winners had the harder game, against West Ham, with the other game between Preston and Swansea, it seemed as if the team that went through from the replay would lift the cup.

Thousands took half-days from work or skipped school, with

the earliest arriving ten hours before kick-off. The streets around the ground were packed three hours before the start time.

Sunderland's record attendance of 75,118 had come in another sixth round replay back in 1933. Had Roker Park in the '60s been able to accommodate that many it was sure to have been broken that evening. But it could not, not least because people were now better fed and thus bigger!

One of those who was there was Doreen Purvis from South Shields. "Back in the 1963–64 season my boyfriend and I had been following the fortunes of the Sunderland team which was pushing for promotion. He was a supporter of some twelve years. I was a recent convert, having started going to matches in 1962. Following the draw at Old Trafford against the mighty Manchester United we thought the FA cup replay at Roker Park would be worth going to. In those days you just turned up at a match. I didn't even know anyone with a season ticket. However, there was a good deal of interest and word was going around that you'd need to get there early.

"We decided that rather than go straight there we would take a half day from work. I took a holiday, Alex simply 'balled up' – a shipyard term for not going back after dinner! After having something to eat we set off mid-afternoon armed with flask, sandwiches and wrapped up well. Even though it was March it was still bitterly cold. We just intended to see if there was anyone there and were staggered to find that there was a queue already at our preferred Roker End. We abandoned our plans of going into Sunderland and joined the crowd. Apart from the odd home-made scarf people were generally dressed fairly soberly. No replica strips, and headgear for the lads was strictly cloth cap.

"As the crowd grew we congratulated ourselves on a wise choice. There was a good atmosphere and the time passed quickly. It started to get cold and dark and thankfully they opened the gates. Not for us women the trips round the back lane for toilet purposes. We had to hang on or find a kindly householder who would let you use their outside lav.

"We were near the front and got a good spot. We were able to enjoy a cup of tea and a sandwich. Of course in those days almost everyone smoked and the air was blue. As the ground filled up we stood our ground but gradually were standing shoulder to shoulder with what looked like a record crowd. You could sense there was some commotion going on as the sound of ambulances was heard. We didn't know till later the extent of what was happening and that the double gates had been broken down.

"Finally we kicked off and every move on goal had us surging forward. The crowd just lifted you up and we hung on to each other in the crush. Dom Sharkey scored just before half-time and we went crackers. Denis Law, one of my all-time favourites – but not that night – equalised in the sixty-second minute. At full time the match was level and we went into extra time. George Best had a very quiet game and we certainly were not aware of watching a future legend.

"Sunderland went 2-1 up as another Sharkey shot was deflected off Maurice Setters for a goal. Sunderland supporters went wild, the pitch was invaded, scenes of celebration ensued. My boyfriend threw his cap in the air and it was never seen again. The noise was incredible, indescribable.

"But, hey, this is Sunderland and after twenty-eight minutes of extra time Bobby Charlton equalised! Hearts were broken and we filed out into the crowded streets to make our way home. We arrived back scruffy, exhausted and drained. Another eventful day in the life of a Sunderland supporter, but the most memorable match of my life."

Paddy Crerand, at right half for United, recalls: "I remember trying to get to the ground in the coach. I thought someone was going to get killed. The coach couldn't get through and it was only ninety minutes before the match. It was wall-to-wall people, totally solid; I think we had to get off the coach and fight our way through to the players' entrance. It was bedlam inside the ground as well."

What Crerand did not know until he was told forty-two years later was that amid the pandemonium two people had collapsed and died. One, a New Zealander, Mr George Smith Young Davison, was on holiday. Just thirty-nine years of age, he appears to have been crushed when the double gates at the Roker End burst open.

The other, Carole Chase Schmullian, was only eighteen and had collapsed running to the ground. One hundred people were taken to hospital, including sixteen with broken limbs. It was difficult for ambulances to get through the crowds.

Afterwards the police were criticised by some who wrote to the papers but with only seventy officers on duty, plus another forty-six on traffic duty, it is difficult to know what they could have done to control a crowd estimated to have touched 100,000. It was in truth a miracle that many more did not perish.

In those days there were no penalty shoot-outs so a second replay was needed and it took place just five days later at Leeds Road, Huddersfield. In between Sunderland had to play Middlesbrough at Roker Park, the second Wear–Tees derby of the season, and it proved a dull, goalless affair. It also took place on a soggy wet pitch that drained the already tired players.

Meanwhile Manchester United had an apparent injury crisis with Setters, Charlton and Law all out injured that day. Best was also rested. Matt Busby assured everyone that he was not trying to pull a fast one. In those days fielding a weakened team would have resulted in a fine from the FA. All four were "genuinely injured", said Busby. Amazingly two days later they were all fit to play in the third match between Sunderland and Manchester United.

Confirmation of the truth comes from Paddy Crerand, who revealed: "Matt Busby rested five players. I know in those days you could get into trouble, but he wanted to beat Sunderland and he was prepared to take the risk of getting fined."

Sharkey put Sunderland in front at Huddersfield three minutes after half-time but Manchester United then rammed home five in the next nineteen minutes – with Law grabbing a hat-trick – to run out worthy winners.

Charlie Hurley remembers: "In the first half we played maybe the best we played against them. It looked very good, and then they suddenly hit us with a couple of goals. We couldn't manage to fight back from there. We were still a very young side. It was a sad hour at the end, but a great experience."

Many years later Sir Bobby Charlton was asked to select the most memorable match of his career – surely it had to be the 1966 World

Cup Final when England beat West Germany 4-2 or the Manchester United victory by four goals to one in the 1968 European Cup Final against Benfica?

But no. Charlton chose the three FA Cup games against Sunderland and the one at Roker Park in particular. And in his 2008 autobiography *My Manchester United Years* he took up five pages on the games, admitting he was shocked after the first at how good Sunderland, a Second Division side, had been.

"The second game at Roker distilled everything I believed was true about the potential of football to capture the imagination of the ordinary working man. There was a fever in the moist air."

Charlton believes it was the three games against Sunderland which revealed that the side rebuilt by Matt Busby after the Munich tragedy in 1958 was destined for great things, rather than the more celebrated 5-1 victory in the Stadium of Light against Benfica in the European Cup two years later. It says a lot about just how well Sunderland played in the three games and reveals, not for the first time, that no ground in England could generate the atmosphere of a packed Roker Park.

Sir Bobby Charlton, of course, is still revered by Manchester United followers. Brian Leng believes Hurley's standing among Sunderland fans today can be compared to Charlton's at Old Trafford, stating "I can't think of any other player in his seventies who gets as much admiration from any set of supporters except Bobby Charlton at Manchester United."

United's eventual victory did them little good as West Ham beat them in the semi-final to set up a date at Wembley with the side that finished third in Division Two that season, Preston North End. West Ham won 3-2.

Despite the defeat Hurley was not too downhearted, saying that he felt "Great, just great. There would be no hangover from that one. We had been the better side most of the time and I thought it was hard that we should go down 5-1. We could get on with the 'other job' knowing that we have looked better than the best in Division One."

Says Paddy Crerand: "The three matches were fantastic games, great atmosphere. In those days the FA Cup was a big leveller, anybody could beat you. Sunderland was doing well, and they had absolutely fantastic support. They must have thought they were going to win. I've seen them when they're like that, I saw it outside Wembley in 1973, and all of them were saying they were going to win. I was telling them you've got no chance but they did beat Leeds and I was wrong."

Hurley did not have time to be disappointed by the cup defeat. He had to rush off to meet his Irish teammates and fly to Spain to play the first leg of the quarter-final European Championship at the Sanchez Pizjuan Stadium in Seville on March 11th. Hurley was once again captain for what was his third big match in six days. The scoreline was the same as at Leeds Road: Ireland were easily beaten with only a single goal reply from Blackburn's Andy McEvoy. Match reports show Hurley did not have a bad game although he was responsible for the first goal when his misplaced pass was seized on and finished in style by Amancio.

Hurley's fourth game in nine exhausting days was at, of all places, St James' Park and on a muddy, windswept pitch. It again ended disappointingly, Sunderland losing 1-0. The goal came after Hurley had fisted away Dave Hilley's shot on the line, an action for which today he would be sent off. Bill McGarry tucked away the penalty. Only 29,220 were there to see him do it because terrible weather and persistent rumours that the match had been postponed caused people to stay at home.

Sunderland fan Harry Clark recalls: "We were standing in the queue outside St James' Park when someone walked past and said the game was off because the pitch was waterlogged. Everyone just walked away and we went back to the station. When I got home I found out that the game had been played and that it was just a rumour that the game was off. My dad couldn't stop laughing when he found out what I had done."

The defeat at Newcastle knocked Sunderland off top spot – to lose out on a trip to Wembley was one thing, but to not gain promotion would be devastating. Two home games provided the perfect antidote. Preston were in third but were beaten 4-0, and in front of 56,675 Rotherham were beaten by 2-0 on Easter Friday.

The following Tuesday at Millmoor, Sunderland were 2-0 down before Crossan scored in the sixty-fourth minute after Hurley's drive had been blocked and it was from a Hurley header across the goal that Crossan equalised. Hurley was at his very best, causing Argus to write that his "second half display equalled the best he has produced in this exciting season." There was even talk that he might replicate the feat the year before of Stanley Matthews in winning the Football Writers' Player of the Year award as a Second Division player.

A Monday evening trip to Brisbane Road helped put to rest the memory of the final match of the 1961–62 season when Leyton Orient were eventually easily beaten 5-2, but not before Hurley prevented the O's from taking the lead.

Alan Williams, of the *Daily Express*, writing in the Coventry v Sunderland programme on December 28th 1968 reminisced: "I well remember that night in 1964 when Sunderland virtually clinched their return to the First Division with a 5-2 win at Leyton Orient. Sunderland were full of tension and Orient with the score at 1-1 some ten minutes before half-time were menacing dangerously. Then in a Leyton breakaway Harry Gregory slipped through a line of defenders who were trying to put him offside.

"It looked a goal all the way. But Charlie Hurley, thinking quicker than any of the other defenders, whipped back and charged the centre forward off the ball and prevented what could have been a crucial goal. There were claims for a penalty. But Charlie had, in my opinion, timed his charge perfectly."

What he did not say was that in the fifty-second minute Hurley produced a marvellous header across the goal to McNab who put Sunderland back in front, a goal which was quickly followed by others from Crossan, Mulhall and Sharkey – his second of the match – before Phillips scored his second for Orient. Orient's largest crowd of the season applauded Sunderland from the pitch.

Afterwards Hurley headed off to Dublin to play his third game in six days. It was the second leg of the European Championship tie with Spain but not a happy night. The visiting right-winger Zaballa heaped more misery on the Irish by scoring twice without reply, taking Spain through 7-1 on aggregate. They went on to defeat reigning champions USSR 2-1 in the final, their only major success until the 2008 European Championships when they beat Germany 1-0 in Vienna.

If Hurley was tired he did not show it as he was at the top of his form just three days later against Southampton at The Dell. This goalless draw meant Sunderland were as good as promoted because with two games left Preston were four points behind with a much inferior goal average.

Hurley was a proud captain when he spoke after the match to say: "This is it. We are there now. This is the happiest day of my life. It is great for the boys because they have done a magnificent job all the way through. It has not been easy and quite frankly at the beginning of the season we were not all that sure how things were going to work out. But we started with a win at Huddersfield and we've gone on from there getting a little bit more confident all the time."

Sunderland were determined to finish in style; they could still win the championship. In their final home game before a 50,827 crowd, again smaller than expected due to advance reports of big queues, they beat fourth-placed Charlton Athletic 2-1, but not before they'd fallen behind and seen their ex-keeper Peter Wakeham pull of a series of incredible saves.

Hurley remembers: "He never played like that when he played for us! He turned on the display of his life. I thought we'd never score. I said to myself, 'I am going to go up there and everything's going to go in the net: me, Peter, the ball, everything; we are not going to lose this game'. Just before I did that we got an equaliser, and despite that Peter still played tremendously. We should have got seven that day; we played ever so well as a team.

"I asked Peter afterwards, 'What were you on to stop us?' He said 'I love playing at Roker Park'. A lot of good pros loved playing at Roker Park. It was a good stage. If you turned on a good display the fans did give you, reluctantly or not, some applause, even if you weren't playing for their side."

Crossan and Herd were the goalscorers on the day but it was what happened after the finish that made it a very special day for all concerned, particularly for Charlie Hurley.

"One of the greatest moments of my career was when we actually got promotion. We did our lap of honour and then we were all sitting in the dressing room afterwards. Syd Collings, the chairman, came in and as he opened the door all you could hear was 'Charlie, Charlie, Charlie, Charlie' and Syd said 'Look, you'll have to go back out again'.

"To go out to that kind of call, that kind of support, was amazing. George Herd only had a jockstrap and a shirt on; some had no boots on. It just showed how important it was for us to go round. We went round for those fans, big shipbuilders, big miners, crying their eyes out. We were shaking hands with these guys and nearly crying ourselves because of the emotion they felt. The pride of actually getting back into the First Division was second to none.

"Alan Brown said after the game it was all down to the players, but I would say it was fifty-fifty. I would have said that the Roker fans were the people who helped us get up there. We went a spell not far off then when we were undefeated for eighteen months at Roker Park. Now that is no mean feat. We played cup sides and everything. So the fans in my opinion deserve a tremendous amount of credit for us actually getting back to the First Division where people say we belong. No one belongs. We had to fight to do it; you have to fight for things in your life, and you don't have a right to anything."

Two days later Hurley heard that he had finished second in the Footballer of the Year award voted on by the Football Writers' Association, gathering 30 of the possible 107 votes, with West Ham's Bobby Moore out in front with 49. The votes of Northern writers had been split with nine going to Denis Law, later voted European Footballer of the Year, while virtually every vote of the southern writers went to Moore. Hurley thus missed becoming the only player from a north-east club to win the award.

Somewhat surprisingly, Hurley dismisses his second place and his comments reveal that the comedian and good bloke he is off the pitch should not obscure the fact that while on it he was a professional footballer whose aim was always to win.

"When I ask people who came second when Bobby Moore won the Player of the Year in 1964 they haven't a bloody clue. I was nearly Footballer of the Year. It would have been marvellous, especially for a Second Division player. I tell people it was a player from the Second Division and they still don't know. They don't care. You only get things in life for winning. Show me a good loser and I will show you a guy that doesn't win a lot."

The following week Sunderland had a chance to claim the Division Two trophy but it meant winning away at Grimsby, and hoping that Charlton would do them a favour by beating Leeds United at The Valley. With Leeds winning with two goals from Alan Peacock, the result at Blundell Park was largely immaterial but the 2-2 draw ensured that Sunderland finished with sixty-one points, two behind the very good Leeds United side that Don Revie was taking back up after four seasons in the Second Division. Despite Leeds winning the trophy, their crowds never compared to Sunderland's. They averaged 29,938 whereas the Roker average was 41,258.

When Sunderland were invited to a reception at the Town Hall, a large crowd turned out to greet them. In his speech Hurley, deliberately ignoring any reference to his own achievements, made special mention of ex-players such as Stan Anderson, Ambrose Fogarty, the injured Brian Clough and the youngsters Brian Usher and Nick Sharkey.

Hurley's season ended with a short international tour, a trip on which one of the players, sick of their treatment at the hands of the amateurish committee men who ran the Irish national team, decided to take matters into his own hands. After a 3-1 defeat by Poland in the Wisla Stadium in Kracow, goalkeeper Noel Dwyer, then playing for Swansea Town, had come on as a substitute for Alan Kelly. But it was what he did afterwards that Hurley recalls with a chuckle: "One of the committee men who picked the squad was a jolly man. He didn't have a clue about anything and I don't just mean about football. Noel Dwyer nicked his passport when we were in Poland and flushed it down the toilet. They wouldn't let the man out; he was nearly in tears.

"He thought he was going to stay there for the rest of his life. He thought Ireland was bad enough but Poland was worse. He didn't get out until the next day. Noel was only taking revenge for the fact that sometimes there were fifteen to twenty committee men on the trip with only thirteen players. It was costing an arm and a leg for the committee men because they were doing all the drinking. We couldn't drink because we were playing; All we got for playing was £30.

"We were wearing collars and cuffs five years after every other national team replaced them with round necks. They must have bought them as job lots because we just couldn't get rid of them. We wore these big old shorts. We were the scruffiest-looking international team you've ever seen. My old heart used to burn in a lot of cases. You don't have to look good to be good, but it feels nicer all the same."

Scruffy or not, three days later at the Ulleval Stadium in Oslo a rampant Ireland side easily brushed aside Norway 4-1. Hurley was the player-manager for this game and he played himself at centre forward. It worked. He scored twice; Giles and McEvoy got the others.

"We played in Poland and got beat. The food was uugh – they brought round this mince with a raw egg in the middle. Some of us ate it, I was one of them, and got food poisoning, the worst ever. I sat on the toilet all night.

"We travelled to Oslo and I shouldn't have played. I said to myself 'Well, I'm pretty useful in the air so I'll go up front'. Fortunately they weren't all that clever and there's me standing up like a bird. Bump, I hit the post. I was loving it, scored one, we went two-nil up, then 2-1. I knocked in another one to make it 3-1. Anyway, I got carried off with cramp in my calves and my thighs – I did well to get to about sixty minutes. I was in a terrible state, but we beat them and I thought 'no pain no gain'.

"If I had my career again I would never in a million years be a centre half and if I'd had a son I'd not have entertained him playing at the back. Scoring goals is what it's all about. I will always remember the Norwich game in the FA Cup as I can remember feeling about a yard above everyone else. It's all about scoring, and I remember that day in Norway as very rarely did Ireland win 4-1 away".

Eleven days later, on the day England beat an Ireland team without the injured Hurley 3-1 in Dublin, came the appalling news that 319 spectators had died after police had fired tear gas into the crowd during a friendly between Peru and Argentina. Some supporters had invaded the pitch to protest at a disallowed home goal and many of those who were killed had been crushed to death when the gates were shut and mass panic set in. It was a stark reminder that many football grounds across the world were no longer safe, with Roker Park almost certainly one of them.

But after six seasons out of the top flight football it could look forward to, once again, hosting First Division football – Sunderland were back!

Chapter Eleven

First Division football but the manager departs

The 1964–65 season should have been the chance for Charlie Hurley and the rest of Sunderland's players to show what a good set of footballers they were – after all, the previous season the Roker Park side had easily beaten the 1962–63 League Champions Everton in the FA Cup and taken the holders Manchester United to three games.

Sadly the season is best remembered for events off the field. Sunderland lost manager Alan Brown only weeks before the kick-off and then slumped towards the bottom of the table before producing a remarkable revival under the leadership of new manager George Hardwick. He was then sensationally sacked for what he later claimed was his failure to get rid of Brian Clough from his role as youth team manager. Hurley himself showed that he was more than a match for the best in the top flight and was to end the season dreaming of a World Cup adventure with Ireland at the 1966 World Cup in England.

Sunderland fans responded to the first season back in the top flight in six years by snapping up a record number of season tickets. In hindsight supporters wondered if the fact that Alan Brown did not strengthen the squad during the summer was because of his confidence in his players to do well in the top flight or an indication that any players he did fancy would be useful if he went to manage elsewhere.

It was a major shock when, with less than three weeks to Sunderland kicking off in the First Division, Brown announced he had accepted an offer to join Sheffield Wednesday, who had finished fourth in the top division the previous season.

At the time there was considerable press speculation. Brown may have been just glad to get away; he had taken some awful stick during his first three years in charge. This had been remarked upon at the end of the previous season by Harry Ditton, in the *News of the World*, who wrote: "Considering all the trials and tribulations Alan Brown went through in his first three seasons at Roker – he reckoned he was the most hated man on Wearside – he must be overjoyed."

All Brown would say was: "I have achieved what I set out to do. Now I must find another challenge."

So it is left to his star man and captain Charlie Hurley to explain what happened: "I don't think people really knew the reasons why Alan Brown resigned. All the lads were on bonuses to win promotion, and for those days I suppose we did really well. Alan told me he got nothing. Now just as the Roker fans played a part so did Alan Brown. He played more than his fair part in us getting promotion because he built the team from scratch. I thought it was very sad. It was a sad day for me and I know it was a sad day for all the youngsters he'd given a chance to."

George Mulhall, who after he finished playing managed Halifax Town, Bradford City and Bolton Wanderers and also enjoyed spells as assistant manager at Tranmere Rovers and Huddersfield Town, says: "Brown was a decent manager; he knew what he was talking about. Those who followed him were not as good and the team suffered as a result."

But being a footballer is basically just a job like many others, so when a manager departs players simply wait for the next one to be appointed and hope to make an instant impression. The wait was likely to be a long one; the Sunderland directors had absolutely no idea who to appoint.

And things then went from bad to worse when Jimmy Montgomery sustained a hand injury that would keep him out when the season started. It meant Sunderland were forced to kick off at home to Leicester City with a goalkeeper who at fifteen years and 156 days was the youngest ever to play in a Division One match. Derek Forster had signed as an apprentice professional only the previous month and had arrived at training to be stunned with news from club secretary George Crow that he was playing against Leicester City in Sunderland's first top-flight game since 1958. It says much that the newly promoted club had not bothered to line up a more experienced reserve team goalkeeper to Montgomery.

Charlie Hurley's first match in Division One, of course, had not gone well; a 7-0 defeat away at Blackpool in October 1957. He had improved as a player considerably since then but nevertheless the match reports generally agreed that he had a poor game on his return. Sunderland, however, looked like they would win the match when Sharkey drove them into the lead with ten minutes left, but Leicester recovered to grab a point when Mike Stringfellow crossed for Keyworth to equalise at 3-3. In goal for Leicester was the man who was to play at Wembley in 1966 when England beat West Germany to win the World Cup, Gordon Banks.

Sunderland's away form the previous season had been impressive with twenty-four of the available forty-two points being gained. But they were now in the First Division and despite Stan Jones knocking a Harvey ball past his own goalkeeper to give them the lead, they were well beaten at The Hawthorns by a flowing West Brom side with Tony Brown grabbing a hat-trick in a 4-1 win. Another away defeat followed, this time 3-1 at Stamford Bridge, from where Argus reported that he felt there had been a significant improvement in Hurley's overall performance from the first two games.

That was not how Len Ashurst remembers it: "Charlie didn't like to be taken down the flanks as he was heavily built and wasn't the fastest. I believe Charlie wasn't one of the best trainers. I think he liked the company of his teammates but because of his weight I think he found training hard work. That day at Chelsea I think Tommy Docherty, who put together a fine side, had spotted how to play Charlie, and Barry Bridges ran him ragged. The ball was sent down the channels and Charlie struggled to get over and get the ball."

Of course every player, however good, gets torn apart on occasions.

Hurley says that he thinks "Len is wrong about this. I was over 6 foot tall and 14 stone. It's true I wasn't a long-distance runner and

I hated pre-season training, but I never had a weight problem and when I wasn't injured I worked hard at training".

Ashurst also offers a different opinion to that expressed by Stan Anderson earlier as to whether Hurley played too many matches outside Division One, saying: "I think it was a tragedy that Charlie played so many matches in the Second Division. He wouldn't have won any more Eire international caps if he'd played in the First, but I think it would have been a challenge. This 'Player of the Century' – now I wouldn't take anything away from Charlie but in a way it's a contradiction in terms because a lot of people who watched Sunderland in the '30s weren't around to vote and the likes of Raich Carter must come into the reckoning. However, so be it. I wouldn't take anything away from Charlie, but that mantle would have been enhanced if he had been playing against the greatest centre forwards of the day, and a lot of them were in the First Division."

It was clear that with Forster having conceded ten goals something had to be done. It came in the shape of Alexander McLaughlin, signed from Kilmarnock at a cost of £12,000. McLaughlin must be one of the smallest players ever to play in goal for Sunderland. As he was only 5ft 8in tall Hurley's ability to head away dangerous crosses was going to be needed!

McLaughlin's debut against West Brom at Roker Park was totally overshadowed by the surprise return of Brian Clough, absent since his injury on Boxing Day 1962. The largest home crowd of the season, 52,177 – the capacity of Roker Park having been reduced after the scenes at the Manchester United cup replay – were silenced when McLaughlin conceded a goal before he had even touched the ball. Tony Brown was again the scorer and although Mulhall equalised Sunderland went 2-1 down when Clive Clark scored.

It was then that Hurley grabbed his first top-flight goal to rescue a valuable point for the managerless side. Brian Usher lobbed the ball into the middle in the fifty-first minute and though Ray Potter in goal got a hand to Hurley's header he could not keep it out.

Leeds United's trip to Roker Park saw Clough remain in the team and he scored what turned out to be his only Division One goal with Crossan firing home two. The home side came from two down to take the lead but it was not enough to win the match as Leeds also hit three. Clough's goal came "when a Hurley header from a corner was helped on by Usher and Clough scored from close range," reported the *Journal*'s Alf Greenley.

Hurley was back in goalscoring mood when Aston Villa came to Roker Park, but the much-needed first victory was still no nearer with the match ending 2-2. It could have been worse, however, as Charlie's goal came in the last minute. It was the result of a magnificent driving run by Martin Harvey who, Greenley reported, "beat two defenders on a sixpence and centred for Hurley to hurl himself at the ball and head a great goal." Hurley had struggled to contain Tony Hateley, a battling hard-working number nine whose son Mark later played in a similar fashion when winning thirty-two England caps during the 1980s and '90s.

There was further bad news in a season already not going well when it became clear that Clough's battle to overcome his cruciate ligament injury was not going to succeed. He was replaced at Highbury by Dominic Sharkey, a good player admittedly, but not of Clough's stature. He scored, but despite a penalty save by McLaughlin Sunderland flopped to a 3-1 defeat.

George Mulhall is an ardent admirer of Clough because "his goals record speaks for itself, but he was very, very arrogant. He could upset people like nobody I've ever met. On the pitch if he was in a good position and you didn't give him the ball he'd tell you about it. Hurley and Clough on the pitch were similar. They both hated losing. They both wanted to win any game they played. Hurley was, of course, the club captain and it was his job to make sure that every player didn't like losing. He was a good captain."

It seems to be around this time that Sunderland fans added to their chant of "Charlie, Charlie, Charlie" at each corner with a new song for their hero. George Forster, one of the founders of the Sunderland Supporters Association in June 1965 and still heavily involved today, recalls: "I cannot recall exactly how the song took off but it went as follows:

Who's the greatest centre half in all the world today?
Who's the greatest centre half in all the world today?

Who's the greatest centre half in all the world today?
Charlie Hurley is his name,
Charlie, Charlie, Charlie Hurley,
Charlie, Charlie, Charlie Hurley
Charlie Hurley is his name.

Hurley was criticised by Argus for having stayed up the field at Villa Park in a search for an equaliser, the *Sunderland Echo* reporter claiming it had added to Sunderland's problems, which he felt were already substantial. The 2-1 defeat had flattered the new boys. Sunderland had four points from eight games. And although their first win came at home to Blackburn Rovers they had only a miserable six points from eleven matches.

Unlike on his Sunderland debut back in 1957, when he'd put the ball into his own net to make it 7-0 to Blackpool, Hurley did at least have the satisfaction of scoring in the right net at Bloomfield Road in September. It came in the twenty-second minute when he jumped magnificently to flash a header across 'keeper Tony Waiters and into the net. This equalised Ray Charnley's earlier goal for Blackpool before a crowd of 31,191, boosted by thousands of Sunderland fans in town for the match and the turning on of the famous Blackpool 'illuminations' in the evening. Not to forget the beer, of course.

Football and beer, in fact, were both celebrated in another song of that period as George Forster again recalls:

Oh glorious, victorious, one bottle of beer between the four of us,
Glory be to God, that there isn't any more of us because
    one of us could drink the bloody lot,
We'll be there; we'll be there,
When the lads are playing football we'll be there,
Wherever the lads are playing football,
Wherever the lads are playing football,
We'll be there.

This was a re-working of a song from the First World War trenches which went as follows:

Gassed last night, and gassed the night before.
Going to get gassed tonight if we never get gassed any more.
When we're gassed, we're sick as we can be.
For phosgene and mustard gas is much too much for me.
They're killing us, they're killing us.
One respirator for the four of us.
Thank your lucky stars that we can all run fast.
So one of us can take it all alone.

Meanwhile, around the country many fans were becoming increasingly frustrated at the actions of a small, but certainly increasing number of supporters who were finding it difficult to behave properly. In the Old Trafford match programme, the Manchester United manager Matt Busby had appealed to the "minority" to behave themselves after the club had received "complaints from spectators about acts of misconduct by some boisterous, ill-mannered fans."

Dickie Rooks deputised for an injured Charlie Hurley as Sunderland continued to stumble, although there was some good news in the performances of John O'Hare, who had forced his way into the first team, making his debut at Stamford Bridge in August just weeks before he turned eighteen. It was to O'Hare that Brian Clough was to turn when appointed manager at Derby County in 1967 and although Sunderland received £22,000 in compensation it was poor reward for the loss of such a young talent.

Sunderland won their second league game of the season, scraping home 3-2 against Burnley, on November 14th but the day is better remembered as the one on which George Hardwick was approached to take over as manager. A former Middlesbrough left back and England captain, he'd had previous managerial experience at Oldham Athletic, PSV Eindhoven, in Holland, and with the Dutch national team. In November 1964, however, Hardwick was a supervisor with ICI. He resigned to take over at Sunderland. No contract was signed.

Hardwick's arrival was a complete surprise to all but the inner circle of decision makers at Roker Park. He appears to have turned up to report on the Burnley match unaware that he was going to be asked to become manager.

It was announced that he would hold a watching brief at Sheffield United the following weekend. It is, therefore, difficult to know whether he agreed or not with the Sunderland board's decision to try and plug the gap left by Clough by bidding to buy Dundee's Alan Gilzean.

Gilzean had scored Scotland's winning goal in a 1-0 victory over England at Hampden Park in the summer and by the time he left Dundee he had made 190 appearances and scored 169 goals, helping them win the Scottish League title in 1962. He would have been a significant signing for Sunderland but it was not to be. Gilzean went to White Hart Lane to become Jimmy Greaves's collaborator in a deadly partnership.

Sunderland's tenth away game of the season – at Birmingham City – brought another defeat. Although twice in the lead, they were beaten 4-3, leaving the club with no points away from home thus far. It remains the worst run of away form in their history, although it was equalled during the 1969–70 and 2007–08 seasons.

Explains Jim Montgomery: "We had a poor away record. I can't really explain it. The Roker home crowd was magnificent. It was often worth a goal head start. We did however have a great away following even in the mid '60s but we just couldn't put it together. It wasn't for the lack of effort."

With Rooks continuing to deputise for Hurley, the eleventh away game finally brought the much-needed first points when Leicester City embarrassed themselves by becoming the first side to succumb to Sunderland, a Sharkey goal winning the match.

But Hardwick was having an effect. Sunderland had won four of his first six games and now had sixteen points after twenty-one matches. In his sixth game at the helm Sunderland produced a wonderful performance to avenge their early season defeat at Chelsea. It was probably Sunderland's finest of the 1964–65 season. Chelsea had been unbeatable on their travels, winning six and drawing four. This run was brought to an abrupt end with Harvey, Herd and Sharkey netting without reply and the Londoners were knocked off top spot in the table.

Hurley was again missing for the eagerly awaited match with champions Liverpool on Boxing Day but he was still at the ground to watch his teammates and for one young boy his presence helped ensure he had a moment never to forget. The tale provides a glimpse of the sort of man Hurley is. It comes from Alan Walsh, a lifelong Sunderland fan from South Shields who now lives in London.

"It was at Christmas. It was freezing and I hadn't taken a warm coat with me. I was mad about Sunderland and like some other young lads at the time I always tried to be the first in the ground. When the turnstiles opened I used to pay my money and dash up on to the terraces. It was so cold I must have collapsed. I can't remember what happened but next thing I knew I was being woken up in a little room next to the players' tunnel. Holding my hand was Charlie Hurley. I thought I'd died and gone to heaven.

"He held my hand while the doctor checked me out and both made sure I was well enough to go and watch the match. By the time I was able to walk back out the teams were coming out of their dressing rooms. As the *Z Cars* music was just about to get started, Charlie took me down the tunnel and with the crowd roaring we were the first ones out. There was an enormous cheer; I actually thought they were cheering for me. It was one of the best moments of my life; Charlie was brilliant."

After being reminded of this incident, Hurley says: "You have to remember when we went outside the entrance at Roker Park we signed autographs for ages and ages. None of this pissing off without doing anything. I thought the world of Sunderland football fans. We used to have lunch in the Roker Hotel then walk down to the ground with the fans; 'Come on Charlie, come on George, we'll do these today,' they'd say. It was the closeness to the fans that inspired you."

Hurley also missed the return fixture at Anfield two days later, Sunderland gaining a small measure of revenge for Liverpool having become the first team to win at Roker Park by grinding out a goalless draw in front of 43,528.

An injured Hurley at least had the consolation of knowing that he would be back at some point, which was not the case for Clough. And according to Hardwick, Clough let everyone know it as Clough "hated every member of the club because they could go out on a Saturday and play football."

Clough was not prepared to let his enforced absence stand in the way of telling the directors what to do. "He told the directors they should resign" at Sunderland's plight, reported Hardwick after he had left the club. It may have just been an attempt to keep Clough quiet but Hardwick put him to work teaching the youngsters and he impressed so much he was made youth team manager.

Johnny Crossan made his final appearance in a Sunderland shirt at Anfield, thus chalking up 99 appearances, during which he scored 48 times. On October 19th 2007 Crossan, then 68, made the long journey from his home in Northern Ireland to join in the celebrations organised by the SAFC Foundation at the Stadium of Light to commemorate Hurley's fifty years as a Sunderland hero.

"I got out of bed at 4 o'clock this morning, I drove to the airport and flew here. I am shattered now, and I wouldn't have done that for too many people. But I think Charlie Hurley was easily the best centre half I've ever seen playing.

"That Real Madrid side I played against for Standard Liege had Santa Maria at centre half. You hear people talking about him but Charlie Hurley was a far better player. He was the most complete player we had. He was a big, heavy guy but he had nimble feet and was extremely good on the ground with the ball.

"In the 1963–64 season I scored, I think, twenty-eight goals. About ten were from a yard out when Charlie came bombing in and the goalkeeper made a save and I was tapping them over the line. Today, if Rio Ferdinand is on 100 grand a week, Charlie would be worth more than that. I've turned up today for him and also because of the Sunderland people. I admire and adore the people of Sunderland. There's not a better place in the world, and I am serious. I played all over the place so I know that when you're winning the appreciation that the people of Sunderland show for a player is tremendous."

Hurley returned for the home game with Blackpool on February 6th and from a well-worked corner he headed the ball across goal for Sharkey to score with just nine minutes remaining.

Hardwick had been forced to change the positions Hurley took up at corners because most teams put two players on him. Instead of attacking the ball and going for goal he was asked to head the ball back towards goal or flick it on. Sunderland forced fifteen corners in the first half against Blackpool and Hurley had caused panic at each one. Argus was full of praise for him afterwards, stating that "the Eire skipper powered Sunderland along, both in defence and attack, it was his inspiring play which created and maintained the gulf between the sides."

That same afternoon an ageing superstar was playing his final match in a career stretching back to 1932. At 50 years and five days, Stanley Matthews had finally decided to hang up his boots after playing for Stoke against Fulham. Incredibly, Matthews is not the oldest man to play League Football. That record belongs to Neil McBain, who aged 51 years and 4 months, played for New Brighton against Hartlepool United on March 15th 1947.

Manchester United attracted 51,336 to Roker Park and Sunderland gained a measure of revenge when they beat them by a single goal from Harry Hood, one of just nine in his short Sunderland career. Suddenly Sunderland were on a roll. They went to London and for the first time since January 14th 1956 they won a First Division match in the capital. And by defeating West Ham it meant they recorded their only double of the season – they had also beaten the Hammers in the League Cup.

Two wins in a row became three when, despite a Jimmy Greaves goal, Tottenham lost 2-1 at Roker Park on March 20th. A fourth victory seemed on the cards when Sunderland took a two-goal lead at Ewood Park but with Hurley badly injured, Blackburn were able to exploit gaps at the back to score three times. The injury meant Hurley missed Ireland's 100th international in midweek, a friendly against Belgium.

Hurley had recovered and was pressed into action as an attacking wing-half when Sunderland drew 1-1 at Goodison Park, which made them undefeated on Merseyside that season! Sharkey's goal was his eighteenth in the league, a fine total especially as they had come in just thirty-one games. It came in the thirty-seventh minute after Hurley had hit a twenty-five-yard pass to him and he'd cleverly beaten Brian Labone, Everton's centre half, to hit a left-foot drive just inside the upright.

Meanwhile off the pitch Sunderland's decline as a shipbuilding port was marked by the announcement that the town had been left off a list of sixty-one ports on which £100 million was to be spent on development. Dark days were ahead.

Everton's youth team had more success against Sunderland than their seniors when they knocked them out in the FA Youth Cup semi-final 5-0 over two games. Nevertheless, reaching the last four was an indication that the policy started back in 1957 with the appointment of Alan Brown was beginning to bring potential first-team players through. A number of those on show in the semi-finals subsequently played professional football including Billy Hughes, Bobby Kerr, Malcolm Keenan, Jimmy Shoulder, Colin Suggett and Colin Todd while O'Hare and Forster had already played first-team football.

The first season back in Division One ended at home to Sheffield Wednesday, now, of course, managed by Alan Brown. A rare Ashurst goal on twelve minutes proved enough to help Sunderland finish in style, their home record reading Played 21 Won 12 Drawn 6 Lost 3.

There was no doubt that Sunderland could compete with, and beat, the best in the land at home and in the 1964–65 season they chalked up their best ever record against the top six, beating five of them with only Leeds, who finished second, managing a point at Roker Park. It was just that they were easy meat when they crossed the River Wear and headed south. Little was to change the following season, or the one after that.

Len Ashurt's view of the season is this: "I think the reason we didn't do well in 1964–65 was because Alan Brown left. Hardwick and later McColl were not in the same street as Brownie. Plenty of his players made a pretty good living after they finished playing. I think he taught good principles and from my point of view he gave me my debut and I am grateful to him for that."

Brian Leng is not so certain, saying that "Brown hadn't made any signings before he left. The team that won promotion needed strengthening if Sunderland were going to do well. There had been record season ticket sales so there was money available. To kick off with Forster in goal facing a side that fielded Gordon Banks was criminal. When Monty was fit again he should have been the first team goalkeeper. Hardwick should also have hung on to Crossan, who went over to Manchester City and did well. Hardwick did turn it round, mind, and deserved another season at least."

Hardwick's record was impressive. In the fifteen games before his appointment Sunderland had won just one match and gained eight points. Under his control they won thirteen, drew three and lost eleven, which brought in twenty-nine points. Had Sunderland managed this later average through the season they would have finished above Spurs in the table in sixth, two points below Everton, who, as a result of finishing fourth, qualified for the Inter-Cities Fairs Cup. It was a decent achievement and it showed what Sunderland could do if properly managed.

This was not the view of Sunderland's directors. Having lost the man who had taken them to promotion they then sacked, or rather failed to offer a contract to, the man who had kept them up. Len Shackleton once left a page blank in his autobiography, claiming that it represented what football club directors knew about football. It seemed the directors at his old club were proving him right.

Hurley remembers the Hardwick sacking like this: "Alan Brown was a very difficult act to follow and for a while Arthur Wright and old Jack Jones the coach ran the show. We struggled. George Hardwick came in and he was a real character was George. I liked him. I think many of the players did. He was very, very laid back. I always remember one game at home when we got beat 2-1, we came in and he was lying under the sun lamp, so he was obviously worried sick!

"We got through the season with no real danger and he took us to watch the cup final. There were speeches afterwards by the directors, saying how he'd done a good job, and then shortly after he was sacked. If ever the old cliché about 'a vote of confidence' was proved it was then."

The sacking was such a shock that it even made the front page of the *Sunderland Echo* – remarkable because this was a time when football was strictly for the back pages.

Hardwick was unwilling to react bitterly at the time, saying he had "no hard feelings against the club... I am naturally disappointed but we have a great set of lads... and a wonderful crowd. I always got on well with the directors too."

However, he did later speak about what he felt had cost him his job – it was the controversial figure of Brian Clough!

In Tony Francis's excellent biography of Clough, he reports that when Hardwick was sacked he approached Syd Collings for an explanation. The board went into a huddle and came back with two reasons: he had been too friendly with the press, and too hard on the players.

Hardwick said that Laurie Evans, then Sunderland vice-chairman, had told him that despite Clough taking the youth team to the semi-finals of the FA Youth Cup they wanted rid of him and "as soon as we get the insurance money he's out of the door."

Hardwick claims to have argued with Evans about this, telling him that "in two years time he'll be my right-hand man." Hardwick may have been a little foolish because he had not even told Clough what he was thinking and as Hardwick later admitted: "I had to play it carefully because he was so unpopular with the senior players."

Nevertheless Hardwick claims he "was fired because I stood by Brian and refused to climb down. Any fool could see that. That's how much they despised him. I don't regret what I did. I had faith in him. Together we could have formed a partnership as successful as the one he had with Peter Taylor."

Hardwick was right to stand by Clough, the board were wrong, but the club had the consolation of collecting £40,000 compensation in insurance. Clough got just £1,500 to go with the £5,000 or so he was to make from his testimonial. It was probably the worst decision ever made by a group of Sunderland directors and the club has suffered since.

On the directors' part at the time, the *Echo* reported that "apart from Mr Hardwick himself there was no comment from anyone else connected with the club", although a few days later Syd Collings admitted that they "had nobody in mind" for the now vacant post.

Hurley was out of the country when much of the controversy raged, having travelled to Ireland to play an important World Cup qualifier. With Tunisia dropping out of Ireland's group only Ireland and Spain were left to contest a place in the finals in England the following summer. It was Hurley's twenty-seventh game for his country and by far the most important he had played in since Atyeo's equaliser for England ruined Ireland's chances back in 1957.

As reigning European champions, Spain were in confident mood. They had, of course, defeated Ireland home and away two years previously, and with Ireland unable to create anything despite the backing of a passionate 42,000 crowd they had no reason to be alarmed. But after seventeen minutes of the second half, Frank O'Neill misdirected a free kick and with no one near him the Spanish goalkeeper Iribar unaccountably let the ball slip from his hands and over the line for an unlikely goal. Dalymount Park erupted.

Johnny Giles was WP Murphy's man of the match and the reporter also reserved special praise for Hurley, stating that "after a season dogged by injury he was back to his old majestic form at centre half – a rock on which most of the Spanish attacks perished – and after this fine display and great Irish victory he was a worthy winner of the FAI statuette for twenty-five international appearances at the official banquet last night."

With Ireland hanging on to the single goal advantage the crowd went home with thoughts of a short trip over the water to watch their team at the World Cup finals in England – if only Ireland could get at least a draw in Seville later in the year.

Eight days later on May 13th there was a shock when Ian McColl resigned as manager of Scotland shortly before World Cup qualifying matches with Poland and Finland. Eight days after that he took over at Sunderland. And four days after that Sunderland signed Jim Baxter. It was a major transfer. In the mid-1960s context Baxter was the Scottish equivalent of George Best although he played in midfield. He was lavishly talented, could dribble with the ball, passed it well and had a strut of arrogance which helped him stand out even in a good team. He also had a Beatles haircut, was reasonably good-looking and liked the good life which, as with Best, was ultimately to send him to an early grave. When he left school he had started down the pit as a coal miner and it was not until he was eighteen that he played for his first professional club, Raith Rovers. In 1960 he joined Glasgow Rangers, where he was to win three League and Scottish Cup medals and four League Cup medals. His nickname was "Slim Jim", ironic in view of the way the pounds piled on once he stopped playing.

In the December before signing for Sunderland Baxter had broken his leg in the dying minutes of a Scottish victory over Austria in Vienna's Prater Stadium. During his time out of the game he took to the good life in a way that could not have done a professional footballer much good. But Spurs, Arsenal, Wolves and Stoke had all expressed an interest in signing him so it was something of a coup for Sunderland to get him, although they had to pay a club record £72,500.

In print Baxter declared himself as delighted, stating that "I couldn't have wished to be going to a better club", but his demeanour told another story and there is a classic picture in which he is being photographed signing for Sunderland with McColl behind him. McColl has a very wide smile on his face; Baxter's face, however, shows him with mouth firmly shut and looking, to put it mildly, a lot less happy. If Sunderland fans or players were disappointed by the 1964–65 season little did they know it was to get a lot worse, and Charlie Hurley was to be among those to suffer most.

Chapter Twelve

Injury and heartache

Before the 1965–66 season got underway Charlie Hurley had his first chance to meet new manager Ian McColl. It did not go well.

"When McColl came I remember him having me in his office because I was the club captain. One of the first things he said to me was 'I don't really need this job, I've got a business at home and I earn good money.' I said, 'Well, I'm going to tell you something here; if you don't need this job then you should never take it because it's one of the biggest jobs in football.' That was it. I don't know if McColl liked what I said or not, but it didn't do me a lot of good. But I had to say what I felt."

The season itself kicked off with two away matches, the first at Elland Road, where Baxter lined up alongside Harvey and Hurley at halfback. Alexander McLaughlin was given his chance between the sticks as Sunderland looked to start the season in better form than the previous one. The fans were overjoyed at the arrival of such a star as Baxter and, convinced that better days were just around the corner, the demand for tickets for Elland Road was enormous. Leeds officials admitted in the matchday programme that they had "been rather worried that some of our own supporters might be left without a ticket". A Norman Hunter goal ensured Sunderland made a losing start in their second season back in Division One.

Next was a trip to Upton Park where West Ham's bumper crowd of 34,772 welcomed the European Cup Winners Cup winners [This tournament played between the cup winners of each European country ran until the end of the 1998–99 season]. West Ham won the trophy at Wembley, beating 1860 Munich 2-0 on May 19th.

O'Hare lined up at centre forward for Sunderland but it was inside forward George Herd who scored the equalising goal in the twentieth minute to cancel out Martin Peters' fourth-minute effort in a 1-1 draw. Argus reported that "Hurley and Harvey showed great determination in pinning down the hard running West Ham attack" and that "Sunderland had put in two sound performances in the first two away games."

This point became three when, in front of almost 43,000 at Roker Park, Sheffield United proved no match for Sunderland – but not before McLaughlin had gifted the Blades a third-minute lead when he dropped the ball to leave Mick Jones with an easy chance.

But this was the day when Baxter demonstrated to the Roker Park crowd what an amazing player he could be. The following day's *Sunday Mirror* headline was simple – "He Was Magnificent". The Scot scored twice in a 4-1 win, including just seconds before half-time after, said the *Sunday Mirror*, "he had the Roker Terraces going crazy when he seized on to a John O'Hare pass just inside his own half. Looking like a thoroughbred among workhorses he streaked a full fifty yards down the centre of the field, then slipped a perfectly controlled shot past the oncoming Hodgkinson."

Three points soon became five when Sunderland maintained their hoodoo on West Ham by beating them at home 2-1. Geoff Hurst had capitalised on a mistake by Hurley to give the Hammers a half-time lead with a nineteenth-minute goal before George Mulhall hammered home the equaliser nine minutes after the interval. Jimmy McNab then dived spectacularly to head the winner in the seventy-second minute. More than 48,000 watched the game.

The Sunderland AFC Supporters' Association had been launched during the summer and already 4,000 had paid their membership fee of five shillings [25p] or two and six [12.5p] for under-18s. One of its aims was "to make the team feel that when they are away they are still at home." If only! Sunderland were terrible away from Roker Park and proved it with their next two performances. O'Hare's goal at Filbert Street could not prevent Leicester winning 4-1 and Aston Villa then won 3-1. Sunderland's Achilles heel remained.

Worse was to follow when Hurley pulled a thigh muscle during a training session and with Sunderland having allowed Rooks to leave during the summer they were without a natural replacement. McLaughlin's poor form saw Jim Montgomery brought back and

Hurley's place was taken by John Parke, who had been signed from Hibernian by Hardwick the previous season for the considerable sum of £33,000. A Northern Ireland international, Parke went on to make 83 league appearances, plus two as substitute, before leaving for Belgium club Mechelen in July 1968.

Although Hurley played against Aston Villa in a 2-1 League Cup defeat at Roker Park it was clear he had been rushed back and he had to miss the next match, a 3-2 home win against Nottingham Forest.

He was desperate to get back on the field as one of the biggest games of his life was just around the corner: the second leg against Spain in the World Cup qualifiers. But he was still missing as Alan Brown's Sheffield Wednesday side helped themselves to two points at Hillsborough in a match in which new signing Neil Martin scored Sunderland's only goal in a 3-1 defeat. Martin, twice capped by Scotland, cost £45,000 from Hibernian. Sunderland had been hoping to make it a double signing but pulled out of the race to sign Wyn Davies from Bolton once the fee reached £80,000. The Welshman joined Newcastle the following October.

Although Charlie Hurley was named in the Irish team for Seville he was unable to turn out and Noel Cantwell, now with Manchester United, dropped back from centre forward to centre half with Shelbourne's Eric Barber coming in to play up front. Hurley could only sit and squirm as Spain recovered from being a goal behind to win 4-1. With a victory apiece the teams had to play-off in Paris thirteen days later on November 10. But unfortunately Hurley's thigh injury stubbornly refused to heal and he could only sit at home as the Republic of Ireland travelled to France.

The countries had argued about where to play. The FAI had suggested either Liverpool or Wembley, venues, of course, where their support would have outnumbered that of Spain. Spain suggested the Colombes Stadium in Paris for the same reason. The venue was vital, especially as both teams were much better at home and the larger support for one team would at least give that pretence.

The Spanish Federation offered to pay the Irish team's travelling expenses if the game was played in Paris. Whether they had worked out that the FAI's finances were in a poor state or not we shall probably never know but it was still an incredible decision by the FAI to agree to take the money and send their team to Paris. One can only imagine what someone like Roy Keane would have said, but this was the 1960s and players simply would not, could not and did not refuse to play for their country.

Spain were backed by around 30,000 of the 35,000 at the match and a single goal from Ufarte sent them were through. Not until twenty-five years later did the Republic reach a World Cup finals.

The 1968 European Cup winner Tony Dunne, who played in Paris, feels that Hurley's absence in the latter two Spanish games "was huge, because you're thinking of someone who basically shuts up the middle of the park and then you only have to worry about the sides. Losing him for Paris was a particularly bad blow. Charlie was someone that you always wanted in your team. When you were without him it was a loss. It didn't matter who replaced him. You felt you were a little bit behind, and that's not to knock the guy who came in."

Dunne played for Manchester United against Sunderland on many occasions, and feels that "Hurley had this little bit of class. He would do his job but he would do one or two other things. He'd control the ball. Now, centre halves were generally there to stop the forwards, and midfield players were there for passing the ball. Charlie would take chances and it would get him into trouble, but he had this little bit of touch in how he played that would usually get him out of it. It was part of his game; he was top class and it was unusual to see."

Warm words indeed from a very good footballer who Hurley's colleague George Mulhall rated, along with Leeds's Paul Reaney, the finest full back he played against during a long career.

Hurley was convinced "Ireland would get through. We had a good bunch of lads – Cantwell, Saward, giant players; Giles who was a great playmaker. It was terrible that the match was played in Paris. Qualifying to play in the 1966 World Cup in England would have put the icing on the cake."

Hurley was finally back for Sunderland's match at Goodison Park on December 4th and he "was kept at full stretch holding together a defensive unit that rocked badly at times," reported Argus. Two goals without reply for the home team meant there was a poor crowd of just 34,417 at Roker Park the following weekend for the visit of League champions Manchester United. George Best was in fine form, scoring twice as United squeezed home 3-2, but not before Martin had given the home side the lead on five minutes. After the game Matt Busby said that he could not remember watching a bad game between the two famous teams.

George Mulhall was a big fan of George Best. "I thought he was superb, and one of the greatest things about him was he would chase back and tackle. Skillwise he would drop the shoulder and go past you. He was in a good team, mind, with good facilities as well. To me George Best and Denis Law were the two best players going forward in the 1960s. Jimmy Greaves's goalscoring record was incredible but I am not so sure he was as good away as at home. I'd like to see his record to compare. The old story with him at the time was to give him a good whack and see what he was made of."

Just before Christmas came the news that the Government was finally acting to curb the excessive speeds of car drivers on Britain's ever-expanding motorways. Hopes that after the initial opportunity to "open the throttle" and "enjoy the open road" drivers would act responsibly and drive with caution had not been met and it was felt necessary to use legal methods to enforce control. A speed limit of 70mph was introduced.

Jim Montgomery was back on January 3rd for the first Wear–Tyne derby in the top flight since 1957–58. Sunderland fans were looking to Baxter as he had a habit of excelling on big occasions. He had played some superb football against Celtic, probably the only occasion in British football that the noise of the crowd beats that during a Sunderland–Newcastle tussle. And Baxter had always enjoyed playing for Scotland against England.

The hopes of the fans were realised. Although Hurley was forced to leave the pitch after twenty-five minutes, Baxter was magnificent and sent Newcastle and their followers home with their tails between their legs, beaten 2-0 in front of 55,000 with goals from Herd and O'Hare. Baxter was also injured, straining a

Charlie Hurley

Charlie was always a fans' favourite but the fans were always Charlie's favourites too.

**With future Leeds and England manager Don Revie who was a member of the Sunderland team
in which Charlie made his debut but who left a year later.**

1959 and Charlie is voted Ireland's Player of the Year.

*Charlie heads the goal that beat Norwich in the fifth round of the FA Cup in 1961
to set up the tie with Spurs.*

Playing for the Republic. Also pictured are Noel Cantwell (left) and Pat Saward.

Charlie Hurley rises high in the 1961 Spurs Cup-tie.

Willie McPheat scores for Sunderland against Spurs in the sixth round of the FA Cup in

1961 after goalkeeper Bill Brown could only parry a header by Charlie Hurley.

The team which won promotion in 1963–64. (top row, from left to right) Cecil Irwin, Martin Harvey, Jimmy Montgomery, Charlie Hurley, Jimmy McNab, Len Ashurst, (front row) Brian Usher, George Herd, Nick Sharkey, Johnny Crossan, George Mulhall. (Sunderland Echo)

Sunderland celebrate promotion by giving Charlie a lift. (from left) Nick Sharkey, Johnny Crossan, Cec Irwin, Hurley on Jim McNab's shoulders, Len Ashurst, Jimmy Montgomery, George Mulhall and Brian Usher.

Promotion brought matches against teams like Manchester United and players like Denis Law who shoots as Charlie closes him down.

Colin Todd: Charlie thought he would put "two or three years" onto his career but it was not to be. (Sunderland Echo)

Jim Baxter, a great player but a divisive presence in the dressing room.
(Sunderland Echo)

The squad for the 1967–68 season. The official photograph shows that not everyone was happy. (back row, (left to right) Jimmy Montgomery, Len Ashurst, Colin Todd, Jim Baxter, Bobby Kerr, Derek Forster. (middle row) George Heslop, Colin Suggett, Allan Gauden, Billy Hughes, Jimmy Shoulder, Cec Irwin, Charlie Hurley (front row) Martin Harvey, George Kinnell, George Mulhall, John O'Hare, John Parke, George Herd, Neil Martin. (Sunderland Echo)

Celebrating promotion with Reading.

The manager of Reading at home with Joan, Tracy and Joanne.

Two great centre halves; Charlie with ex-Arsenal and England defender and later London Evening Standard writer Bernard Joy.

Charlie before the Republic's game with England at Lansdowne Road on November 14th 1990 - next to him is the Patron of the International Club Mr Justice Liam Hamilton and former Taoiseach Jack Lynch.

Joan and Charlie.

thigh muscle, and played the last half-hour of the match hardly able to run. Nevertheless he was involved in the second goal in the sixty-sixth minute, with a wonderful forty-five-yard pass to Hellawell. He knocked it into the middle and O'Hare sent a twenty-five-yard right-footed drive into the corner of the net.

Two days before a 1-1 draw at Old Trafford on January 6th, achieved without Hurley and Baxter, Sunderland had learned which games they would be staging as part of the World Cup. Roker Park and Middlesbrough's Ayresome Park had been chosen over St James' Park for matches in Group Four featuring Chile, Scotland's conquerors Italy, North Korea and the USSR. Roker Park would also host a quarter-final tie in a competition composed of just sixteen teams. Sunderland received around half of the estimated £100,000 they spent on improvements to the ground from the Labour government.

After missing six games, Charlie Hurley was fit for the match at Ewood Park against Blackburn Rovers and then for the St James' Park derby on March 5th. The programme for this game showed that hooliganism and bad behaviour were not something that affected English football just from the 1960s onwards. A feature on "Tyne–Wear Battles for Gallowgate" recalled the calling off of the match back in 1901 which, "within seconds, led to coats off and free fights raging. They fought like maniacs. Down came the club flags. Up came the goalposts and the palings, to be used as weapons. Nets were torn to shreds. Police were roughly manhandled.

"Fifty policemen, batons drawn, lined up to meet the charge, but the throng could not be tamed. It was late in the day when dozens were in hospital before riot on the pitch ended. But the arguments and fighting still went on in the streets. Many were the drunks in City pubs that night. And many battle-scarred supporters of Sunderland staggered homeward in the early hours."

Thankfully it was a lot more sedate in 1966 and the Sunderland fans in the crowd were safe to return home having seen their side beaten 2-0. Both goals came from Colin Suddick, whose team was in control of the game after his first in the thirty-third minute although it was not until the eighty-third that his second finished the match.

Three days later one of the most famous murders in Britain was committed when Ronnie Kray shot rival gangster George Cornell in The Blind Beggar pub in Whitechapel in east London, while in Ireland those opposed to England's continuing presence blew up and destroyed Nelson's Pillar in Dublin.

Hurley had a fine match as Sunderland overcame third from bottom Blackpool at home in their next game, Argus reporting that "he was unbeatable in defence and stirred up panic in the Blackpool defence every time he surged forward for corners and free kicks." John O'Hare snatched both goals in a 2-1 win, sweeping in Baxter's cross for the winner. According to Argus, Sunderland were "now at the stage where the result is more important than the spectacle."

There was still an outside chance of relegation but a 2-2 draw with league leaders Liverpool and a win against Chelsea at Roker, even though they had won ten and drawn two of their seventeen away games, made things easier. But a point at Highbury following the home game against the Gunners did not make Sunderland safe. Charlie Hurley scored his only goal of the season at Highbury, a header from a Herd free kick.

Sunderland could still be relegated when they made the short journey from London to play Northampton Town two days later, and defeat left them fourth from bottom on the last day of the season.

With Blackburn already relegated the table read:
Fulham 35 points from 41 games
Sunderland 34 points from 41 games
Sheffield Wednesday 33 points from 36 games
Northampton 33 points from 41 games
Aston Villa 32 points from 39 games

So Sunderland faced the prospect of the drop in only their second season back in Division One. Thankfully they were at home to Everton, whose minds were clearly distracted by the knowledge that they would shortly be running out at Wembley in the FA Cup final against Sheffield Wednesday. Sunderland won comfortably enough 2-0.

With Villa winning and Northampton losing, the latter returned to Division Two, and they promptly crashed straight through to Division Three and two seasons after that into the Fourth Division.

Sunderland ended the season on thirty-six points, one less than the previous season, but four places lower in nineteenth. Average gates had also fallen considerably to 33,159. Home form had remained good, but not as good as in 1964–65 although twenty-eight points was not bad. Away from home only eight points had been won and only one victory achieved, at Blackpool on September 18th.

Most players hurried off on holiday but Hurley, of course, would have been overjoyed to have been playing competitively that summer. Instead Ireland played a series of friendlies which included a thrashing by West Germany. There were only 16,091 at Dalymount Park to see goals from Franz Beckanbauer, Helmut Haller and Wolfgang Overath with two – all of whom played in the World Cup final against England later in the summer – give their side an easy 4-0 victory. It would undoubtedly have been a lot more had Hurley not been playing.

Certainly that was the view of Tom O'Shea, writing in *The Irish Press*, when he stated "before the game Charlie Hurley was given a public welcome on his return to the team after injury. Afterwards the crowd could thank him for the fact that we were not completely overrun. The big Sunderland man stood head and shoulders above everyone, cutting out the dangerous Uwe Seeler and putting any life there was into our attacks."

Of course, this was not the first time Hurley had marked a top class West German forward out of a match. In 1960 in Düsseldorf, Haller had been so tightly marked during a famous Irish victory that he went into the Irish dressing room after the match to throw his shirt at Hurley, saying he might as well have it as he'd had hold of it virtually the whole game! "You didn't swap shirts in those days," remembers Hurley. "And I liked to keep mine!"

While Germany's near neighbours Austria had failed to qualify for England they were still too good for Ireland, winning 1-0 in Vienna with a goal from Walter Seitl before 50,000.

This was a rough match in which the Austrians, perhaps after reading the West German match reports, targeted Hurley for particular attention but little good it did them as, according to Tom O'Shea: "Hurley had a brilliant game"; but then again he nearly always did.

Hurley's final game of the season was before little more than 5,000 in Liege as Ireland beat Belgium 3-2. "Hurley was impregnable in defence," wrote O'Shea.

The victory was a particularly proud one for Charlie Hurley as he and Noel Cantwell had taken joint charge of the team on the tour, and had, oddly for the time, played both matches without recognised wingers.

Tom O'Shea of *The Irish Press* pays this tribute to Charlie Hurley:

> *"The last time I met Charlie Hurley was in Dublin Airport in November 1989. The previous night Hurley had become the first winner of the FAI Hall of Fame Award before a gathering of footballers past and present. The next day he was in the airport at the same time as the Republic of Ireland squad headed for Malta to complete the mission that was to bring them to the 1990 World Cup Finals in Italy for the first time ever in their history.*
>
> *"Hurley, tall and proud, had no reason to feel overshadowed by this team – he was well entitled to bask in the glow of success that they had brought to the country he represented with such distinction forty times.*
>
> *"He could remember clearly the days when he played for 'Eire' – as he always refers to his country – with a team that seldom knew the meaning of the term 'full strength' but had battled bravely at home and abroad in campaigns that always ended on the edge of success. It was the nearly team.*
>
> *"All of the players had been present at the previous night's gala event. He was proud that so many remembered him – but not surprised. Hurley, who was as big in heart as he was in stature, said: 'Why wouldn't they? I never shirked a game*

or tried to find an excuse for not turning up no matter where we played. If I was fit, I was there'.

"And that often meant leaving Sunderland after a Saturday afternoon game, making his way to the overnight ferry to Dublin for Ireland on the Sunday afternoon. It was usually a trip into the unknown – it wasn't until he joined up with the team a few hours before kick-off that he even knew the make-up of the team. Yet this unsatisfactory approach never turned him off playing for his country.

"Jack Charlton, the Republic of Ireland manager during that great period of Irish football, asked Hurley to join them in Malta and maybe go on to some of the World Cup games in Italy. Charlie said no. He said: 'This is their time, not mine'.

"Though Charlie left Cork when he was just seven months old – settling in London with his family – he always knew he would play for Ireland. He recalled how his father said to him from the age of six, 'you will play in the green of Ireland'.

"Hurley's importance to Ireland could never be overstated. Big match previews rated the chances on whether Charlie was in or out. It was the era of the 'moral victory' – a draw or a one or two-goal defeat could be made to look like a triumph, given our lack of resources and preparation.

"It, too, was a time when football officials picked the team. They often named players out of position and were accused of club favouritism and a lack of deep knowledge of the game. It was something akin to the football legislators providing the conductor for the band that provided the music on the day of the game.

"But Charlie was always philosophical. He reckoned you had to make the best of every situation. Hurley had a good relationship with the rest of the Irish squad.

"And though Ireland never seemed to be going anywhere on the world stage, Hurley never lost his enthusiasm to line out in the green. The late Joe Wickham, general secretary of the FAI, often recalled how he would get regular phone calls from Hurley asking when Ireland's next game was.

"Hurley's great attributes were his height, physique and strength and, despite his size, he could play neat and delicate football. He could look fearsome going into a tackle, but would come away with the ball and set up an attack with a pinpoint pass.

"In the '60's Hurley wrote a weekly column for The Sunday Press *in Dublin and he was always full of ideas about how the game should be played. He also admired those with dedication and one of his most memorable columns was about how Brian Clough fought back from a bad injury, spending hours running up and down the terraces at Roker Park to build up his strength.*

"He loved the glamour and crowd worship that was part of the football scene but he never lost touch with what it was all about. As he left Dalymount Park after an international, youngsters looking for autographs invariably surrounded him. As other players sought a quick exit, Charlie would line them up and stay until everyone got his signature. He would say: 'You must never forget the real fans. These youngsters make their dads bring them to the games – and that is what pays my wages'.

"Hurley made his first appearance for Ireland when he was playing with Millwall. It was against England in 1957 in the World Cup at Dalymount Park. Ireland scored first in this second leg game but in the last minute their hopes were shattered when England scored. Desmond Hackett, of the Daily Express, *described the moment: 'The deafening silence could be heard in the centre of Dublin at Nelson's Column.' Hurley had not been selected for the first game, which England had won 5-1. He watched that game from the terraces.*

"Hurley was to remember many disappointments in his years with Ireland but he always preferred to look at the bright side. His greatest memory he told me was an away win over Czechoslovakia in 1967. He recalled: 'As usual we were short of several of our top players and on our way to the game the Czech crowd was making signals at our bus suggesting

that they would win 10-1. I was player-manager and we were under severe pressure early on. We gave away an own goal through John Dempsey who played for Chelsea. Then I switched the formation to 4-4-2 and we went on to win 2-1 with goals from Ray Treacy and Turlough O'Connor. It was a marvellous occasion for all of us.'

"The Irish team was always a mixture of full-time professionals playing in England and Scotland and part-timers from the local League of Ireland. It could make life difficult for the manager, but Hurley, on the occasions that he assumed the job, always worked hard to get the mix right. At the end of the 1966 season, Ireland embarked on a two-match tour of Austria and Belgium.

"Hurley captained the team and along with Noel Cantwell planned the strategy. The Vienna game was played in hot, sunny conditions in Prater Park. The Austrians left the Irish team standing alone in the heat for a good ten minutes before they made their appearance – it was their way of softening up the Irish. Ireland played a resolute defensive game and conceded only one goal. Hurley commented afterwards: 'They kept coming at us in waves. It was like playing heading out.'

"They moved on to Liege for the second game and Hurley and Cantwell decided on a 4-4-2 formation. It worked a dream and Ireland won a thriller 3-2. Afterwards the two Corkmen, Hurley and Cantwell, reckoned it was they who showed Alf Ramsey how effective 4-4-2 could be.

"Hurley scored two goals for Ireland in his long career. This was on a two-match tour of Poland and Norway. Hurley got a touch of food poisoning before the second game. But Ireland, as usual, was short of players and he was forced to play at centre forward. He says: 'I got two goals and then had to be stretchered off'. That was against Norway in Oslo when Ireland won 4-1.

"When I met Charlie that time in 1989 he had one mission to complete while in Ireland – to find his fortieth cap. He told me: 'I treasure every award I won in the game and I

needed this to complete my collection'. The cap was finally found in the archives of the FAI offices and was immediately forwarded to Hurley.

"It was typical of a man who brought great honour to the game to club and country. He was a colossus in his time; a player of rich ability and a man who, though he loved all that his great football ability brought, never forgot his family values or the fans that put him on that pedestal.

"He was the people's player."

Chapter Thirteen

Bust-up with Baxter

Three weeks after England had kicked off the World Cup final against West Germany Sunderland began their third campaign back in Division One with a home match against Arsenal. The first team playing staff had been expanded with Colin Todd, Bobby Kerr, Billy Hughes and Colin Suggett coming through from the successful youth teams of the past couple of years.

With Charlie Hurley fit and Jim Baxter starting the season with number nine on his back, a home crowd of just over 38,000 were hoping to see Sunderland maintain their highly impressive home form of the last six seasons. Their opponents had sacked England legend Billy Wright at the end of the previous season and appointed club physiotherapist Bertie Mee as manager. At the time it seemed an astonishing decision but five years later Mee was to lead Arsenal to the League and FA Cup double.

In Mee's first game he saw his side win fairly comfortably 3-1. Baxter at least had the pleasure of scoring Sunderland's goal although in truth Jon Sammels in Arsenal's midfield dictated the play.

Despite the increased interest in football after England's World Cup success, the Football Association still thought it wise to limit the number of live matches on television, deciding that the FA Cup final would be the only live game to be shown in the 1966–67 season. This the FA justified on the grounds that *Match of the Day* would be featuring Saturday evening highlights and five independent TV companies would screen extracts from matches in their areas on Sunday afternoons.

With Jack Charlton injured there was no chance for supporters to compare the quality of Hurley against the man who had played magnificently for England during the World Cup when Sunderland played at Leeds. It was probably just as well because Hurley had a poor game, giving away a penalty, converted by his Irish teammate Johnny Giles, in the thirteenth minute and being too slow to react to a bouncing ball in the area in the thirty-sixth minute, which allowed Albert Johanneson to score the winner after Allan Gauden had equalised for Sunderland in the thirty-third minute.

There was satisfaction, though, when a point was brought back from a hard-fought tussle at Chelsea with Gauden again the scorer but for Hurley there was only the agony of another injury. Plagued the previous season, he now found himself with his knee in plaster while the bloom was still on the grass.

There were rumours that Hurley's knee injury was likely to keep him out of the team for at least two months and comments that he would be lucky to ever play again. This forced him to speak out publicly, saying: "This is nothing. I've had this one before in my other knee and got over it no bother. I know I will be playing again in a few weeks."

Mind you, his football problems were nothing compared to Ronald 'Buster' Edwards who, after running away from the police for three years and fleeing to Mexico, finally surrendered himself for his part in the "Great Train Robbery" of August 1963. During this more than £2.6 million was stolen [equivalent to over £40 million today], making it probably the largest robbery by value in British history until the Securitas depot robbery of 2006 in Kent. It occurred when the Royal Mail Glasgow to London travelling Post Office was stopped at Sears Crossing, Ledburn near Mentmore in Buckinghamshire by a fifteen-strong gang. Edwards' story was later dramatised in the 1988 film *Buster* starring Phil Collins in the title role.

Charlie Hurley and his wife Joan suffered a personal tragedy which put his injury into stark perspective. "We lost a baby in October 1966," says Joan. "She was a week late. We had the rhesus factor problem that you don't have these days. Women who have a baby now and the blood is incompatible have injections to stop it forming with antibodies. We didn't even have time to give her a name. I was ill and that was an awful time for Charles and I."

Hurley's absence at least offered an early opportunity for an emerging talent, Colin Todd. 'Toddo' had not even signed professional forms for Sunderland when he made his full debut against Sheffield United in the League Cup replay on September 20th 1966. A cultured player, Todd is more than forty years later still involved in football as manager of Randers FC in Denmark.

He had chosen to join Sunderland rather than Newcastle, the team he watched as boy, or the other local club, Middlesbrough, because "their policy for young players was the best of the three local clubs. I had the chance to go to all three. I opted for Sunderland and it was the right decision because I got in the first team at seventeen.

"I lost my dad when I was fifteen and not long after it was Charlie Ferguson from Sunderland who came knocking on the door. Obviously I was delighted to sign for Sunderland; I just wanted to go into football. I did all right at school. Not great, but I coped. Once I got into football I was determined to make a good living out of it and I have."

When Sunderland next crossed the River Tyne it mattered little that they were without Hurley to face Wyn Davies who was making his debut. Sunderland, with Baxter sublime, took the Magpies apart to record their first away win in the League in over a year. If anything the goals from the three Scots, Martin, O'Hare and Mulhall, were poor reward for a one-sided match that left Sunderland fans in the massive 57,643 crowd – up 41,000 on Newcastle's previous home match against Manchester City – in ecstasy as their team won 3-0.

Argus gave particular praise in his after-match report to Colin Todd, writing that "despite his lack of experience Todd did not look out of place" on the field. He never did. Years later, when he was at Derby County, Clough attempted to buy Frank McLintock from Arsenal. The Scotsman was stunned to discover that he was to take Colin Todd's place as Roy McFarland's partner but Clough had not lost a grip on his senses, stating "Todd is such a good player he could play anywhere. I'd use him all over the place."

The 1966 game at St James' Park was Colin Todd's favourite game in a red-and-white shirt. "It's a great feeling to beat your local rivals. The 3-0 win at St James' Park was fantastic and the whole team played very well."

The match took place at the end of a week in which the national news had been totally dominated by events at Aberfan in Wales, where a slag heap of colliery waste had slid down the Merthyr Mountain destroying houses, a farm and much of Pantglas Junior School and parts of the adjacent senior school. Pupils, who had just left the assembly hall where they had been singing "All things bright and beautiful" were engulfed. In total 144 people were killed, 116 of whom were between the ages of 7 and 10.

Sunderland suffered its own tragedy the day after the match at Newcastle when seven men lost their lives on the 10,000-ton cargo ship *Toronto City* being built at Doxford's shipyard. The men were trapped by fire in the propeller shaft tunnel and perished. Five were married and they left behind a total of thirty-two children.

Fortunately the injury to Hurley was not as serious as first thought, allowing him to make his comeback in the green of Ireland in a European Championship qualifier against Turkey at Dalymount Park on November 16th when he again captained the side.

Reporting on a 2-1 home victory in the *Irish Independent*, WP Murphy wrote that "the return of Charlie Hurley was a personal triumph for he played a real captain's part not only as a defender, but as an inspiration to the front-line, with his determined efforts to get a goal from corners and free-kicks. He was a mighty figure in this Irish victory, he had on either side of him two excellent lieutenants in the Manchester pair, Brennan and Dunne."

Three days later Hurley was warmly welcomed back by a 32,526 Roker crowd when Burnley were the visitors. His return, playing for the first time alongside Colin Todd, did not initially go smoothly and he and Montgomery together made mistakes that helped gift Burnley two of their three goals to leave them 3-1 in the lead with just twenty-five minutes left. It looked like Burnley might repeat their four-goal victory of the previous season before Sunderland recovered to score three more, including two from Mulhall, and capture both points. Funnily enough the next time Sunderland recovered from being 3-1 down at home to win 4-3 also came against Burnley at the end of the 1971–72 season.

On the Monday Sunderland, in the form of a Jim Baxter XI – the Scot had taken the captain's mantle from Hurley – were the opponents when Bishop Auckland, ten times winners of the FA Amateur Cup, officially switched on their floodlights. Jack Charlton, a man never slow in expressing his dislike of all things Sunderland, was allowed to play at centre half instead of Hurley.

Back in the League Charlie Hurley had to go in goal at Old Trafford after Jim Montgomery was injured. Later Jim Parke replaced him and not surprisingly United won 5-0.

Hurley was to play his third consecutive match for Sunderland, and it transpired his penultimate game of the season for the club, when Spurs came north in early December. And it was the man Sunderland tried to sign the previous season, Alan Gilzean, tremendous in the air, who stole both points for the Londoners with what else but a headed goal. Sunderland had now played ten times at home and lost four. If there was any consolation it came from Hurley's performance and the knowledge that he was starting to return to full fitness. This was a relief for supporters but McColl had other ideas and decided to keep George Kinnell in the team and leave out Hurley.

Hurley's silence at the time led some Sunderland fans, and others with a keen interest in religious politics, to wonder whether the thorny issue of sectarianism might have been behind McColl's decision. After all he was an ex-Rangers man and therefore a Protestant and the man taking Hurley's place was another Protestant. Hurley, of course, was a Catholic.

Manchester United's Paddy Crerand, who played with Baxter in the Scotland side and against him for Celtic against Rangers in 'Old Firm' clashes is, however, sure that any fall-out had nothing to do with religion, saying: "Jim didn't have a sectarian bone in his body. I knew him very well and he was not like that. When Jimmy was at Ibrox there was a restaurant called Ferraris on Buchanan Street in Glasgow and the Celtic team would go there for lunch. Jimmy would come up afterwards. He was very pally with myself, Billy McNeill and Mick Jackson – we were his pals and we all played for Celtic".

Colin Todd admits that "there was a clash between Baxter and Hurley, but it was not about religion. Charlie took a great pride in himself as a person and a player, Jim was not so bothered, and Jim was a drinker. I am not saying that Charlie didn't have a drink but he did it in the right way, in moderation. Drinking of course was very, very rife then – it was the same at Derby: Cloughie would have you drinking on a Friday before the match.

"I thought Baxter on his day was a genius. He could play, he could take teams apart, but I don't think that we saw the best of him at Sunderland mainly because the drink caught up with him. I don't care what you say, if you don't look after yourself you suffer."

Clearly the conflict was about how to live your life and approach your profession. Hurley was respectful and determined to look after himself and his family while Baxter was determined to enjoy himself. In many ways Hurley wanted to maintain traditions while the Scotsman wanted to jump on and be part of the "swinging sixties", an era when authority was to be challenged.

For more than forty years Hurley remained silent on what went on behind the scenes during this period and it took some persuading for him to reveal what happened, but here for the first time is how he views events.

"A short period of time after I was injured, and I was out of the team, he [McColl] bought Kinnell, who was a cousin of Jim Baxter. Nice lad George, big honest player, nowhere near as good as me but that's neither here nor there. McColl also gradually got rid of a lot of players that Alan Brown had and unfortunately it didn't do us any good.

"There was a wee bit of a split among the players, but I was the club captain and I tried to keep the atmosphere right. But it was very difficult because for a period of time I wasn't even in the team so you don't have the same influence.

"Now McColl unfortunately thought the sun shone out of Baxter's backside, so Slim could do nothing wrong whatsoever. I would love to have had the ability on the ball that Jim Baxter had, but that's all I would have wanted from him.

"Mr McColl and Baxter was the worst thing that ever happened to Sunderland, a right bunch of piss artists. In the team that got promotion there were no piss artists; when Baxter came I thought the club would be finished. I said he was ruining things.

"At the end of that season McColl asked me whether I wanted to go on tour [it was to Canada] and I said there are two or three bastards going. He knew I meant Baxter and Kinnell but asked me who was the third and I said 'You work it out' as it was him. As a manager he should have told me to go. I told Jim, 'I hate you as much as you are a good footballer' and he said 'How good do you think I am?' and I said 'I know how much I hate you!'

"If we had a practice match – I was in the reserves and I'd tell Jim how much I didn't like him. McColl didn't like that as he didn't like trouble. There wouldn't have been any if he'd been a good manager. I knew he was going to be rubbish.

"We had this particular practice match and we were winning 1-0 at half-time and I scored the goal. McColl changed our team and put in a load of kids and we got thrashed. Baxter was taking the mickey so I said to one of the youngsters I would play against him and he was to take my position.

"I told him [Baxter] to be very careful. I smiled but I told him I was going to get him. He tried to be funny and I went 'bang'. I went straight through him, right across his shin. He was carried off and at the end I went in to see the physio Johnny Watters who was a great mate of mine. It was Johnny Watters who kept my old left knee going.

"I walked in and as Baxter lay on the treatment table asked 'How's he doing?' Great big bruising and Johnny said, 'Oooh not too good' and I asked, 'Is that broken?' and he said, 'No but not too far off'.

"So I said 'I've done it wrong again' and I told Baxter 'Let me tell you something, you bastard: I will be on your tail every chance I get. That is only the start. I can't stand you. You are very bad for this football club and I can't let something that's been very good to me go down without a fight. So keep your eyes over your shoulders'. Baxter had a magic left foot, great footballer on his day but he was an animal."

It has to be said that animosity and fights among teammates, as Bill Lloyd makes clear in chapter three, are nothing unusual in football. Since Hurley's days we've seen Derek Hales and Mike Flanaghan kick each other during Charlton Athletic's defeat to Sunderland in the 1975–76 season, observed Eyal Berkovic's head make contact with John Hartson's left boot in training at West Ham and laughed at the petty scrap between the then Newcastle midfielders Kieron Dyer and Lee Bowyer. Nevertheless Hurley's intent to do serious damage to one of Scotland's one-time greatest footballers is a step up from these incidents and reveals just how sickened he had become at the mere sight of boozing Baxter.

Without Hurley in the side, Sunderland continued to play fairly impressively at home but very poorly away. One of those home victories was the sweetest of all – a 3-0 win over Newcastle with Bobby Kerr snatching two. But there was the other side of the coin for Kerr the next week when in a 1-1 FA Cup draw with Leeds United at Roker a tackle with Norman Hunter saw Kerr suffer a broken leg. Sunderland went on to lose a controversial second replay match at Hull City's Boothferry Park when Leeds were awarded a very dubious last-minute penalty.

Although Hurley was not turning out for Sunderland, Ireland's team manager Johnny Carey still picked him for his country and in the latter part of the season he played and captained the Republic on another three occasions in the qualifying round of the European Championships.

Unfortunately they lost all three matches. The first was at the Mestalla Stadium in Valencia where Spain would have won much more easily than 2-0 had it not been for an excellent performance in goal from Preston's Alan Kelly. Giles, Cantwell and McEvoy were all absent through injury and the makeshift side were simply not good enough, although Hurley had a decent match himself: according to WP Murphy his "gigantic figure was a real bulwark against the Spanish attack."

Ireland were also disappointing when losing 2-1 to Turkey in Ankara and for once Hurley played poorly in an Ireland shirt. This may not be entirely surprising; the match on May 19th was only Hurley's second competitive game of 1967 and as a result "the not too imaginative Turkish forwards were able to create a surprising number of opportunities," reported Noel Dunne in the *Irish Independent*.

Two days later Czechoslovakia won 2-0 at Dalymount Park, where a number of those who turned out in a tiny crowd of just 6,500 slow-handclapped the side in the second half after goals from Juraj Szikora and Vojtech Masny had given the away side a comfortable lead. Colm Smith, writing in the *Irish Independent*, reported that "coach and captain Hurley was one of the few to emerge with any credit."

Meanwhile off the pitch at Roker Park the problems on the terraces were starting to cause concern – some younger fans were starting to ape their counterparts at other clubs and club officials and the Supporters' Association urged fans to bring back the "Roker Roar" and ditch obscenities aimed at the referee and opposition teams. Older fans were particularly angry at the singing before the match of "God save the team" rather than Her Majesty. Charlie Hurley, however, had more important things to think about, namely whether he still had a career left at Sunderland.

Chapter Fourteen

McColl and Baxter leave

Had psychologists examined Sunderland team photographs for the start of each new season in the 1960s they would be struck by the different expressions displayed on the players' faces. In the early ones most of the first team like Charlie Hurley are smiling widely. However, the picture released for 1967–68, featuring twenty players, suggests all of them had just lost a pound and found a penny. It is not a pretty sight and hinted at some possible personality clashes.

George Forster, from the Supporters' Association, witnessed first hand an incident that casts a light on events at the club, recalling that "we used to have some wooden huts in the ground from which we'd sell scarves and programmes. One summer I spent two weeks along with others painting them and I was able to watch the team running round the outside of the pitch at Roker. I used to see Baxter drop out and sit and have a natter with McColl while everyone else ran round. He'd then join in after missing a few laps. I got the impression that Baxter was McColl's favourite."

Jim Montgomery explains: "Jim would often come in for training after having a skinful the night before. He could run it off as he was naturally fit, but it wasn't unusual for him to puke up as he did so. We never saw the best of Jim Baxter; great bloke when not drinking but not so nice when he was."

Sunderland found they had to travel to Elland Road for the first fixture of the new campaign. McColl had bought Ralph Brand from Manchester City for £5,000 during the close season, and he would be linking up with Jim Baxter. They were part of the team that had crushed Hurley's Ireland side at Hampden Park in a World Cup qualifier back on May 3rd 1961, Brand scoring two that day.

McColl also let John O'Hare go to the Baseball Ground as one of Brian Clough's first signings. Clough's managerial spell at Hartlepool after leaving Sunderland had gone well and he left behind the nucleus of the team that was to gain Pools' first ever promotion in May 1968. Len Shackleton had played the role of go-between and had convinced Derby chairman Sam Longson that Clough was the man to revive his club's fortunes – and Shack's judgement was spot on as Clough took Derby to promotion and later the First Division title in 1972.

Hurley was missing from the opening game for the first time since the Second Division defeat against Lincoln City in 1958. McColl had announced that Kinnell was his preferred choice at centre back and as he was also made captain it seemed Hurley's days at Sunderland – only months before his testimonial – were numbered. Kinnell played well at Elland Road and scored Sunderland's goal in a 1-1 draw.

Fulham, with an ageing Johnny Haynes still turning out in midfield, had been easily beaten at Roker Park at the end of the previous season and they proved no more difficult to beat at the start of the new one as Suggett, Martin and Brand – his first goal for the club – scored without reply. Baxter, however, was ordered off with Fulham's Parminter after the two had a vigorous dispute.

Johnny Haynes is best known as the first footballer to earn £100 a week. In fact he was paid that only during the playing season, his wages dropping to £85 in the summer. He was a marvellous player who made 594 league appearances for Fulham, scoring 147 times. He also amassed 56 England caps, 32 of them when he played in Division Two. He captained his country on 22 occasions. One of his best ever performances of many was his role in the defeat of Scotland at Wembley by nine goals to three in 1961. A road accident forced him to cut short his international career, otherwise he would have been competing for a place in the 1966 World Cup squad. He was a modest man, prepared to accept the referee's whistle, and always tried to play football with intelligence and passion.

After ten matches Sunderland were at the wrong end of the table with only eight points and as Hurley had failed to start any of the games he asked for a transfer, saying simply that he hoped to move on. Ambitious Hull City were keen and Cliff Britton, their manager, had been in touch about signing him in the weeks leading up to his testimonial match on October 4th. At this, some of the best British footballers of the time appeared, including Chelsea's Peter Bonetti, Charlie Cooke, Peter Osgood and Eddie McCreadie and West Ham's three World Cup winners Bobby Moore, Martin Peters and Geoff Hurst. The game ended 5-5 and more than forty-one old and new stars turned out, which showed the respect in which Hurley was held in the game.

The crowd, however, was a very disappointing 19,629, causing Argus to state that "the attendance was a poor reflection on the Sunderland supporters, but for those that did go to Roker Park the fare was anything but poor."

Before the match McColl announced that Hurley would play against Manchester City. With Sunderland having lost three matches after being defeated 5-1 at home by West Ham and conceding seven goals without reply it was hardly surprising. In his report of the game, Argus reckoned that he was the main factor in the 1-0 victory, with Alf Greenley in the *Journal* saying it "was vintage Hurley."

Joe Mercer's team had started their second season in the top flight in fine form and to the surprise of virtually everybody, except perhaps the most die-hard City fans, were even starting to challenge their near neighbours United in the top half of the table. No one at this stage could, however, believe they might go on to win a League they had won only once, in 1936–37, a year after Sunderland last won it.

Hurley remained in the team for the third round League Cup tie at Everton and when the Scousers raced into a 2-0 lead things looked over for his team. But Kinnell, playing at inside right, Martin and Mulhall scored to overturn the deficit and take Sunderland through to play Leeds United in round four.

When Sunderland travelled to Coventry City, they were covered by the *Match of the Day* cameras and those watching could clearly hear the travelling fans' chants of "Charlie, Charlie" before each Sunderland corner. When Nottingham Forest were beaten it was clear that Hurley's return had produced a revival in Sunderland's fortunes with seven points from ten in the league as well as the Goodison Park League Cup success. The returning Jim Baxter had an outstanding game against Forest, earning ten out of ten in the *Journal* – a game Montgomery rates the Scotsman's best in a Sunderland shirt.

In the 1960s Sunderland's home programmes were dull and rarely had much information. It was therefore an indication of just how angry supporters were when the chairman Stanley Lambert used his Supporters' Association column to note the team's success with Hurley at number five and state that "Charlie is still a firm favourite with all Sunderland supporters." Roughly translated this meant "Hurley is better than Kinnell. What is McColl doing not playing him?"

And Hurley proved it in the next home match, a 1-1 draw with Liverpool, in which according to Bob Cass in the *Journal* he mastered Tony Hateley while Todd had a fine match against Roger Hunt.

One of Hurley's favourite matches – one etched into Irish football folklore – took place in November 1967, a 2-1 win by Ireland in Prague that he remembers with great pride, a wicked sense of humour and a twinkle in his eye.

"I felt this was the best result ever when I was player-manager which meant doing everything. We had no Noel Cantwell and there was no Johnny Giles. It was always very strange. You'd find that when we had a difficult away trip players would find these strains. They'd play on a Saturday but couldn't play on the Sunday and then they'd be all right for the following Saturday. We knew what it was all about. You've also got to remember that we got £30. England got £50; everything was on the cheap.

"We were driving to the ground in Prague, and the Czechs were saying ten-nil with their hands, and one of their players was saying five-nil with his hands before the match. We had three players I didn't know – one of them must have borrowed his brother's jacket and he had trousers up above his shoes. I asked one of the officials who he was and he said 'I don't know' – and he was one of the selectors! I said, 'If you don't know then how the heck do I know who he is!'

"He had these big heavy boots on and he looked like he'd never played football in his life. But we only had twelve players so he had to play. I told him I wanted to go out and niggle their centre halves. We kicked off and suddenly this big centre half is chasing this little centre forward. The ball's up the other end and he's gone up and kicked the guy. He didn't even wait until the ball was around! Anyway this little fella's a revelation. He couldn't play, but the big Czechs were chasing him all over the pitch and we got to half-time. It was no score, a miracle as they'd given us a pounding.

"I was playing 4-4-2. At half-time I said 'Well done, Pat' and he stuttered, 'Am I doing a good job, Mr Hurley?' I said, 'Great son, keep up the good work. Those two guys are not liking it, you might get hurt' and he stammered back, 'I don't mind getting hurt as long as we win'. I said, 'You're doing terrific, keep at it and if you talk to them as well that'll even put them off even more!' Anyway, second half John Dempsey's scored an own goal: one-nil down; we didn't need that at all.

"We had no chance so I went 4-2-4, and we beat them by scoring two goals in the last ten minutes and the little fella who'd given their centre halves a chasing scored the winner. His name was Turlough O'Connor. You'd have thought all the supporters were all dead. All you could hear was a few Irishmen going "Come on Charlie" and singing all the songs.

"After the game none of us could believe we'd beaten them. It was the greatest win I'd ever had. In came the officials and there were loads of them as usual. I stood up and said 'One of the reasons why we won today, Pat, was because you upset those two big centre halves'. He stammered and said 'I'm very pleased, Mr Hurley' and I said I would recommend he got another cap.

"I can still see everyone sitting in the dressing room stunned. We should have got murdered. Spain got through to the finals of the European Championships because of that win. Spain sent us two crates of their finest wine; unfortunately they sent it to Ireland not to the players, and we never saw a bottle.

"In Czechoslovakia we had twelve players and fifteen officials. Still it was good fun despite at times being completely disorganised. It was amazing the times those guys put a green shirt on and became a different character. An Irishman who gives his lot will always take some beating. I come from a big family; I added something to it, I made them proud and I wouldn't have missed an international match for anything, and especially that one."

Ray Treacy, who scored the equaliser, was a young West Bromwich player. He also created the winner when he passed to O'Connor, a Fulham reserve, with just minutes remaining. Hurley played in a back four missing the Manchester United duo, Tony Dunne and Shay Brennan.

"Hurley Shows The Way – Eire, brilliantly led by Sunderland's Charlie Hurley brought off one of their most important victories" – *The Newcastle Journal*.

Back at Roker Park, Sunderland could claim only one point from the next three league games. A young Leeds side, superbly led from midfield by Billy Bremner, who Ivor Broadis in the *Journal* commented was "deft and clever: quick feint to evade the tackle and unerring despatch", then brushed Sunderland aside in the League Cup.

This meant that it was an angry crowd which assembled for the home game with Chelsea at the start of December. The Londoners, of course, had lost on their previous three visits, failing to score and conceding seven goals. Not this time; Sunderland were two down in ten minutes and despite a valiant effort ran off beaten 3-2. After the game a number of mainly younger fans assembled outside the main stand to demand McColl's resignation. Bob Cass reckoned in the *Journal* that "unless Sunderland dig deep into their pockets in the next few days team alternatives will only mean the same old faces and that cannot be the answer."

There was considerable press speculation about who might be brought in to replace McColl with ex-Leeds man Peter Lorimer recalling that throughout the 1967–68 season there "were strong rumours that Don Revie was about to leave Elland Road, with Sunderland supposedly the club to which he was going."

McColl decided on drastic measures and when Nottingham Forest offered £70,000 for Baxter, still only 27 and keen to collect the five per cent of the fee then on offer for a player who had not requested a transfer, their bid was accepted. McColl was desperate to refashion a team which had struggled around the bottom of Division One since its promotion in 1964. With the money, he bought Gordon Harris from Burnley, Ian Porterfield from Raith Rovers, Calvin Palmer from Stoke City and Geoff Butler from Chelsea.

According to Jim Montgomery: "Jim Baxter would have been a far better player if Alan Brown had been the manager. He wouldn't have let him get away with not looking after himself like McColl did. McColl wasn't a patch on Brown. Brown didn't stand for any nonsense, and he was a far better coach. There was a very good atmosphere among the players under Brown; we were more like a family than a football team. That wasn't the case with McColl or Hardwick. Brown also brought in shadow play in training and was prepared to try new things."

It was still, however, to be some time before goalkeepers worked with specialists. "We would go and stand in the corner till the coaches shouted us over. We had to learn by watching other 'keepers, of which Gordon Banks was the best at the time. There were also no such things as dieticians or psychiatrists working with us. That was years away."

Only 21,189 bothered to turn up for the 2-2 draw with Leeds, but according to Argus they saw Hurley "firmly in command in the middle and doing an excellent covering job." The match itself was another rough affair, the *Journal's* headline imploring both sides to "End This Club 'War'" and commenting that "the time will come when the kicking will have to stop. Some drastic soccer tourniquet is essential to prevent the constant bad blood between these two sides getting completely out of hand."

Sadly the short trip to Newcastle saw Sunderland lose 2-1, Wyn Davies opening the scoring for Newcastle after knocking over both Montgomery and Hurley in an aerial challenge before hammering home the loose ball. Colin Suggett then equalised before Albert Bennett scored the winner with a twenty-yard shot. Hurley's struggle with Davies, which helped make him Sunderland's man of the match according to Ken McKenzie in the *Journal* with nine out of ten, helped towards Sunderland recording thirty fouls in the match.

And things seemed to go from bad to worse in the return fixture four days later when Hurley was penalised for a legal tackle on

Davies in the thirteenth minute, allowing Ollie Burton to give Newcastle an early lead from the spot. After that, however, Hurley showed he was never one to shirk a fight and, inspired by his dominance, Sunderland hammered three goals in just over half an hour: Suggett scored in the thirty-second and thirty-fifth minutes and Bruce Stuckey, signed earlier in the season from Exeter City, got the other two minutes after half-time. This might well have proved enough but a knee injury to Hurley just before the hour saw him replaced by Kinnell. His commanding presence was badly missed and with three minutes left, following another Burton penalty, the Newcastle centre half John McNamee headed home from a corner to make it 3-3.

It was while Hurley was on the sidelines that McColl's reign ended. The club had not won in eight home games when he left after a defeat by Second Division Norwich City in a third round FA Cup replay on January 31st 1968. Less well noticed that day was that for the first time Sunderland fans had engaged in some poor behaviour that involved stealing scarves and roughing up those they'd taken them from.

"Ian McColl wasn't strong enough and because of the Rangers tie-up, he had his arm around Jim Baxter most of the time and Jim had his cousin with him, George Kinnell. Jim used to say 'bags' to him when we were going anywhere and George would rush to get Jim's bag to take on the bus," says George Mulhall.

There was a shock when it was announced that the new man was an old man, if you get what I mean. The new manager was Alan Brown. The appointment happened so quickly that when Sunderland ran out at Sheffield Wednesday three days after the cup exit the home programme contained the confusing message that "Sunderland would like to put one across Alan Brown, their former manager." Perhaps themselves confused, Wednesday's players lost out to a single Brand goal.

Hurley feels that Brown made a bad move, stating: "I reckon you never go back and in my opinion Alan should never have come back. He left something and he thought there was something still there. There wasn't. The players had grown up, they were mature and they weren't his players. Alan found it quite difficult. I got back in the side and Colin Todd came in. He was very, very quick. I was glad he did so well. He was a lovely lad. I gave him a lot of advice and he listened. I thought the arrival of Colin Todd would put two to three years on my career but little did I know that I was going to be given a free transfer within eighteen months."

Despite the managerial change Sunderland were favourites to go down but they brought back three points from a 3-0 victory at Nottingham Forest which was followed by Hurley making his first appearance of the year when they ground out a goalless draw at The Hawthorns. Hurley was a tenth-minute substitute.

In the next game Sunderland finally won at home, beating Stoke City, but not before a major scare when Montgomery was injured in the tenth minute and was forced to leave the field. Hurley came on as substitute and Calvin Palmer went in goal. It was, therefore, a highly satisfying 3-1 victory against a team that started the day level on points with Sunderland.

Charlie Hurley's return had been helped, as it often was for much of his Sunderland career, by the work of the Sunderland physiotherapist John Watters. Backroom staff are often the unsung heroes at a football club but Hurley has no doubt of Watters' importance to him and the Roker club, saying "Johnny Watters was the perfect guy to have as a physio because the treatment room is the place no one wants to be. He kept my old knee going. A real bullshitter was Johnny and he talked that much I'd say I was fit just to get away from him. A lovely man though.

"Mind, he should have talked a little more to one or two others at times to get them to play, We used to have one or two players and you'd find that if we were playing Liverpool away on the Saturday, they'd be training during the week and suddenly say their backs had gone. You'd see them playing in the little league cup away but not at Tottenham or Liverpool. It was always an away game, the away from home back syndrome!

"Johnny had a good sense of humour. He would get the butcher, the baker, the candlestick maker in his treatment room. You could smell who was in there. They didn't have a lot of money; it was just a case of 'Right, John, I've got a bad back and what do you want, a kipper or a bit of haddock?' And he'd ask, 'what's your injury?' and if it were bad it'd cost them two kippers!

"I remember one time when Alan Brown banned smoking in the dressing room and John was always puffing away at this old pipe; I'm not even sure there was any tobacco in it at times. This day he was smoking away while doing my thigh, puffing on the old pipe. He heard these steps coming like the old sergeant major and out went the pipe and into his pocket. And he shuffled around to the back so the Bomber couldn't see but the Bomber knew because there was smoke coming out of John's pocket. He didn't stay long – just enough to ask how I was – because he knew if he stayed any longer John would catch on fire. These are the little things that at a club are very important; rules are not broken, they are just moved around a little. Everyone knew John smoked a pipe, including Alan Brown. But as long as you showed respect by hiding it then that was fine – because the Bomber was a very tough disciplinarian, he wouldn't take any crap from anyone."

Victories by 2-1 over Wolves and then Arsenal eased the pressure and in the latter match, during which Argus reported "Hurley was harder than ever in his tackling", Charlie scored his final goal for Sunderland, typically a header, this time from a Mulhall corner in the sixty-second minute. It took his total to twenty-six league and cup goals.

Says Len Ashurst: "The fans loved Hurley for his heading and his goal record was excellent. During his time at Sunderland every team had wingers in their side. We had Harry Hooper and George Mulhall and they generally took the corners. They looked for the big man, who usually stood on the edge of the box and made a run diagonally to the twelve-yard area. That's how Charlie got virtually all of his goals. He was brilliant at it. It's what the crowd loved about him and it set him aside, with the exception of John Charles, from other centre halves in his day. Both were similar and both got a lot of goals with their head."

The fate of the League title lay in north-east hands. Sunderland's final match of the season took them over the Pennines to play Manchester United. Matt Busby's side were lying second to Joe Mercer's team across the city. To win the league United had to do better in their game than City, who were playing at Newcastle United.

It was generally accepted that Manchester United would have little problem in beating Sunderland, which would leave City needing to win at St James' Park to clinch the title. Sunderland had different ideas and in the fourteenth minute they took the lead when Bruce Stuckey drove the ball to the near post where Colin Suggett cracked it into the net on the half-volley. George Mulhall then scored a perfect header from a Suggett cross to put Sunderland further ahead and, despite a goal from George Best, Sunderland won the match fairly comfortably. It was an all-round team display that it could be argued was the best away from home by any Sunderland team Hurley played in during his career.

George Mulhall remembers: "We played exceptionally well and it was one of the finest Sunderland games I played in. We had played some good games in the Second Division and also in the FA Cup but the quality of opposition on that day – Best, Charlton, Crerand, marvellous players. I scored the winner with a header; I got up and headed it back across the goal right into the corner. The players used to call me 'Chandelier' for my heading abilities, or at least some of them. That was a really good header, that one."

Sunderland's dominance was not reflected in the *Match of the Day* coverage and the *Guardian* newspaper was not the only paper to criticise the BBC's forty-five minute highlighted coverage of it, remarking, "It is said that the camera cannot lie – but the skilful sub-editing of the television film conveyed a totally misleading impression of what actually happened – on the day Sunderland were far and away the better side."

It turned out that a victory for Manchester United would not have been enough as City won 4-3 at Newcastle and in front of large numbers of their own supporters hoisted aloft the League Championship. United did at least have the consolation of seeing their team knock out Real Madrid in the Bernabeu four days later on the way to European Cup success against Benfica at Wembley.

Charlie Hurley had a very good game at Old Trafford. One of his opponents that day, Paddy Crerand, is among a large number of fans: "He was a tremendous player, Charlie. He was also unusual in those days for a centre half because he could bring the ball down and pass it out of defence to set up attacks. He was also great in the air; perhaps the one thing he lacked was a bit of pace. He wasn't the quickest, but he was a clever player and sometimes if you're clever you can get away with it. Look at Bobby Moore; he couldn't run to save his life but that didn't matter."

Chapter Fifteen

Thanks, Charlie, it's time to go

The final day win on the previous season at Old Trafford had capped a remarkable comeback by Sunderland, who had looked odds on to be relegated. But sixteen points from the last twenty-four, including six from three away games, had helped them to finish at the giddy height of fifteenth. The major factor in Sunderland's revival had been the decision to get rid of Ian McColl and replace him with Alan Brown but Hurley's inclusion in the side had also helped in the final matches of the season.

The question was, could Sunderland take this into the 1968–69 season? It began at Stoke City where, despite a Gordon Harris penalty, they slumped to a 2-1 defeat. Brown had started with both Hurley and Kinnell in the line-up, with Hurley wearing number four and playing the more attacking role of the two. Colin Todd was now an established member of the back five, but was expected to get forward and support his midfield players.

There was a crowd of 49,807 at Roker Park for the first derby with Newcastle and although over the years since the war there had always been arguments and occasionally one or two hotheads at these games, what happened this time marked a change for the worse. The Fulwell End, where the youngest and loudest tended to congregate to try and imitate the Liverpool supporters on the Kop, were accused of engaging in "dirty words" as well as the "throwing of bottles, darts and other objects" and while some Newcastle fans also did not behave themselves the events off the field appeared to unnerve the Sunderland team on it.

The Supporters' Association was clear that they "did not want those who use filthy words and who resort to violence." Those involved did not care and they converted the Tremeloes' song *Helule, Helule* to reflect their mood with "Hoolie, Hoolie, hooligan! Hoolie, hooligan."

On the pitch, Hurley had a real problem dealing with Wyn Davies in the 1-1 draw and again had a large number of free kicks awarded against him as he struggled not entirely successfully to control the Magpies' number nine.

"Davies was a big, bony character. I remember his elbows. I think he was the only player I played against who could jump higher than me. His strength was in the air but on the floor he knew enough to play it simple. It was a real battle. It was hard, it was no holds barred and we didn't look too clever either," laughs Charlie Hurley.

Martin Harvey had replaced George Kinnell, sold to Middlesbrough for £20,000, which meant Charlie Hurley moved back to his favoured number five spot for a 1-1 draw at Wolves and the big man was in fine form in a 0-0 draw at Arsenal. Not for the first time the programme editor lauded him in print, stating: "Long one of the best footballing centre backs to grace a football arena."

The game with Leeds – a 1-0 defeat – was suffused with the usual ill-feeling as George Mulhall remembers: "Alan Brown said, and I shouldn't be saying this, 'Look, if any of you have a right kick at one of them then I didn't see it'. I never heard him say anything like that at any other match. No other teams played the game so cynically."

The Leeds game may have been spiteful but it was the result at the Boleyn Ground in October 1968 that sticks in the memory of every Sunderland fan, as well as those from a lot of other clubs.

West Ham had made a good start to the season but had failed to win in their previous six league games. They had also failed to beat Sunderland at home since 1926. Hurley had played three times at the club he had turned down before signing for Millwall in 1953, each time facing Geoff Hurst, and the England World Cup hero had failed to score on each occasion. This day, October 19th, was very different. Hurst scored six, and West Ham eight. Sunderland suffered their record defeat, subsequently equalled when they lost at Vicarage Road to Watford in the early 1980s.

Alan Brown, who it must be said was not generally known for his humour [although compared to managers today when everything is so serious he was a bundle of laughs], at least raised a smile in the after-match press conference when he said: "It was an even game. We conceded four in each half."

The match report in the following Monday's *Echo* was headed "World Class West Ham In Brilliant Form" and as Argus stated "was only told with casual references to Sunderland as amidst opposition of such quality they were never in the hunt" although "Hurley and Harvey earned a lot of sympathy for having to take such a hiding in a no-chance defence. Montgomery had eight goals rammed past him which gave him no chance."

According to Charlie Hurley: "Hursty was bleeding dynamite; he used to time his runs to the near post brilliantly. They had a very good side. Eight-nil flattered us."

Geoff Hurst himself feels that "arguably that was my best league game ever for West Ham United. If I am not mistaken no one has scored six goals in a top-flight match since and that was close to forty years ago."

Crowds at Roker Park were falling each week, and there were only 33,151 in to see the European Cup holders Manchester United, even though Sunderland had won 3-0 at home to Coventry City following the West Ham debacle. Sunderland took the lead when Harris scored in the first half and there were only two minutes left when World Cup hero Nobby Stiles hit a powerful shot from the edge of the area that the diving Hurley managed to deflect past the despairing dive of Montgomery to concede an own goal.

"It was a bitter moment for the Sunderland defence, most of all Hurley who had given a tremendous display in the middle," wrote Argus afterwards.

Most of the national newspapers agreed the following day that Hurley had been as good as any player on the field, with many selecting him as their man of the match.

On October 30th 1968 Hurley made his thirty-seventh international appearance. But a single Wlodzimierz Lubanski goal was enough to give Poland victory in a friendly in the Slaski Stadium in Katowice. His thirty-eighth appearance was against Denmark in a World Cup qualifier at Dalymount Park on December 4th but at 1-1 after fifty-one minutes it was called off due to fog. He captained the side on both occasions.

If Jimmy Greaves could not emulate Geoff Hurst when Sunderland travelled to Tottenham Hotspur he did manage to score four as Sunderland were well beaten 5-1. An injury to Martin Harvey on seventy-three minutes, when the score was only 2-1, was the key to such a heavy defeat. This took Greaves's record to ten goals in nine games in matches against Sunderland since 1964. However, a look behind the figures shows that until that day in November 1968 Greaves did not do that well when Hurley played for Sunderland.

Hurley had previously faced Greaves just three times before then and Greaves had scored only once. In the other five games when Hurley was missing through injury Greaves scored five times. In 1968 Hurley was coming to the end of his top-flight career and Greaves exploited his lack of pace and scored a goal that was shown on TV replays for many years, running through from the halfway line to take the ball round Montgomery and finish in fine style. Hurley had the satisfaction of playing against Greaves once more, at Roker Park in February 1969, and Greaves again failed to score – it was some feat to prevent a genius like Greaves from scoring in three out of the five games.

Hurley has no doubt that "the best sniffer ever was Jimmy Greaves, better than Denis Law. I did well against Greaves, mind. He played at Roker Park one time and we won 3-2 and he scored two that were disallowed for offside, and I said to him afterwards 'Tough luck there, Jim' and he said 'Charlie boy, if I'd been at home I'd have got them both'. What a good player, great touch and a decent bloke as well. Law must have scored half his goals from within six yards, he poked his goals in, no runs and dribbles. He was brave, mind, around the box."

Fortunately not all London clubs found Sunderland such easy pickings. Chelsea, lying sixth in the league, were beaten 3-2 in a thriller with Bobby Kerr outstanding. Hurley was not far behind as according to Argus he "took the eye with his command in the air and one or two challenges which reminded the opposition that he really meant business."

Revenge was in the air just before Christmas when West Ham came to Sunderland, and goals from Calvin Palmer and Gordon Harris in the first twelve minutes at least wiped the smile off the faces of Ron Greenwood's players in a 2-1 victory.

The *Sunday Express*'s Tony Hardisty, in an article headed "Super Hurley foils Hurst", reported that "West Ham were attractive as ever, but could never create really clear cut chances against a defence in which Charlie Hurley was superb."

The key moment in the game came in the second half as West Ham pressed for an equaliser. Argus's report in the Monday *Echo* that week captures some of the qualities that made Hurley such a favourite for Sunderland fans from that generation.

"Geoff Hurst broke rapidly to outpace Colin Todd to hit a fierce shot from just inside the penalty area but Charlie Hurley who had made a beeline down the middle dived in to take the full weight of it in his face and turn the ball away for a corner. After receiving treatment Hurley took all the danger out of the situation by clearing the corner with a powerful header."

It was wonderful stuff that this author as a young man can still remember from the enormous cheer that went round the massive Roker Park ground for the next few minutes, leaving Argus to report that "against the magnificent Hurst, Hurley turned in another great display in a run of form which equals the best in his eleven years with the club."

Hurley recalls: "The ball was hit so hard by Geoff and it hit me full in the face. It was rock hard and hurt like hell. It knocked me flying; my face was sore all that night."

Sir Geoff Hurst has nothing but praise for Hurley, saying: "I played a few times against Hurley. He was a terrific footballing centre half. He was very, very good in the air, but he was also very good on the ball and not that many centre halves in that era were. I loved playing at Roker Park and I scored a few goals against Sunderland, which was always nice. The place had a fantastic atmosphere; Sunderland and Newcastle have very passionate fans. I loved playing in big games and before big crowds; it brought the best out of me. Sunderland is a fantastic club, they've got great support and they always treated the opposition team well. It's the same today."

Yet another London team, Fulham, now of the Second Division, came to Sunderland for the third round of the FA Cup. Sunderland were lying twelfth in Division One and when Bobby Kerr drove a cracking shot from the edge of the penalty area to give the home side an eighth-minute lead the vast majority of the 27,000 present were looking forward to seeing them build on it. Fulham, however, were no mugs and stormed back to win 4-1 with the thirty-four-year-old Haynes largely running the show. Argus criticised Hurley, stating that "he was more commanding in the Fulham penalty area than his own."

According to Jim Montgomery: "Charlie really struggled in that last season he played for Sunderland. His knees would creak; he didn't have full flexibility in them, and his time had come to an end. It's difficult when that happens. When I left in the 1976–77 season to move to Birmingham it was a massive wrench. It happens but it hurts. Charlie was no different. He'd had a magnificent career at Sunderland and it was only right that in 1979 he was voted the Player of the Century as he was a tremendous player. He did, however, have some very good players alongside him during his career including Jimmy McNab and Martin Harvey among others.

"When I first got into the side I was only 11st and 2lb and Charlie looked after me, making sure as best he could I was protected from a battering. He was magnificent in dealing with crosses. The most difficult part of a 'keeper's job is to come out and collect crosses. Stopping shots is easy, well it was for me anyway, but to decide to come for a cross means deciding whether you can get the ball from among a load of bodies and if you don't it can end up in the net and you look a bit daft. I was always a little cautious, but you have to remember that after Charlie I had another fantastic header of the ball in front of me in Dave Watson. And I'd like to think I didn't do too badly in my career, however."

Too true; 623 games, a record never likely to be beaten for Sunderland, a good number in which Monty was the outstanding player on the field. If England had taken him to Mexico in 1970 they might well have retained the World Cup.

Charlie Hurley is a big fan of the Sunderland number one, stating: "Montgomery was the best shot-stopper I ever played with and he should have played at least some games for England. But maybe he was around at the wrong time and Sunderland weren't a prominent club in those days. He was an excellent goalkeeper, was Jimmy."

Another injury meant Hurley sat out five games. His replacement, Ritchie Pitt, was only seventeen and he was to suffer four defeats in his first four games. Thankfully Pitt, who went on to represent the club at Wembley in 1973, had a happier fifth game which brought a much-needed one point in a 1-1 draw at St James' Park, where Colin Suggett scored his last goal of 24 in 83 league appearances in a Sunderland strip.

Despite the point, earned mainly courtesy of another magnificent Montgomery display, Sunderland had only picked up four points from their first ten games in 1969 and when Pitt was injured playing against Bournemouth in the Youth Cup semi-final Charlie Hurley was brought back into a side that suffered a 1-0 defeat against Ipswich at Portman Road.

This was followed by two 0-0 home draws, including one against already relegated QPR where, according to Argus, "the tarnished image of Hurley, who had his worst game ever for the club, was as typical as anything of the sub-standard offering which came from every position with the exception of the goal."

It was no surprise that Pitt replaced Hurley for the match with Manchester City at Maine Road, which Sunderland lost 1-0. But Dennis Tueart and Bobby Kerr ended any doubts about Sunderland staying up when Wolves were beaten 2-0 in Hurley's last Sunderland league game at Roker Park. Argus's match report praised the Irishman, stating that he "played well defensively and was always a menace in the Wolves penalty area from set positions."

Hurley played his final first team match at Turf Moor against Burnley. Playing alongside Hurley that night was Colin Todd, who has this to say on his ex-teammate: "Charlie was a very majestic player. He used to dominate the opposing teams' centre forwards. He could also pass it, he could get the ball down, and he could play centre forward. You mentioned Beckenbauer; he was probably a bit more mobile than Charlie. But Charlie had a very good feel for the ball and he was very strong. He was vital when coming up for corners. If he had a weakness it was that he wasn't the quickest of players.

"Mind you, I think I extended his career by a couple of years. I was the runner at the back and he was a big help with his advice but no one can teach you how to think, how to anticipate. You've either got that or you haven't. I listened carefully to what he had to say, mind, but you have your own ability and nobody can teach you everything about the game."

Hurley admits that he "was very, very sad that night at Burnley, but I felt very proud of what I'd done for Sunderland football club. I became something good for the fans. I had a fantastic career. I have never stopped loving that football club".

Sunderland won the match 2-1, so Hurley signed off with a win.

On May 17th 1969 it was announced that Hurley, along with George Mulhall and Ralph Brand, were to be released on free transfers. Also given their notices were three members of the backroom staff Arthur Wright, Jack Jones and Bill Scott.

Joan Hurley was sad to leave Sunderland. "The people were always very friendly towards us. I made some good friends with other players' wives, especially Valerie Ashurst and Sylvia McNab who I still see fairly regularly. Charles and I were very upset when Jimmy McNab died; Charles read the eulogy at his funeral.

"I didn't go to all the games, but I can recall the Roker Roar, especially at the Everton FA Cup match: it was deafening. We also had a good social life, Wetheralls was always a good night and we had a friend, Norman Levi who owned La Dolce Vita in Newcastle that we visited. Also, as Charles was a professional footballer, he got a very long summer break and that was great as we could do lots of things together as a family. We had a very good life in Sunderland and every time we've been back since we have been very well treated. Bob Murray and his wife Sue were always great towards us at the football club."

Mulhall admits that "I was maybe a bit annoyed when I got released. Brown had gone away and then come back. We all played a lot of games but the free transfer I got worked out really well for me, although Sunderland did get relegated the following season.

I went to South Africa to play in Cape Town for two years. It was great – we visited all the major cities. We did that in England, mind – that's one of the joys of being a professional player. At Sunderland we also had some good times after the games as well. You could write a good book about those I can tell you, but I'm not going to!"

Charlie Hurley had meanwhile made his thirty-ninth international appearance when, as captain and player-manager, the Irish lost 2-1 at home to Czechoslovakia in a World Cup qualifier. It was one of his poorest performances in the green shirt, with many in the 33,000 crowd possibly agreeing with *Irish Independent* reporter Noel Dunne that we "may have seen the last of Charlie Hurley. Few players have given better service to this country than the big popular Sunderland 'king' but his reign had to end sometime and now no longer the commanding and awesome figure to opposing sides he used to be his time seems nigh."

In fact Hurley did turn out once more, on June 8th just after he signed for Bolton. He was asked by the selectors to play at centre forward but, well past his best, his presence was a handicap for his teammates and as Noel Dunne reported, he "did the right thing by taking himself off and bringing on Frank O'Neil at half-time."

With forty caps stretching over twelve years Hurley had every reason to feel more than satisfied with his efforts for Ireland and he had done his dad from Cork proud.

Chapter Sixteen

Burnden Park and the end of a great career

So Charlie Hurley had to sit by the telephone and wait for offers in the summer of 1969. He could have been player-manager at Norwich City but he didn't want to start a coaching career and the job went to Ron Saunders.

Then the phone rang and on the other end was one of English football's legendary names, Nat Lofthouse, the Lion of Vienna, one of the great post-war centre forwards.

"One of the reasons I was given a free from Sunderland was for services rendered. You could make a good killing and I was sitting waiting for the phone to go. It wasn't red hot, a few down Torquay way and the south-west before I got a call from Nat Lofthouse. He asked if I was fixed up yet? 'Oh yes, three or four,' I replied and he likely knew I was lying. 'Would you like to come to Bolton for a couple of years,' he asked. 'We've always thought highly of you and what are you looking for?'

"I said a bit more than I thought he'd be willing to pay and he said he'd speak to the directors and get back to me, which he did that evening. He said they would pay what I asked for and it made it worth my while. It was sad for me. Bolton was a bit ramshackle compared to Sunderland but they were a lovely bunch of lads."

Bolton Wanderers suffered badly from the lifting of the maximum wage. From the early '60s players who previously had little financial incentive to move to better-supported clubs were aware that these could now afford better money than those with smaller gates.

In the season before Hurley's arrival, the columns of the *Bolton Evening News*'s Saturday sports paper, commonly known as the

Buff, were full of letters from supporters concerned about Bolton's decline. Some of them might have done better to actually go to the game, where a struggling side in the lower reaches of Division Two managed to stay just outside the relegation zone for much of the season, watched by crowds that averaged just over 10,000, with only 6,357 at the Oxford game that finished 1-1.

Even worse, only 4,927 witnessed Ronnie Phillips's thirty-ninth-second goal that was at least good enough to ensure safety in a 1-0 home win against Hull City. A letter in the *Buff* from George Blake of Farnworth probably summed up the situation by stating: "It's over, the most depressing season in the history of the Wanderers" while D Rothwell urged supporters to turn out at Burnden next season. Bolton finished eight points clear of Bury, who were relegated in twenty-first place. The club were urgently seeking two new directors who could put some money up for some "big name signings."

W Dingsdale of Wigan thought that "Bolton Wanderers could take advantage of star players on the transfer list such as Hurley and Mulhall at Sunderland, Clayton at Blackburn..." hoping that one or all of them might prove a catalyst for success in the same way that Leeds's signing of Bobby Collins in the early '60s and Derby County's signing of Dave Mackay had later proved.

He must have been pleased to hear the Wanderers chairman Harry Tyldersley stating at the end of May 1969 that the club had "opened negotiations to bring Charlie Hurley to Burnden Park. I must stress that Charlie does not want a player-coach appointment yet. He wants to continue purely as a player. His experience would do wonders for our defence, and I am sure the players would respond." The supporters appeared to be generally in favour.

On June 7th 1969 a smiling Hurley was pictured in the *Evening News* signing for Bolton Wanderers. He made his debut in a pre-season friendly at Fellows Park, won 1-0 by Walsall.

The *Buff* reporter Frank Booth was not expecting too much from a side managed by 1958 FA Cup hero Lofthouse, stating: "With all the goodwill in the world, I suggest that the Wanderers will do well to finish in a good position in the Second Division."

So it was a welcome start to the season when Bolton crushed Hurley's former club Millwall 4-1 in a match watched by 10,075. They saw John Byrom grab a hat-trick. Booth commented that "Charlie Hurley held the defence together well and took everything in the air."

The team was: Eddie Hopkinson, John Ritson, Paul Hallows, Warwick Rimmer, Charlie Hurley, Arthur Marsh, Terry Wharton, John Byrom, Roy Greaves, Dave Hatton, Ron Phillips. Sub: Gordon Taylor.

The substitute that day, Gordon Taylor, now the PFA Chief Executive, says that "there wasn't enough money. Bolton had been unable to bounce back. They nearly did so in 1965 but finished third in the period when there were two up and two down and by 1969 virtually all the players were up for sale."

Hurley had agreed to write a weekly column for the *Buff*, and he provided some interesting snippets in his first season at Burnden Park. On August 23rd he wrote that: "Bolton offers a new challenge. Here is a club of great tradition. A club that I believe can be great again. And I believe I can help them."

When Bolton beat Preston 4-0 Booth reported: "Hurley was again superb at centre half. He blotted out Irvine and Ingram completely, Hopkinson had little to do in goal." Six points were gained from the first four matches but an injury at Cardiff in the next game meant Hurley was forced to watch the next few games of a Wanderers side further weakened by the sale of Dave Hatton to Blackpool for £40,000.

The Irishman was back for a dull 1-0 home defeat against Portsmouth that left Bolton with ten points from the first ten games, and according to Booth he then had a poor game at Huddersfield which Bolton lost 1-0.

Things went from bad to worse both for Bolton and the ex-Sunderland star. At Ayresome Park Booth criticised him for "misskicking completely, leaving Hickton to nip in and take the ball on and hit it past Hopkinson" to give Middlesbrough a forty-fifth-second lead in a game that finished 4-0. When Oxford grabbed a point in a 1-1 draw at Burnden Park Bolton were left in nineteenth place and a 1-0 defeat at Norwich City saw the club fall into the relegation zone, having gathered only four points from thirteen games. Hurley, meanwhile, had some minor satisfaction from scoring his first goal for the club in a 3-2 home defeat by Watford in October.

In his column, Hurley referred to the lack of atmosphere at Burnden Park, "except at the Lever End as this is the only hint we have that we are playing at home and this is very important to the younger players."

QPR were chasing promotion back to the top flight when they arrived at Burnden Park but in what turned out to be one of the most exciting games at the famous stadium Bolton came from 1-0 down to win a thriller 6-4. Things began to look up even more when they signed England World Cup winner Roger Hunt from Liverpool for £32,000 in December and announced that further major transfers were likely. Hunt was set to line up alongside Bolton's most impressive performer of the first half of the season, John Byrom, who had grabbed eighteen goals before Christmas.

In his column Hurley spoke of his admiration for Hunt, stating that he was as good as Geoff Hurst "but not as good as Greaves", a view he maintains to this day.

On Boxing Day, Hurley grabbed his second Bolton goal, scoring the first in an impressive 3-1 win against local rivals Preston North End at Deepdale before 24,934 spectators.

Hunt's FA Cup debut attracted the largest Bolton home crowd of the season, but the 20,447 saw Watford win 2-1 courtesy of two Barry Endean goals. It was to prove an inauspicious start. Hunt was past his best.

With the Mexico World Cup on the horizon, Hurley used his weekly column to urge England to pick Jimmy Montgomery rather than Peter Bonetti and tipped Brazil to win with Italy their closest rivals. How right he was, although had Montgomery been picked England may have turned out to be Brazil's closest rivals as the Sunderland man would have played in the ill-fated quarter-final against West Germany rather than the Chelsea number one.

Hurley, however, had much more important things to be concerned about than either Bolton's poor form or the 1970 World

Cup. Joan had given birth on January 6th 1970 to a second daughter, Joanne, and doctors did not think she would survive.

Hurley recalls events with tears of joy years later but at the time there wasn't much to smile about: "We had lost a child, a girl, who was born dead, when we lived in Sunderland, and my wife should never have had another one. Joan had a relapse and had to go into hospital. She started bleeding only seven months into the pregnancy and they had to bring the baby on, and Joanne was born.

"My wife collapsed. We could have lost everything. The big guy, the top doctor, came up and said to me, 'I don't think you've got much chance with this baby'. This broke me up and so I said 'You're wrong, absolutely wrong' and I went down to see her. She was sitting with a dummy in her mouth and she had something to help her breathing. I went down morning, noon and night, I talked to Joanne. It was a horrible part of my life. I didn't, couldn't, play football. I said to Nat [Lofthouse], 'Look, I can't play football' and he said I should do whatever I wanted, that I was good to have around the club and that he appreciated what I'd done for the club.

"I went down to the hospital and asked the nurse for some gloves so I could touch her. I pinched her bum and she went 'Aagh' and, gospel truth, I cried my eyes out. She never looked back after that. I dashed up to see Jo and said she was going to be all right. She asked how did I know and I said I just knew.

"I've told loads of people about pinching her bum. I told that tale at her wedding. I've got a fabulous daughter and every now and again I pinch her bum to remind her. After three months she had to go back to the hospital to see if there were any mental defects and thankfully there weren't. She now has two beautiful daughters of her own."

Joan Hurley says: "I can't praise Nat Lofthouse and Bolton enough. Once Joanne survived, she quickly recovered and soon started putting on some weight and so we were able to bring her home."

Hurley was back for the home match with Middlesbrough and enjoyed a measure of revenge for the walloping earlier in the season, snatching Bolton's second in a match which finished 2-1.

The other goal was scored by Hunt, his first for the club. Hurley's goal came after Byrom forced the 'Boro 'keeper to drop the ball to leave him with a simple tap-in. "It was one of the softest goals I've ever scored," he said after the game.

Hurley had been replaced during his difficult period by John Hulme and in his column of March 7th Hurley praised his young understudy, who was part of the Bolton side that went to Loftus Road and hammered QPR 4-0, truly a case of "Can we play you every week" as Bolton completed an impressive double.

According to Hurley, Hulme was very good, "purely a stopper and very good at it. He got in and when I'd gone there I'd taken his place. He got upset. I took him out for lunch and we sorted things out. I told him he was a great defender and that his job was to stop people.

"By the end of it he said that he'd heard a lot about me, but he couldn't take it 'because you took my place, but I know that I got it all wrong'. I said I wanted him to take my place in the team but I wasn't going to make it easy for him. He was a good professional and when I became manager of Reading I signed him – he was actually my first signing as a manager."

On March 28th Hurley played impressively as Bolton won 1-0 at Sheffield United, where Byrom again scored. The Lancashire side were now six points clear of relegation, and an excellent Easter period, when five of the six points on offer were gratefully accepted, finally pulled them away from the bottom two. Byrom was quite rightly awarded the Player of the Season award, having rattled in twenty-four goals.

An ageing Charlie Hurley may not have had his best year but Frank Booth summed up his contribution perfectly in the *Buff* by stating that "Hurley helped to steady down the defence and his influence has helped many of his colleagues, especially the younger ones, to really find their feet".

Hurley's eighteenth season of league football – 1970–71 – started with him out of a Bolton team that began badly, although in September a 2-0 victory at Blackburn, courtesy of goals in the last six minutes from Gordon Taylor and Byrom, showed that on their day Wanderers could beat most sides.

On October 3rd, almost thirteen years since Hurley made his debut for Sunderland, he returned to Roker Park for the first time as part of an opposing squad. Teenager Paul Fletcher scored an impressive goal as Bolton lost 4-2. But Hurley, selected as substitute (only one in those days), did not get on. Nevertheless the *Buff* reported that "Charlie Hurley received a tremendous reception from the crowd on his return to Roker Park". He was back for the following weekend's match, which saw Bolton crush Charlton 4-0. Byrom scored twice but with reported losses of £28,290 on the year till the end of March and gates of little more than 8,000 at home there was a deep sense of gloom at Burnden Park.

Gordon Taylor is full of praise for Hurley, saying: "I moved to Birmingham at Christmas 1970 and it proved a good move as they were a club on the up and it restored my career. I'd been at Bolton for ten years and things weren't going well. They'd put a lot of youngsters in and had Roger Hunt and Charlie, but they were at the end of their days. That's not being cruel. Charlie was a legend and he had all these Republic of Ireland caps. He was a real gent. He had the highest of standards and he used to regale us with stories from Sunderland, about how one of the manager's favourites Jim Baxter was a good footballer but who didn't represent to Charlie how a good footballer should act.

"In training Charlie was very committed and he was still up for a game. He was a big character in the area and he became well liked. I'd liken him to a military general. He was a natural leader. He was strong, he was big, he had presence but he was on his tiptoes, the way he ran with his elbows up. He had such a distinctive running style although he wasn't fast.

"The crowd liked him. You could not but like him. You knew why he had been so popular at Sunderland. He gave his all, very committed. He was very professional – he didn't suffer fools gladly. He was very good socially off the field as well. He had a natural sense of humour. I have only seen him once or twice since then but if we bumped into each other I know we'd be pleased to see each other.

"To tell you the truth he was different class. If you had eleven Charlie Hurleys in your team then you'd have no problems. He was a real good ambassador, the old type of ambassador. He'd been at the very top and Bolton was battling but no way was he a big-time Charlie."

Without Taylor or Hurley, Bolton crashed out of the FA Cup in the third round, beaten 3-0 at York City. The following week Lofthouse stepped down to become coach with Jimmy Meadows, the Blackpool chief coach, replacing him.

Charlie Hurley could have had the job but he knew he would be leaving at the end of the season. "Nat called me into his office and said, 'Look you've got good experience and the players respect you so would you do the job?' But we'd already made up our minds to move south."

Birmingham, with Taylor in the team, were to crush Bolton 4-0 at St Andrews with an emerging talent, Trevor Francis, grabbing all the goals. Meadows had dropped Hunt and Hurley followed, although little good it did as Bolton's terrible run continued with a 3-0 defeat at Leicester City.

There was now a real possibility that one of the founder members of the Football League would drop into the Third Division for the first time. And it looked almost certain when the Wanderers directors decided to take the £60,000 on offer from Burnley for Paul Fletcher. Bolton fans were outraged and the *Buff*'s Frank Booth attacked the sale, reminding supporters that "Nat Lofthouse and chairman John Banks had stated that the club's policy was to rely on youth. The fans were led to believe and I was led to believe that the club had turned the corner financially."

Trouble again flared, this time at Burnden Park, before a 0-0 home draw with Hull as fifty fans battled on the pitch. QPR then hammered Bolton 4-0, Rodney Marsh rattling in a hat-trick against a defence without Hurley. Bolton travelled back, bottom of the league and looking doomed. Desperate, they brought back Lofthouse to replace Meadows but to little effect as, again without Hurley, they lost 3-0 at Carlisle. On April 17th Bolton were taken apart by Charlton, losing 4-1 to confirm their relegation.

Over the two seasons Hurley made 43 appearances for Bolton, scoring three times, and on May 25th 1971 the club, who had appointed former Blackpool and England right back Jimmy Armfield as their new manager, announced that Charlie Hurley was being given a free transfer, thus ending a playing career that had started seventeen years earlier on January 30th 1954 and during which the Irishman had performed with honour for Millwall, London, Sunderland, Bolton and the Republic of Ireland against some of the best players and sides in the world.

Chapter Seventeen

Management at Reading

After being released by Bolton, Charlie Hurley was keen to stay in football. So when Reading's Jack Mansell was sacked on October 14th 1971, just months after the club had suffered relegation to the Fourth Division, Hurley, along with fifty-seven others, applied for the vacant post.

After deliberating into 1972, the Reading board decided it was between Charlie and ex-Manchester United centre half Bill Foulkes. What appears to have tipped the scales was Hurley's natural charm.

Hurley recalls: "I had three interviews. First one not too bad, second more serious. I then picked up a paper just before Christmas and it said Billy Foulkes was favourite to be appointed Reading manager, and that he was being interviewed on the Wednesday. I'd received a letter to be interviewed for the third time on the Friday, so I was quite pleased. People always remember the one who goes last rather than the one who goes first. I remember going for my interview and I paid for my lunch. I went into the toilet and Frank Waller, the Reading chairman, followed. He said it was a very difficult decision for them. They didn't know who to go with – 'you or Billy Foulkes'. I said, 'If you want to pick the wrong one then pick Billy Foulkes' and he laughed. I think it got me the job. It was a real gamble. I got a call about the Sunday – it was pretty quick – saying 'The job's yours'. That was the start of a managerial career."

On the day of his appointment, Hurley said: "There is ample scope for development here. I am sure that I can do some good here. I am a great believer in discipline, hard work and the need for players and management to be professional". It was reported by David Dibben in the *Reading Evening Post* that "he had not been given a contract and will work on a 'do or die' basis. He has been given a salary of £5,000 plus. It is understood that Hurley's time with less prosperous and successful clubs gave him the edge over Foulkes."

Hurley took over a side struggling fourteenth in the Fourth Division. Physiotherapist Jimmy Wallbanks picked the side for the FA Cup third round tie at Blyth Spartans, where Hurley saw his new players competing for the first time. Three days after the 2-2 draw he picked the following side for the first time as Reading crushed Blyth 6-1 at Elm Park: Steve Death, Alan Wooler, John Harley, Stuart Morgan, Dennis Butler, Peter Harman, Tony Wagstaff, Ray Flannigan, Gordon Cumming, Les Chappell, Dick Habbin.

Harman got a hat-trick, taking Reading through for a fourth round tie with League and Cup holders Arsenal at Elm Park. The game naturally attracted a capacity home crowd but Reading lost 2-1.

Things got better. A 2-1 victory at Griffin Park in a local derby against Brentford was two of twelve points from eight matches before Reading returned to their pre-Hurley days by losing four in a row. They ended the season in sixteenth place, causing Dibben to write that "if Charlie Hurley is going to produce the goods next season then he plainly has a monumental task ahead in the summer."

Things did improve in the 1972–73 season and when Reading ran out at Field Mill to play table-topping Mansfield Town they lay eighth in the league, having lost just four matches in eighteen. After grabbing a creditable 1-1 draw, Hurley said he was "proud of the way we played. We gave Mansfield an object lesson in how to play football. It was the best we've played since I've been manager."

He had strengthened his defence by signing John Hulme, making him skipper. After twenty-one league games Reading had conceded only eighteen goals. The problem was that they were not scoring many themselves and when they lost at Newport County on Boxing Day to a Steve Aizlewood goal they had scored just twenty-two in twenty-three matches.

All was forgotten when Reading beat Doncaster in the FA Cup third round to set up an emotional return for Hurley to Roker Park to play Sunderland.

Inspired by a decent away following and exhilarated by the reception Hurley received before the game, Reading stunned a Roker crowd of close to 34,000 by taking the lead when Les Chappell rose to meet a Gordon Cumming corner before a Dennis Tueart effort ensured a replay. Man of the match was Steve Death, with Dibben remarking that "in fifteen years of watching Reading it was easily the best goalkeeping performance I have ever seen."

Extra class told at Elm Park but as Sunderland later beat Manchester City, Arsenal and Leeds to win the FA Cup, Reading had done remarkably well to force a draw in the first match.

Hurley remembers: "I always said that if we beat Sunderland at Roker Park I would do a lap of honour. Now it would have been very emotional for me. I love Sunderland, but then I was manager of Reading. I used to tell my players, never thinking I was going to go up to Sunderland with a football team, 'You don't know what it's like to be a hero – if we ever go to Roker Park just see those fans out there'.

"And then we were drawn against Sunderland at Roker Park and there was a mass of fans all round the ground, chanting 'Charlie, Charlie' and it was amazing for the Reading players. The respect I got from them. They thought I was giving them a load of bully, but to realise what I was saying was true thrilled them.

"In fact the reception I got was better than I thought it might be. The players went out to see what type of boots to wear and when they came back in they said 'Look, Boss, you'll have to go back out because the fans are going crazy'. So I went out and gave a wave to the fans. It was a great tonic to the players because I didn't give much of a team talk. I said, 'Now you've seen the sort of reception I've got. To get that type of reception you have to do a bit. The Roker fans don't suffer fools gladly, you've got to have earned your stripes. Now I don't want you to go out there without the biggest fight you've ever made, you're representing me. Be sure that if you don't fight you won't play for me any more. That's a fact. This is my patch'.

"We gave a very good display in fact. Stephen Death the goalkeeper was magnificent. He was a great lad. Sunderland came down to Elm Park on the Wednesday. We had a full house. Sunderland had a good side: they had Tueart, little Bobby Kerr, Dave Watson and we knew we had our work cut out. We played very, very well for twenty minutes but Sunderland finished up winning 3-1. It was thoroughly deserved. I was very annoyed afterwards. It was said that Sunderland were 200-1 to win the cup and I didn't have a fiver on me, a fiver...

"The thing about that day was after the match in the directors' room I was having a drink with Bob Stokoe. Both sets of directors were there and someone came upstairs and said 'Look, Charlie, you are going to have to come downstairs because the whole of the offices are packed with fans chanting your name. You'll be the only one to get them out without any trouble'. I said, 'No problem', walked down, signed a few autographs, shook a few hands, kissed a few women – they were younger ones then, now I have to kiss the older ones – and I said 'Come on, you'll have to go now' and they went outside. I went back upstairs into the boardroom and we all looked down at the road outside and there was a mass of fans just chanting 'Charlie, Charlie'."

When the matches against Sunderland were followed by three league wins and a draw in four consecutive home games it appeared that Reading were set to mount a late successful promotion run, but only if they could reproduce their home form in away matches. However, by capturing only three points from their next seven away games any hope of promotion had long gone when the season ended with a 0-0 draw against Crewe Alexandra at Gresty Road.

Reading finished seventh, just four points behind promoted Newport County in fourth. They had conceded only thirty-eight goals, including just seven in twenty-three home games, which should have been a platform for promotion. David Dibben felt that "Charlie Hurley faces a massive rebuilding programme if Reading are to make a worthwhile promotion effort next season. His defence is basically solid with skipper John Hulme and Tommy Youlden or Barry Wagstaff in the middle. But the creation of moves, the running off the ball and the ability to win tackles leaves a lot to be desired. And up front, Reading seldom seem to have the punch to turn a chance into a goal. Les Chappell has the ability – he's proved it before – but new players Bobby Hunt and

Percy Freeman are not contributing £16,000 worth of attacking flair."

Reading started the 1973–74 season well and did not suffer defeat until the fifteenth game, a home reverse to Gillingham. Making his debut that day was Hurley's former Sunderland teammate Bruce Stuckey. He had left Sunderland in 1970, returning to Devon to join Torquay, and Hurley had signed him for £12,500. Stuckey was an old-fashioned winger and Hurley's idea was that he would provide the crosses which would boost the goals tally. It worked quickly; in the next game, at Valley Parade, Hurley's side scored three goals away from Elm Park for the first time that season. The problem was they conceded four. Having let in only one away goal in 690 minutes they lost four in thirty minutes just after half-time, letting slip leads of 2-0 and 3-2.

When Reading lost 3-2 at Barnsley on February 3rd 1974 they slid to twelfth and a long way off promotion. Against this background Charlie Hurley had taken the decision to buy Robin Friday from non-league Hayes and on February 10th 1974 he scored two goals on his debut in a 4-1 home victory against Exeter City. It was to be the start of a short but thrilling career for the club in which he made 135 appearances and scored 53 goals.

Friday should have been playing in the top flight. He clearly had the ability; the problem was his temperament. Drinking and smoking to excess, Friday was happy to start fights with both opponents and teammates, including some he considered his friends. But Reading's form improved with Friday in the side and with only three defeats in the last eighteen matches they were able to improve one place on the previous season. But they were a long way behind fourth-placed Bury, who had eight more points.

When the season ended Hurley gave four players free transfers, including Bobby Hunt and Tony Wagstaff. Fees were wanted for Gordon Cumming and Brian Bromley, whom Hurley had bought at the start of the season for £10,000 but who had failed to command a first team place and was thought to be available for £6,000. Dibben meanwhile reported that "those players offered new contracts are thought not to be happy with the terms offered."

It is unlikely that Reading could have afforded to pay them a great deal more because at the start of the following season – Hurley's third full season in charge – the club revealed their finances were in poor shape. They had debts of more than £79,000, despite the average gate in 1973–74 rising by almost a thousand on the previous season to reach 6,318, boosting receipts to £81,028.

The situation, however, would have been considerably worse had it not been for the efforts of the Reading Supporters Club. They raised and donated £25,200, equivalent to almost a third of the money taken at the turnstiles.

Some cash was available to strengthen the side and Hurley was able to buy John Murray from Bury at the start of the season for £4,000 and announced he was "quietly confident of returning the club back to Division Three."

Murray scored the first goal of the season as Reading ran out 2-0 winners at home to Cambridge United on the opening day of the season. Star of the show, reported David Dibben, was "as usual, Robin Friday who entertained the crowd and frustrated the Cambridge players with his own highly individual brand of skills."

At first it seemed that Reading were going to maintain their fine form from the end of the previous campaign and after nine games they were second, just a point off the top. They had even managed to win away games at Scunthorpe and Exeter City and by the season's end they had taken both points on eight occasions away from home. However, this time their home form let them down, as they lost four and drew six of their twenty-four matches at Elm Park. Friday was crowned "Player of the Year" in his first full season as Reading finished seventh, five points behind promoted fourth-placed Lincoln City.

The 1975–76 season was to be the finest in Charlie Hurley's short managerial career as he took Reading to their first promotion since 1926. He could, however, have walked into a much more lucrative post early in the season when, following a fine start, it was reported on Thursday October 16th 1975 by Dibben "that Charlie Hurley had again been linked with the vacant post at First Division Sheffield United, stating that he had previously been offered the post when former team boss John Harris became general manager in 1973 but had turned it down because he felt he didn't have enough experience." The Blades were bottom of the league with only three points from the twelve matches.

Charlie Hurley says: "I was offered the Sheffield United job but at the time I wanted to make sure Reading got promotion. Johnny Short, who was from Millwall, was up there and he'd said to the board that I was doing well, knew my stuff, was a good person and I was a football fanatic. I turned it down; Reading looked like getting promotion. I didn't even go for an interview, which was silly, as it would have put some pressure on the Reading people. I am not saying I was right; I was just too honest for my own good. I should have taken the chance, but my wife didn't like the idea of moving, especially after we'd settled in Hoddesdon where we still live today. Most players these days just go where the jobs are if it's up the ladder. Even if they do badly they get paid off and do rather well from it.

"George Mulhall did well and it was clear that when he was at Sunderland he was looking ahead to staying in the game when he finished playing. I never looked that far in advance and this might have been a mistake on my part. I was enjoying my time at Reading and it was an unfortunate decision. In all fairness the Reading fans were fantastic when I got them promoted. When you make so many people happy it also makes you happy."

Joan Hurley says: "We'd moved back south because I wanted to have a few years with my parents before they died. Charles's parents also lived close by in Essex so it meant we could see them as well. Also we had, because of Charles's work, moved a few times and we wanted some stability in our lives. It was the right move; Charles's mother died in 1978, my father died in 1983, one year before Charles's dad and my mother passed away in 1985. Charles was very close to his parents and he is very close to all his brothers and sisters."

It was Jimmy Sirrell who took the United job, moving from Second Division Notts County, although his new club were doomed to play his old one the following season as Sheffield United, were relegated from Division One in last place with just twenty-two points.

Hurley must have wondered about the wisdom of his decision to stay at Elm Park when his players heard a section of the Reading fans humming the "dead", or "funeral", march during another home victory, this time 2-0 against Huddersfield.

After the match Hurley was so angry that he rapped the fans involved, sparking a furious debate in the *Evening Post* letters page in which some supporters criticised the style of Reading's play despite the fact that in 1975 they had won thirteen and drawn four of their first seventeen home games, scoring twenty-eight goals and conceding just seven.

One of the Reading players took up the issue in his *Saturday Evening Post* column. This was Irish international and ex-Millwall midfielder Eamon Dunphy, signed by Hurley during the close season. Having experienced promotion with Charlton and Millwall, Dunphy was, according to Hurley, "someone who can put his foot on the ball in the middle of the park."

He had been joined in the Reading squad by experienced forwards, Ray Hiron from Portsmouth and Jack Whitham, once of Liverpool.

Dunphy said that he had been warned about a "notorious section of the fans" but even he had to admit that "he'd never heard a successful team subjected to the kind of abuse we heard last Saturday… if the crowd start getting at the home players you can be sure life would be a lot easier for the away team. The home players, reluctant to become the focus of the crowd's frustration, will either start to hide or get rid of the ball as quickly as possible in the general direction of their opponent's goal."

The crowd's attitude had no immediate affect on the Reading players. They proceeded to win nine and lose only one of their next thirteen league games and on January 17th they lay third, just a point off the top. More importantly they had a ten-point gap over fifth-placed Bournemouth.

Then calamity struck. Reading slumped to three away defeats, including hammerings by 5-1 at Swansea and 4-1 at Exeter. A 0-0 draw at home to Torquay was at least offset by a narrow victory at home to Hartlepool but when another away defeat at Huddersfield was followed shortly after by the first home defeat of the season, to

Doncaster Rovers, and by two draws, Reading had shuffled out of the top four with only eleven games left.

Interviewed about the promotion season for the book *More than a Job?*, put together many years later by Reading fan Roger Titford, Dunphy is quoted as saying that "there was a great sense of Reading never having got promotion for fifty years and the weight of that got heavier as we got nearer. Charlie Hurley had had several goes at it and one of the things I remember most was the scepticism in the town. While in the early stages it didn't matter to us, it didn't affect us, in the later stages it began to eat away a little bit at us."

That might have been the case for some of the players but not it would seem for the inimitable Robin Friday. In his finest display in the blue and white hoops, he tore apart a Tranmere Rovers side also fighting for promotion in front of 10,961, Reading's biggest crowd so far that season. Two-nil up, Friday mesmerised the Tranmere defence to score perhaps the greatest goal ever seen at the now long-gone Elm Park and a photograph of referee Clive Thomas with his hands on the back of this head in amazement rather than pointing back to the centre spot as the ball enters the net tells its own story. Tranmere were brushed aside 5-0.

It proved the turning point and despite a late season 4-1 loss at Northampton, the Reading side knew that if they could snatch a draw at Cambridge in the penultimate game they would be promoted. Initially everything went to plan. Two-nil ahead and cruising, Reading leaked a goal and Hurley decided his defence needed strengthening. Dunphy was asked to make way. According to Hurley his former international teammate was not impressed.

"He was very self-centred, you see, Eamon Dunphy, everything was about him. He was a very good footballer. But at 2-1 I thought we needed a big iron man in defence to hold the fort. I took him off, we got a draw and won promotion. Afterwards everyone was celebrating but in the dressing room he came up to me as he wasn't happy. I said to him, 'We came here to get promotion, and we've got it, what's your problem? I stuck on a big defender who wasn't scared of anything, you weren't stopping them, I needed someone who was'. I said, 'I don't want to hear another f****** word from you'. I told him he'd played his part and that was good, so he should just shut up. Go and ask the other players how they felt, I said. He didn't."

Three days later Reading beat Crewe 3-1 in front of a packed Elm Park crowd which invaded the pitch at the end, calling for Hurley and the players to take a deserved bow from the main stand. Reading went up into the Third Division by finishing third, their home form proving vital with nineteen wins and just a single defeat from twenty-three matches.

Despite Hurley's success in winning promotion, Dunphy clearly did not rate him as a manager. He was quoted in *More than a job?* as saying: "Reading should never have been in the 4th Division with the resources at Charlie's disposal and the players he had there when I arrived. They wouldn't have got promotion if Gordon Cumming and myself hadn't been there. We were the two key people in terms of leadership and in terms of performance... Charlie just used to say 'come on' and that shite. He knew nothing, we did it for him, that's the job I did for him, get them organised on the pitch, get the dressing room spirit up."

Having gained promotion at the fifth attempt under Hurley, Reading now had the task of staying up, which became immediately a lot harder than it should have been. This was because when the new season's terms were offered many players were incensed, feeling they should have been more handsomely rewarded for their efforts.

One of them, centre back Geoff Barker, quit football to become a sales rep, and although he returned after the halfway point of the season, stating he missed football too much, his actions reflected some of the players' anger. Many refused to commit themselves to another season at Elm Park.

Just weeks before the big kick-off Friday asked for a transfer, stating that "there doesn't appear to be any ambition at the club." John Murray and Tommy Youlden followed suit while Cumming, Death and Dunphy were still refusing to sign until it was pointed out that a new Professional Footballers Association regulation meant that if no new deal were signed by August 12th a player would have to continue on the previous season's terms. Death still refused to sign and on the opening day of the season had to be persuaded out of bed by a local journalist, who took him to Gillingham where he had a storming match.

Despite Friday's genius on the field Hurley reluctantly decided to let him leave. His off-field antics, unwillingness to train and constant need for managerial attention were proving too much. Although heavily criticised at the time when Cardiff snapped him up for £30,000, Hurley's instincts proved correct as the Hammersmith-born Friday's impressive start at his new club gradually gave way to long absences and eventually his loss to the game. Cardiff manager Jimmy Andrews said later that "at the time I didn't know what his major problem was so I bought him... for a period I handled it but I'm afraid Robin was a hopeless case. He was lost and by the end he was uncontrollable."

Friday's career and Hurley's major role in it is featured in a book by Paul McGuigan and Paolo Hewitt, *The Greatest Footballer You Never Saw*, published in 1998, eight years after his death from a heart attack at just 38. He remains an idol for many Reading fans and was selected as their "Player of the Millennium".

Hurley remembers: "Robin Friday – he was the biggest talent I ever signed. He was a nutter. That's an understatement, but he was a naturally gifted player. He was tremendous. One time on the training ground I whacked him one and he put the fists up. I apologised and said 'I'm wrong but I will see you in the office after training'. He told me to f*** off but I insisted and said he wouldn't be training any more if he didn't turn up. He said he could go anywhere and I said the only place he'd go would be in the reserves and that he was too good for that. 'Do yourself a favour and come up to the office," I told him. He came to my office. But by the end even I couldn't control him. We sold him cheap but he was determined to leave; we'd have got nothing for him if I'd waited."

Nevertheless, the loss of such a fine talent, combined with the uproar among the remaining players, was bound eventually to take its toll, even though when local rivals Swindon Town were crushed 4-1 at Elm Park on October 2nd the Biscuitmen rose to the giddy heights of third, level on points with leaders Shrewsbury Town.

According to Hurley: "After we got promoted we started well, too well in fact. I thought we'd had a lot of luck and was worried. I knew that things wouldn't continue. I was after two players. One was Alan Devonshire, who was playing for Southall, and I managed to get the board to agree to buy him, but when I went back they'd sold him. The manager there had been told by West Ham to let them know if anyone was sniffing around. He did and they got £10,000 for him I believe; it was no contest. The other was Cyrille Regis, who I watched at Hayes, good player, but Reading felt he wasn't the sort they wanted at the club at the time. This was a time when racial attitudes weren't what they're like now."

Regis signed for West Bromwich Albion for £5,000 and both he and Devonshire had glittering careers during which they became full England internationals.

Foiled in his attempts to strengthen the side, Hurley could not stop Reading slipping down the table, and when they played out a dull goalless home draw with Crystal Palace on New Year's Day they were in trouble. Instead of Regis, Hurley bought Pat Earles for £15,000 from Southampton to play up front. After a home defeat to Wrexham on January 15th Reading were seventeenth, just two points off the drop.

On January 22nd they lost 2-1 at home to Gillingham, causing Dibben to comment in the *Evening Post* that "things look bleak with three of the next four away". Charlie Hurley stated: "I've got the hardest fight on my hands I've ever had in my soccer career, but like my players I'm going to fight all the way."

However, when another defeat at Bury was followed by a 3-1 loss at Sealand Road against Chester City, in a match in which Dunphy returned to the side for the first time since November, Reading were plummeting fast and were now firmly ensconced in the bottom four.

A 0-0 draw with Shrewsbury in which Dibben felt that "the best example was set by the hard-working Dunphy" provided some small crumb of comfort for the dwindling band of regulars, who were, judging from *Evening Post* reports, still supportive of Hurley's efforts.

However, on February 12th Reading were taken apart by Walsall, suffering a 6-1 thrashing, in which they conceded five goals in half an hour at the start of the second half. Dibben was scathing, stating: "Reading were completely outplayed by a side also deeply in relegation trouble". Fans had to dig deep to remember that the last time their side had been so comprehensively beaten in the league was by a similar scoreline at Shrewsbury in October 1960.

Hurley's plight was probably not helped by reports that he had just received a "vote of confidence" earlier in the week!

Reading were third off bottom, and after drawing with York City, they stumbled 4-2 against Northampton. Hurley was apoplectic, saying afterwards that "In all my life I have never seen defending as bad as that" as he dropped Paul Bennett, Geoff Barker and John Turner to the third team.

Reading were now twenty-third, one off the bottom, and it got worse when Bury took both points with a 3-1 win at Elm Park. It was reported after the match that Hurley had decide to quit at half-time, stating: "I was disappointed with that performance. I wasn't getting the response from the players I wanted."

So after just over five years in the manager's seat Hurley decided to go. Reading had just twenty points from thirty-two matches, were bottom of the league and staring relegation in the face. Assistant Manager Maurice Evans was immediately appointed to take over, doing a decent job but ultimately failing to keep them in the Third Division.

Hurley explains what happened: "What I did was go to see the directors and say I needed some money to strengthen the side or else I'd quit. They called my bluff and I quit. I would have possibly have been wiser financially to either keep my job or if the worst happened and I got sacked then I'd have got a bit of money. As it was I got hardly anything."

Little did he know it but after almost quarter of a century the Irishman's football career had just come to an inglorious end.

"I was a fool, I should have taken the Sheffield United job, but hindsight is a wonderful thing. I was good as a manager. I am a very sad football man," laments Hurley.

Chapter Eighteen

Aftermath and missing football

Charlie Hurley's decision to quit as Reading manager on February 26th 1977 was a selfless decision, giving Maurice Evans a fighting chance to pull off a famous escape. But although Reading took fifteen points from their last fourteen matches, a 3-0 home defeat against Rotherham proved just too much.

Principled it may have been, but, as Hurley says, financially it was not the best decision he ever made. Having managed Reading for five years without a contract it meant he walked away with no significant payout. True, he had done pretty well from a quarter of a century in football, including five as a manager, but not well enough to be able to retire and put his feet up in comfort for the rest of his life, especially with a seven-year-old daughter to bring up.

"I feel Charles was a little impetuous with his decision at Reading. Sometimes he makes decisions too quickly. I certainly didn't know he was going to quit. I think if he'd waited he may have been able to turn things round," recalls Joan.

Hurley's record at Reading, combined with the decision not to take the chance to manage at a higher level when First Division Sheffield United came calling in 1973 and later in October 1975 was such that clubs were unlikely to be beating down the door to employ him as manager.

So later in 1977 he took a job working for Anson Packaging.

"I worked as the sales manager for twenty-two years for the company after I left Reading until I retired in 1999. It was a sales packaging firm. Ted du-Jardin owned it. I was related through Jo's sister's husband, one of those things. They asked me to come on board. They knew I was honest and they knew I was a grafter. I didn't particularly like it because football was my love. I don't have that many regrets, but the one I do have is that I left football. I got to know people and I got a lot of business for the company but I always kept looking at my stupidity, which was not to have left Reading to go to Sheffield United.

"You had to bring in a certain amount of business. Ted was a great fan of mine as a player, but I also did well for them. Quite a few people were football fans, so I had a sort of 'in'. It didn't mean you'd get the business but you got a hearing. I got a lot of business because I'd been a famous footballer. I got pleasure out of being successful at something I didn't like, but sometimes my honesty let me down. As a professional person I did a job, but having been in a job I adored then it was tough and it was my own fault!

"Joan and I have done all right, and my daughters are both very happy, but what an idiot I was – and I was good as a manager. What I did at Reading and with Robin Friday demonstrates that. I am a very sad football man; Reading didn't sack me. I left. I was great with the players. You have to treat each one differently; rollick some, and cajole someone else. I was successful at Reading; oh dear, what a fool.

"Despite the mistakes I am still a very happy man, however. I am quite happy for people to say 'Oh, you were a good footballer'. Nothing wrong with that, but I also like it when people say that I am just an ordinary bloke. I've had a good life, I am seventy-one now and my old joints aren't too bad despite the fact that I took some stick when I played. I am eternally grateful to Millwall Football Club, who stood by me in 1955 when I suffered what could have been a career-threatening injury.

"Mind you, the best bit of luck I had was meeting my wife. That was in the Tottenham Royal. We used to go dancing; there were four of us. We'd go in the car; my best mate Wally used to drive us. It was a long way from Rainham, and she didn't know I was a footballer. I wanted the best, Wally was brave and so I kept him away from her. I went to the 3.00pm dancing; it was take your partners for the foxtrot which was good because I could only really do the foxtrot, my quickstep wasn't quick enough to get in front of the other lads to get a dance [laughter] – I waited. I could do the waltz, and the foxtrot is 1-2-3-4, 1-2-3-4. Anyway, someone grabbed her before I got there, so I stood behind a post and I went round and she'd gone. As soon as the next time came round and I heard 'fox...' then I was in. I didn't say a lot as I wasn't that brave. You didn't even get a kiss on the first date in those days.

"That night I had two or three dances. I was the only one with a car so I decided to go on my own one night, but as Joan had a mate I thought I'd take Wally. We were able to drive them home, had a kiss and cuddle. She lived in Hoddesdon, Joan Gale – she still looks terrific. After I moved to Sunderland I used to come home every fortnight, and getting married in 1959 was the best thing I ever did. We've had a terrific marriage, still have."

The Hurleys' two children, Tracy and Joanne, speak warmly of their parents although the former has seen less of them than she might have wished due to work commitments.

Tracy, who was born in Sunderland in June 1960, says that "living in Sunderland was nice. We used to go to Seaburn beach, especially when my aunt and uncle came up in the summer holidays. I don't know why but the weather seemed to be better in those days. I went into the rock pools and I remember people saying 'Hello, Charlie' but it wasn't like nowadays when footballers get mobbed. I ate candyfloss. It was a good time. I was very sad when we moved, because I thought the people there were nice.

"I watched a couple of matches at Roker Park and I remember going to watch Dad train on a couple of occasions. I remember the crowds being massive and there was no trouble. I do vaguely remember the crowd swaying in one end. It was called the Roker Roar. I went with my mam; she's not that interested in football. My dad was around a lot as a football player because he really only trained in the morning. My dad was very disciplined. You didn't put a foot out of place. He didn't stand for any nonsense. When I got older I fell out once or twice with him. Dad was the hard cop, mam the soft cop.

"I think I did suffer educationally because of the need to move around when my dad moved for work. My best days at school were the ones in Sunderland. I left school at age sixteen to work in the office of a furniture shop. I didn't do that well at school. When I was in Bolton I had passed my eleven plus to go to grammar school but when we moved to Reading I had to go to a comprehensive. If I'd stayed in Bolton I probably would have done better.

"We moved to Hoddesdon when I was seventeen and I started work at the head office of Tesco, until I met my husband Garry Titchen who also worked there. We got married in June 1983 and I've moved around a lot as Garry's job has meant he's had to do so. Firstly it was with Great Universal Stores in Bradford; I moved there in 1984. Garry's now a sales director for a children's wear designs company in Bolton called Drew Brady. I am working part-time in Bollington in a medical market research company and I do telephone sales.

"My relationship with my parents is good, but I did move away twenty-four years ago and therefore we have not had the relationship I would have liked. And they've obviously missed out on their grandchildren, James aged sixteen, Matthew thirteen and Emma eleven, growing up, because they only see them a few times a year rather than a few times a week. I know that my dad really misses that, especially having two grandsons, and my middle one really loves football. He said if I'd lived nearer he could have done some coaching with him. It would have been nicer to live closer. I am aware of how popular Dad is up in the north-east. It's like he's still playing; it was lovely to see all those people around in October 2007 when they held the Fiftieth Anniversary Celebration"

Joanne lives in Hertford, less than twenty minutes' drive from her parents' house in Hoddesdon.

"My dad is my best friend. I am extremely close to him and as a child I went everywhere with him so we have a very close relationship. He's a very strict man as well, a firm hand with lots of love. You were brought up to respect him and my mam and I feel that came from his own strong Irish family background. My dad has always called me 'tup', short for tuppence, and always has to this day.

"One of the best things we've always done is to go fishing, which we started when I was about twelve. It's river fishing, trying to catch roach or perch, the little ones – we still go even now although not as much. It's always been such a laugh; it's competitive, mind, and I always have to get him to say how much he's caught because if

I say what I've caught he always seems to have one more! When my Nan was alive we were out at 5.30 or 6 in the morning and then we went to hers at 2pm; that was my mum's mum. We'd have crusty white bread with boiled bacon sandwiches. It was a regular Saturday morning thing. I've won most times for fish caught.

"My dad has always been there for me; right through senior school he'd pick me up. He's very kind and warm to people. He loves chatting with people, he's a people's person and is very approachable. My parents' relationship is very loving and warm, its very rare to see. My dad didn't talk about his sales rep job. Coming out of football made his life totally different, he learnt everything from scratch but I think he enjoyed some parts of it. He has a great sense of humour, my dad; he's very witty and charming. He's very down to earth and humble, not at all big-headed.

"Obviously as you get older there is a distance that emerges as you start to take your own decisions, rightly or wrongly. I left school at sixteen and worked at a pharmaceutical company in human resources for seventeen years. When my first marriage broke up and I got divorced it was an extremely bleak period, but during it both my parents were superb and the two grandchildren love them a great deal."

Joanne is now married to Simon Wakeling, who says: "Charlie's two granddaughters in Hertford are Katherine who was born in 1995 and Charlotte born in 2002. The grandchildren idolise him – Charlotte calls him 'gaggy'. He picks her up from school and she literally runs out of school into his arms. I am aware that the Sunderland fans love Charlie. I was in the Legends Bar with him and a fan I'd guess aged sixty to sixty-five came over with his son who was around forty years of age and both started shaking Charlie's hand and saying 'I can't believe it, this giant of football' to me. I just replied, 'Be yourself' as what you see in Charlie is what you get," says Spurs fan Simon.

One of Charlie Hurley's closest friends, Norman Howe, who helped establish the former Sunderland Players' Association, says that whenever he's out with him in Sunderland and in other parts of the north-east it is almost always highly entertaining. "Charlie is always well dressed, but that doesn't mean he isn't approachable, far from it. He will give his time freely to anyone. I have seen him seek out people who he feels may be a little shy and scared of coming forward to speak. I have also seen examples of people going completely crazy when he enters the room. I have seen grown men get up, sometimes even on the table, and start singing 'Who's the greatest centre half the world has ever seen?' and then belt out his name," says Howe, who has been watching Sunderland since he came down from Scotland in the late 1940s.

Of course, good bloke that Charlie Hurley is off the pitch it is what he did on it that mattered most to Millwall, Sunderland and Ireland supporters and for what he is best remembered.

And in November 1979 during the centenary celebrations for Sunderland Football Club he was selected by members of the twenty-one branches of the Sunderland Supporters' Association as the 'Sunderland Player of the Century'. It was a fitting tribute to a magnificent career at the club from 1957 to 1969.

Charlie Hurley remembers: "I couldn't believe it at the time. I look back – Shack, Buchan, Ford, Carter – I am too modest to say I am the greatest player ever to play for Sunderland. I got a call from the club; they said I'd been voted Sunderland's player of the century. They had to tell me twice. All I heard when I went up there was 'Shack, Shack, Shack'; now when I go up there they call me 'The King'. I am embarrassed to tell the truth.

"I would like to say that to be voted the greatest player to play for Sunderland in one hundred years is without a doubt the greatest honour I have ever had in football, when you think of the fantastic amount of footballers that played for Sunderland. I think without a doubt I was a very good player, but I think I was there at the right time when they were picking the best player. A lot of the great players were dead and buried. I still can't believe I was the greatest player to play for Sunderland. What an honour!

"Usually, in all fairness, it is a goalscorer that gets this sort of award. At my 70th birthday do Stan Anderson came along. He was a great player – Stan Anderson's football brain was brilliant and it was him that helped make me.

"I've never ever been any different, and you've got to emphasise in this book that I am a fan of the Sunderland fans, I really am. I've been so grateful to them. Even today people see me and come up and shake hands with me; it's fantastic. When you hear the fans signing 'Charlie, Charlie, Charlie Hurley', it's incredibly humbling. It's over fifty years since I signed for Sunderland, and they say to me 'Oh, you're Charlie Hurley, my granddad and my dad told me about you'. I only know that people treat me ever so well; the club have been good to me, Bob Murray was excellent to me."

The award in 1979 arrived twenty years after Hurley had won his one and only trophy during his actual playing career, the 1959 Caltex Trophy for the Republic's Footballer of the Year. Since 1979, however, he's been inundated with awards, causing him to remark that "I get better each year. No one knows how good I will be if I get to a hundred years old!"

Bibliography

History – inter/national

Churchill – A major new assessment of his life in peace and war,
    Edited by R. Blake and Wm Roger Louis [Oxford University Press
    1993]

Our Hidden Lives – the remarkable diaries of post-war Britain,
    Simon Garfield [Ebury Press 2004]

The Irish War – the military history of a domestic conflict, Tony
    Geraghty [Harper Collins 2000]

Culture and Consensus, England, art and politics since 1940, Robert
    Hewison [Methuen 1997]

Britain 1914 – 2000, Edited by Derrick Murphy [Collins Educational
    2000]

An introduction to Modern British History 1900–1999, Michael Lynch
    [Hodder and Stoughton 2001]

Teach yourself The History of Ireland [Contemporary books 2005]

Sixties Britain: Culture, society and politics, Mark Donnelly [Pearson
    Education Ltd]

From Rationing to Rock, The 1950s revisited, Stuart Hylton [Sutton
    Publishing 1998]

The Blood Never Dried, John Newsinger [Bookmarks Publications
    2006]

Local History

Easington the way we were, Eileen Hopper [Easington Village Parish
    Council 1996]

Changing Tide – the final years of Wear Shipbuilding, Ray Nichols
    [Sunderland and Hartlepool Publishing and Printing Limited 1990]

A Wearside Mining Story, John E McCutcheon [1960 Self-published]

The Durham Miners' Millenium Book, David Temple [TUPS Books in
    association with Durham National Union of Mineworkers 2000]

Canny Aad Sunlun, Maurice Boyle [Northeast Press Limited 1995]

Alice in Sunderland: An entertainment by Bryan Talbot [Jonathan
    Cape 2007]

Sunderland Today 1963 [Sunderland Evening Echo 1963]

Bibliography

Crimes of Yesteryear – murders and mysteries from Wearside and old County Durham, Nigel Green [Sunderland Echo 1990]
Them were the days....or were they? Life in Sunderland's East End in the 1930s [compiled by the East End History Project 1986]

Football – Sunderland
All the Lads – a Complete Who's Who of Sunderland AFC, Garth Dykes and Doug Lamming [Sunderland AFC 2000]
The History of Sunderland AFC 1979–1986, Bill Simmons and Bob Graham [Bob Graham 1986]
The Official History – Sunderland AFC 1879–2000 [Sunderland AFC 2000]
50 Post War Seasons of Sunderland AFC, Mel Kirtley [Wearside Books 1996]
Clown Prince of Soccer, The Len Shackleton Story, Colin Malam [Highdown 2005]
The People's History – Sunderland 'til I die, Alan Brett and Andrew Clark [The People's History 1999]
The People's History – Football in Sunderland, Peter Gibson [The People's History 2002]
Chalford Oral History Series – Roker Park voices, Compiled by Alan Brett and Andrew Clark [Chalford 1997]
The Battle for a Town, Sunderland AFC v Sunderland Albion, Paul Days [Imagination Corporation Ltd Publications 2007]
Sunderland AFC Centenary 1879–1979, The story of Sunderland, Arthur Appleton [Sunderland AFC 1979]

Football – autobiographies and general
Purnell's Encyclopedia of Association Football [1972]
Hotbed of Soccer, Arthur Appleton [Sportsmen Book Club 1961]
Through the Turnstiles, Brian Tabner [Yore Publications 1992]
Clough – a biography, Tony Francis [Stanley Paul and Co 1990]
A Pictorial History of Soccer, Dennis Signy [Paul Hamlyn 1968]
The Hamlyn Book of World Soccer [Hamlyn Publishing 1973]
Martin O'Neill, The Biography, Alex Montgomery [Virgin Books 2003]
Big Ron, Ron Atkinson [Andre Deutsch 1998]
Bestie – a portrait of a legend, Joe Lovejoy [Sidgwick and Jackson 1998]

Careless Hands: The forgotten truth of Gary Sprake, Stuart Sprake and Tim Johnson [Tempus 2006]

Sam Bartram: The Story of a Goalkeeping Legend, Mike Blake [NPI Media Group 2006]

True Grit – The Autobiography, Frank McLintock with Ron Bagchi [Headline 2005]

The Jimmy Hill Story, Jimmy Hill [Hodder and Stoughton 1998]

The Greatest Footballer You Never Saw: The Robin Friday Story, Paul McGuigan and Paolo Hewitt [Mainstream Publishing 1997]

Peter Lorimer: Leeds and Scotland Hero, Peter Lorimer and Phil Rostron [Mainstream Publishing 2002]

You're not singing anymore, Adrian Thrills [Random House 1998]

John Charles: Gentle Giant, Mario Risoli [Mainstream Publishing 2003]

Boots, balls and haircuts, Hunter Davies [Octopus Publishing Group Ltd 2003]

Biting Talk – Norman Hunter: my autobiography, with Don Warters [Hodder and Stoughton 2004]

Harry's Game: The autobiography, Harry Gregg with Roger Anderson [Mainstream Publishing 2002]

Ron Reynolds: The life of a 1950's Footballer, Dave Bowler and David Reynolds [Orion Books Limited 2003]

Jimmy Greaves: The Heart of the Game [Time Warner Books 2005]

Bobby Charlton: My Man Utd Years, with Jim Lawton [Headline 2007]

Paddy Crerand: Never Turn the other cheek [Harper Sport 2007]

The Way it Was: My Autobiography, Stanley Matthews [Headline 2001]

Billy Wright's Book of Soccer [Stanley Paul 1958]

More than a job? The player's and fan's persective, Roger Titford, Eamon Dunphy [Further Thought Publishing 1992]

Niall Quinn – the autobiography [Headline 2002]

Index

164, 165, 190, 191, 202, 214,
215, 224
Bury 12, 109, 114, 123, 218, 230,
231, 237, 238
Busby, Matt 4, 44, 61, 78, 144, 145,
149, 150, 164, 178, 205
Butler, Geoff 202, 227
Byrom, John 219, 220, 222, 223

Cantwell, Noel 40, 41, 42, 65, 74,
81, 87, 113, 132, 135, 176, 177,
182, 185, 194, 199
Cardiff City 57, 82, 88, 133, 142,
219, 236
Carey, Johnny 64, 82, 115, 138,
194
Carrow Road 119, 120, 134
Carter, Raich 8, 161, 244
Celtic 105, 178, 191
Chappell, Les 227, 228, 229
Charles John 4, 29, 33, 95, 117,
133, 205
Charlton Athletic 18, 25 ,29, 37,
69, 79, 140, 153, 155, 194, 223,
224, 233
Charlton, Bobby 1, 3, 61, 145, 148,
149, 150, 206
Charlton, Jack 43, 122, 183, 187,
181
Charnley, Ray 55, 163
Chelsea 19, 24, 25, 28, 29, 44, 47,
59, 60, 83, 129–131, 141, 160,
165, 180, 185, 188, 198, 201,
202, 211, 220
Chile 87, 105, 109, 179
Chisholm, Ken 39
Clayton, Ronnie 40, 86, 218
Clough, Brian 3, 69, 73, 78, 87, 92,
99, 104, 105, 107, 108, 109, 111,
113, 114, 115, 117, 118, 119,
120, 122, 123, 124, 128, 137,
138, 155, 158, 161, 162, 164,
165, 166, 167, 171, 184, 189,
196, 197
Colchester 37, 116
Collings, Syd 47, 115, 154, 171
Collins, Bobby 4, 117, 122, 123,
188, 218
Cork Evening Echo 13
Coventry City 34, 36, 37, 41, 127,

128, 152, 198, 210
Crerand, Paddy 54, 105, 106,
148–150, 191, 206
Crewe Alexandra 229, 235
Crossan, Johnny 4, 5, 120, 126,
129, 130, 134, 142, 144–146,
152, 153, 161, 167, 170
Crystal Palace 22, 31, 34, 237
Cullis, Stan 28, 46, 63
Cumming, Gordon 227, 228, 230,
235
Cummins, George 49, 64
Curtis, Dermot 40, 49, 64, 80, 87
Curtis, George (Sunderland trainer)
44
Curtis, George (Coventry City) 127
Czechoslovakia 4, 74, 75, 105, 109,
110, 184, 195, 200, 216

Daily Express 41, 69, 71, 72, 77, 82,
152, 184
Daily Mail 30, 56
Daily Mirror 39, 42, 87, 90, 100, 113
Dalymount Park 30, 39, 40, 41, 43,
64, 80, 81, 105, 109, 172, 181,
184, 190, 195, 211
Daniel, Ray 12, 39, 57, 58, 95
Davies, Wyn 39, 176, 189, 202, 209
Davis, George 138, 139
Death, Steve 227, 228, 235
Den (The) 18, 19, 21, 26, 34, 45,
49, 116
Denmark 42, 49, 189, 210
Derby County 54, 73, 87, 110, 112,
126, 136, 164, 189, 192, 197, 218
Dillon, John 102, 104
Ditchburn, Bill 29, 38
Docherty, Tommy 131, 160
Doncaster Rovers 227, 234
Dougan, Derek 62, 125
Douglas, Bryan 50, 86
Dunne, Tony 40, 113, 177, 190,
195, 201, 216
Dunphy, Eamonn 233, 234, 235,
237
Dwyer, Noel 89, 155

Eastham, George 84, 85, 96, 97
Eastville 69, 104
Edwards, Duncan 40, 65, 188

Other football books from SportsBooks

Raich Carter: the biography
Frank Garrick

The definitive biography of one of the greatest players to pull on a Sunderland shirt. The great inside right had his career ruined by the Second World War but he was the only player to win FA Cup medals before and after it. He also starred when Sunderland won their last League title in 1935–36.

1899807 18 7
Price £16.99
Hardback

Ha'way/Howay the Lads
Alan Candlish

The rivalry between Newcastle and Sunderland is legendary. This book give a report of every game.

1899807 39 X
Price £14.99
Paperback

Modern Football is Rubbish
Nick Davidson & Shaun Hunt

The authors are going through a midlife crisis as far as football is concerned. Now they've reached early middle-age they are wondering what has happened to the beautiful game. Where have all the muddy pitches gone they wonder. They wallow in nostalgia for 3 pm Saturday kick-offs and cup upsets and they rant against inflated egos, spiralling salaries and satellite TV. And they wonder about men in tights and gloves.

9781899807 71 0
Price £7.99
Paperback

The World at their Feet: Northern Ireland in Sweden
Ronnie Hanna

The story of Northern Ireland's first trip to the World Cup finals when, despite being the smallest country, they reached the quarter-finals. Ronnie Hanna also wrote *Six Glorious Years: Following Northern Ireland 1980–86*

9781899807 74 1
Price £7.99
Paperback

Memories of George Best
Chris Hilton & Ian Cole
Malcolm Brodie, of the *Belfast Telegraph* who covered George Best throughout his brilliant and ill-starred career, called this "the best Best book ever". The authors talked to many of the Manchester United star's contemporaries to find out the true story of the wayward genius.

9781899807 57 4
Price £14.99
Paperback

From Sheffield with Love
Brendan Murphy
Published on the 150th anniversary of Sheffield FC, the world's oldest football club. The book charts the rise of organised football in Sheffield and Nottingham, the two oldest centres of the game.

9781899807 56 7
Price £8.99
Paperback

The Irish Uprising
Andy Dawson
The story of Roy Keane's first season at Sunderland, which ended with promotion to the Premier League.

9781899807 60 4
Price £10.99
Paperback

Wembley
Glen Isherwood
Everything you need to know about the 'old' Wembley. Every match ever played at the world's most iconic football venue is detailed here as well as appearances, scorers etc.

1899807 42 X
Price £14.99
Paperback

Accrington Stanley: the club that wouldn't die
Phil Whalley
Fan and writer Phil Whalley charts the comeback of Accrington Stanley the club which re-signed from the Football League in the early '60s. After going bust they re-formed in 1968 and began an astonishing climb back to the League.

1899807 47 0
Price £16.99
Hardback

Europe United: a history of the European Cup/Champions League
Andrew Godsell
The story of the European Cup on its 50th birthday.

1899807 30 6
Price £17.99
Hardback

Growing up with Subbuteo: my Dad invented the world's greatest football game
Mark Adolph
The author writes about the colourful life of the man who invented Subbuteo and turned it into a world-wide success.

1899807 40 3
Price £7.99
Paperback

Fitba Gallimaufry
Adam Scott
All you need to know about Scottish football and a lot you don't!

1899807 45 4
Price £9.99
Hardback

Ode to Jol: A Spurs fan's diary
Alasdair Gold
A very funny look at what turned out to be Martin Jol's last season at White Hart Lane.

1899807 43 8
Price £12.99
Paperback

The Complete Centre-Forward: Tommy Lawton, the authorised biography
David McVay & Andy Smith
Tommy Lawton was one of England football's greatest strikers despite, like Carter, losing six years to the war. He went on to manage Notts County and his colourful career and life shine through.

1899807 09 8
Price £14.99
Hardback